HOLINESS

Scholars have defined holiness in many ways. These range from the vague and ethereal adjective 'numinous' to practical matters of ritual purity. When both a sheaf of grain and God can be called 'holy', how should we understand the elusive meaning of this word?

Hannah K. Harrington presents an in-depth exploration of holiness in the context of rabbinic Judiasm, based on a holistic yet detailed understanding of the relevant texts and Scripture. The rabbinic concept of holiness is placed alongside other notions of the sacred in the Graeco-Roman world, providing a much-needed comparative view of this core subject during a key period in the development of the Jewish religion.

Holiness will be of interest to students and scholars of biblical studies, Graeco-Roman religions and Jewish studies.

Hannah K. Harrington is Professor of Old Testament at Patten College, Oakland, California. She received her Ph.D. in Near Eastern Studies from the University of California, Berkeley, and has written numerous articles on the Dead Sea Scrolls and rabbinic Judaism.

RELIGION IN THE FIRST CHRISTIAN CENTURIES
Edited by Deborah Sawyer and John Sawyer,
Lancaster University

The aim of the books in this series is to survey particular themes in the history of religion across the different religions of antiquity and to set up comparisons and contrasts, resonances and discontinuities, and thus reach a profounder understanding of the religious experience in the ancient world.

Also available in this series:

WOMEN AND RELIGION IN THE FIRST CHRISTIAN CENTURIES
Deborah F. Sawyer

THE CRUCIBLE OF CHRISTIAN MORALITY
J. Ian H. McDonald

SACRED LANGUAGES AND SACRED TEXTS
John Sawyer

DEATH, BURIAL AND REBIRTH IN THE RELIGIONS OF ANTIQUITY
Jon Davies

TEACHERS AND TEXTS IN THE ANCIENT WORLD: PHILOSOPHERS, JEWS AND CHRISTIANS
H. Gregory Snyder

MAGIC IN THE ROMAN WORLD: PAGANS, JEWS AND CHRISTIANS
Naomi Janowitz

HOLINESS

Rabbinic Judaism and the
Graeco-Roman world

Hannah K. Harrington

London and New York

First published 2001
by Routledge
11 New Fetter Lane, London EC4P 4EE

Simultaneously published in the USA and Canada
by Routledge
29 West 35th Street, New York, NY 10001

Routledge is an imprint of the Taylor & Francis Group

Typeset in Garamond by Exe Valley Dataset Ltd, Exeter
Printed and bound in Great Britain by
TJ International, Padstow, Cornwall

British Library Cataloguing in Publication Data
A catalogue record for this book is available from the British Library

Library of Congress Cataloging in Publication Data
Harrington, Hannah K.
Holiness: rabbinic Judaism and the Graeco-Roman world/Hannah K. Harrington.
p. cm. – (Religion in the first Christian centuries)
Includes bibliographical references and index.
1. Holiness–Judaism. 2. Holiness–Biblical teaching. 3. God
(Judaism)–Attributes. 4. Rabbinical literature–History and criticism.
5. Sacrifice–Biblical teaching. I. Title. II. Series

BM645.H58 H37 2001
296.3–dc21

2001019756

ISBN 0–415–14986–X (hbk)
ISBN 0–415–14987–8 (pbk)

This book is dedicated to my dear mother, Constance M. Karajian, and to the memory of my loving father, Dr Samuel L. Karajian.

CONTENTS

FIGURES AND TABLES

FIGURES

TABLES

ACKNOWLEDGMENTS

This work would not have been possible without the support and guidance of several, special people. I want to thank Prof. Jacob Milgrom (Professor Emeritus, University of California, Berkeley) for giving me his insights into the priestly system of holiness. This has provided the solid basis necessary for understanding the rabbinic concept of holiness. I consider it a privilege to have received his tutelage in graduate seminars as well as his counsel in post-doctoral work. Also, Prof. Daniel Boyarin (University of California, Berkeley) corrected parts of the manuscript and I thank him for his helpful advice.

I am also deeply grateful for the support of my friends, especially Dr Rebecca Skaggs, Academic Dean of Patten College, Oakland, CA where I am Professor of Old Testament and the late Dr Priscilla Benham, who was President of Patten College for many years. Dr Skaggs and Dr Benham were an invaluable source of encouragement to me during the process of writing this book. Dr Bebe Patten too has been a source of inspiration to me.

Many thanks go to several people who were helpful in supplying illustrations for this book. I want to especially thank Dr Karen Ensor, Alex Allan, and the Judah Magnes Musem for allowing me to use photographs free of charge. Also, Peggy Zemens, Library Director at Patten College, helped to supply needed information regarding the illustrations.

Finally, I wish to thank my family for its unfailing confidence in me. My mother, Constance Karajian and late father, Dr Samuel Karajian, gave me my first lesson in holiness in a practical sense. My loving husband, Bill Harrington, has been a constant source of encouragement to me and provided listening ears for many discussions, often over small details. His patience is unequaled and greatly appreciated.

ABBREVIATIONS

1 En.	1 Enoch
1QH	Qumran, *Thanksgiving Psalms*, Cave 1
1QM	Qumran, *War Scroll*, Cave 1
1QS	Qumran, *Manual of Discipline*, Cave 1
2 Bar.	2 Baruch
2 Macc.	2 Maccabees
4 Ezra	4 Ezra
4 Macc.	4 Maccabees
4Q274	Qumran, *Tohorot,* Cave 4
4Q284a	Qumran, *Purification Rule*, Cave 4
4QFlor	Qumran, *Florilegium*, Cave 4
4QMMT	Qumran, *Miksat Ma-aseh ha-Torah,* Cave 4
11Q13	Qumran, *Melchizedek*, Cave 11
11Q19	Qumran, *Temple Scroll*, Cave 11
Aesch., *Eur.*	Aeschylus, *Euripides*
Ar., *Lys.*	Aristides, *Lysistratus*
ARNa	*Abot de-Rabbi Nathan - first version*
ARNb	*Abot de-Rabbi Nathan - second version*
Arist.	*Letter of Aristeas*
b.	Babylonian Talmud
Barn.	*Epistle of Barnabas*
Cant. R.	*Canticles Rabbah*
CD	Cairo (Genizah text of the) Damascus (Document)
Civ. Dei.	*De Civitus Dei (City of God)*
Cyr. *Cat. Myst.*	Cyril of Jerusalem, *Catechesis Mystagogica*
Ench.	*Encheiridion*
Eur., *El.*	Euripides, *Electra*
Eur., *Hipp.*	Euripides, *Hippolytus*
Eus.	Eusebius
Hist.	*Church History*
Vit. Const.	*Vita Constantini*
Exod. R.	*Exodus Rabbah*

Gen. R.	*Genesis Rabbah*
Gk.	Greek
Heb.	Hebrew
Hekh. Rab.	*Hekhalot Rabbati*
Heracl., *Fr.*	Heraclitus in *Die Fragmente der Vorsokratiken* (Diels)
Herm. Sim.	*Hermas Similitude(s)*
Herm. Vis.	*Hermas, Vision(s)*
Ign., *Rom.*	Ignatius, *Letter to the Romans*
Jos.	Josephus
Ag. Ap.	*Against Apion*
Ant.	*Antiquities*
Wars	*The Jewish Wars*
Jub.	Jubilees
Just., *Dial.*	Justin Martyr, *Dialogues with Trypho*
Lat.	Latin
Lev. R.	*Leviticus Rabbah*
LAB	*Liber Antiquitatum Biblicarum*
Lact., *Div. Inst.*	Lactantius, *Divinae Institutiones*
Luc., *De Syria Dea*	Lucianus, *De Syria Dea*
m.	Mishnah
Mart. Pol.	*Martyrdom of Polycarp*
Mek.	*Mekilta*
Mid. ha-Gadol	*Midrash ha-Gadol*
Mid. Teh.	*Midrash Tehilim*
Num. R.	*Numbers Rabbah*
Orig., *Ag. Cels.*	Origen, *Against Celsus*
Philo	
Flacc.	*In Flaccum*
Fug.	*De fuga et inventione*
Heres	*Quis rerum divinarum Heres*
Sp. Laws	*Special Laws*
Vit. Mos.	*De Vitae Mose*
Pesikta R	Pesikta Rabbati
PRE	Pirke de-Rabbi Eliezer
Pl.	Plato
Crit.	*Crito*
Resp.	*Respublica*
Soph.	*Sophista*
Plut.	Plutarch
Phoc.	*De Phocione*
Tranq. An.	*De Tranquillitate Animi*
PRK	*Pesikta de-Rab Kahana*
Pss. Sol.	Psalms of Solomon
Ro.	Roman
Sen., *Moral Essays*	Seneca, *Moral Essays*

Sen., *Moral Epist.*	Seneca, *Moral Epistles*
Sh. Ar.	*Shulkhan Arukh*
Sif. Deut.	*Sifrei Deuteronomy*
Sif. Num.	*Sifrei Numbers*
Sif. Zuta	*Sifrei Zuta*
Sir.	Ben Sira (Ecclesiasticus)
Soph., *Ant*	Sophocles, *Antigone*
t.	Tosefta
Tanh.	*Tanhuma*
Targ. Jon.	*Targum Jonathan*
Test. Benj.	Testament of Benjamin
Test. Job	Testament of Job
Thuc.	Thucydides
Xen., *Hell.*	Xenophon, *Historia Graeca*
Wis. Sol.	Wisdom of Solomon
y.	Jerusalem Talmud (Yerushalmi)
Yalk.	*Yalkut*

Tractates of the Mishnah, Tosefta, Jerusalem (Yerushalmi) or Babylonian (Bavli) Talmuds

Ab.	Abot
Arak.	Arakin
AZ	Aboda Zara
BB	Baba Batra
Ber.	Berakot
Bets.	Betsah
BQ	Baba Qamma
Dem.	Demai
Ed.	Eduyot
Erub.	Erubin
Git.	Gittin
Hag.	Hagigah
Hal.	Hallah
Hor.	Horayot
Hul.	Hullin
Kel.	Kelim
Ker.	Keritot
Ket.	Ketubot
MQ	Mo'ed Qatan
Ma'as. Sh.	Ma'aser Sheni
Mak.	Makkot
Meg.	Megillah
Men.	Menahot

Naz.	Nazir
Ned.	Nedarim
Neg.	Nega'im
Nid.	Niddah
Oh.	Ohalot
Or.	Orlah
Par.	Parah
Pe'ah	Pe'ah
Pes.	Pesahim
Qid.	Qiddushin
RH	Rosh Hashana
San.	Sanhedrin
Shab.	Shabbat
Sheb.	Shebi'it
Shebu.	Shebu'ot
Sheq.	Sheqalim
Sot.	Sota
Suk.	Sukkah
Ta'an.	Ta'anit
Tam.	Tamid
Ter.	Terumot
Toh.	Tohorot
Yad.	Yadayim
Yeb.	Yebamot
Yoma	Yoma
Zeb.	Zebahim

INTRODUCTION

What did it mean to be holy in the first Christian centuries? Many people have mixed views on the concept of holiness. Some see it as a Judeo-Christian phenomenon. Others regard the sacred realm as a universal construct. The definition of holiness too is variously understood. Some see it as a moral category, others as a social classification. Some regard it equivalent to religious experience, while others regard it as simply a state of being outside of the norm. What is needed is a systematic presentation of the matter, and nowhere is the topic so integral to religion as in the rabbinic Judaism of the early centuries of the common era. This period provides rich soil for explaining the concept both in the broad, pagan domain of Graeco-Roman culture as well as in the more narrow but extremely fertile valley of rabbinic Judaism. In the latter we find the components of a complete system of holiness compiled from the prolific teachings of the rabbinic sages. It is this material upon which the following study is based. The rabbinic concept of holiness provides a detailed model for comparison and contrast with the notion of the sacred in both paganism and Christianity.

SCHOLARSHIP ON HOLINESS

General scholarship

Scholars from a variety of disciplines have been intrigued with the notions of holiness and purity. Each has contributed a special dimension to the present state of research. Anthropologists from Emile Durkheim to Mary Douglas have demonstrated that the realm of the holy, or the sacred (I use these words synonymously), is a cross-cultural phenomenon. It seems that universally, human beings mark out certain areas, persons, times, and rituals as sacred and fear them

1

as extraordinary, powerful, and/or mystical. Graeco-Roman historians and religionists have unearthed numerous sacred temples and statues across the Roman empire which reveal the concern for the holy throughout the Roman empire. Greek and Latin texts and inscriptions confirm the regard for the sacred with numerous restrictions on holy personnel and sites.

Biblical scholars have advanced the understanding of holiness to a great degree by insisting that universal models alone do not get at the heart of what it means to be holy in a given culture. Here one must delve into the language of the particular texts which a group preserved. The most standard text on biblical holiness in the early part of this century was written by Rudolph Otto, *The Idea of the Holy*.[1] Otto regards holiness as sort of a *mysterium tremendum*, an awe-inspiring energy which brings people to God. In a probing analysis of Scripture, Otto presents holiness as a divine power, which he calls the "numinous," which awes and overwhelms human beings. However, Otto sidesteps the aspect of holiness so prevalent in Leviticus and Numbers which is based upon the Temple cult. The fact that animal sacrifices are labeled holy, and some even "holy of holies," by the biblical priests is not explained.

Probably the most productive and integrative of Bible scholars on our topic has been Jacob Milgrom. In an extensive commentary on Leviticus, Milgrom analyzes the biblical data to uncover a system of holiness and purity which resonates within its ancient near eastern context but has a unique ring of its own as well. He explains the system of the biblical priests in a systematic manner, filling in gaps of the text by means of the Bible's own inner logic as well as its ancient near eastern context. Milgrom brings into relief the classifications inherent in the system and the way in which they are maintained. Milgrom is nevertheless keenly aware of the ethical undergirding of the biblical system and constantly seeks to uncover the ethical in the ritual. Rationales and motives of the priests are examined, providing an outstanding model for any other scholarship on holiness in any context.

Other biblical scholars who have contributed to the clarification of the data on holiness include Baruch Levine, who has done major linguistic work on holiness, Philip P. Jenson, with regard to classifications in the priestly system, and John Gammie, who has compiled a broader study of holiness by examining it in the different genres of biblical literature.[2]

The matter of holiness in the New Testament has traditionally been considered a topic of proper social and sexual conduct. With the demise of cultic ritual in Christianity, early interpreters began to regard holiness as a matter of ethics having nothing to do with ritual sanctification by means of sacrifices or purity rituals. The latter categories were reinterpreted in light of the person and ministry of Jesus Christ with the end result being that they were rendered out-of-date and superseded by the atoning death and resurrection of Christ. Matters of Israelite cult and ritual were often used as effective teaching tools to illuminate theological aspects of Christianity even though they were considered obsolete in actual practice. In modern times, New Testament scholars have become increasingly interested in early Christianity's own holy rituals and the way in which they contributed to the social stratification of nascent Christian communities.[3] As this book hopes to prove, rabbinic scholars too can contribute to this endeavor. Much of the early Christian teaching on holiness shows an affinity with its rabbinic Jewish counterpart and some ideas are clarified by comparison with similar notions in rabbinic Judaism.

Rabbinic scholarship

As far back in time as the New Testament itself, the Pharisaic tradition, which gave rise to Rabbinic Judaism as it is known from the Mishnah, Talmudim and other sources (see below), has been criticized for its emphasis on cultic ritual over matters of ethical goodness. In response to this critique and continuing criticism from Christians of Jewish rituals, noted rabbinic scholars at the turn of the century, such as Solomon Schechter, wrote essays and handbooks on Judaism which emphasized the ethical dimension of holiness in Judaism. George Foot Moore's two-volume work entitled *Judaism* as well as Ephraim Urbach's work, *The Sages*, are both invaluable reference sources for those wishing to know the principles and even details of rabbinic Judaism, but neither focuses on the ritual nature of sanctification in much detail.

However, when one examines the Mishnah, the primary source of rabbinic Judaism and the earliest redacted rabbinic document (ca. 200 CE), issues of holiness take up over one third of the material, and sanctification is clearly by ritual means, i.e. sacrifices, purity rules, cultic festivals, agricultural offerings, etc. Thus, it appears that the traditional Christian critique is correct. Judaism's road to holiness is by ritual means. Indeed this seems to be the attitude of Jacob Neusner, who has done the majority of recent work on holiness in rabbinic Judaism. Neusner has written the most extensive modern commentary on the Mishnah in addition to translations of and commentaries on other rabbinic sources, including the two Talmuds. One of his major contributions has been to bring into relief the ritual character of sanctification in rabbinic Judaism in a positive, healthy light without apology. Another benefit is his analysis of each aspect of holiness and purity as part of a coherent, rabbinic system rather than a collection of random laws.

One of Neusner's main themes is that the Mishnah authors tried to help the Jewish people deal with the calamities of 70 and 135 CE in which so many lives were lost, the Temple was destroyed, and Jews were banned from Jerusalem. The Mishnah's main focus, according to Neusner, is filling in the religious vacuum of the loss of the Temple. The Mishnah's solution to the problem is to ignore the vacuum and insist that holiness continues within the daily private life of Israel. It is not dependent on the cultic structure:

> That sanctification, as a matter of fact, from the viewpoint of the system now endured and transcended the physical destruction of the building and the cessation of sacrifices. For Israel the people was holy, enduring as the medium and the instrument of God's sanctification.[4]

Unfortunately, in his successful effort to show that the Mishnah is preoccupied with the sanctification of Israel, that this holiness is maintained by means of purity and the cult, and that the presence of impurity does not automatically indicate the presence of sin, Neusner makes the untenable conclusion that holiness by rabbinic definition is not a moral category at all. He refers to it as simply a means to social classification via public and private rituals: "Virtue and holiness constitute distinct classifications, the one having to do with morality, the other with ontology. . . . [R]epresenting uncleanness as part of a hierarchical classification of social entities constitutes the correct systemic reading of the matter."[5] In fact, Neusner regards the moral dimension of holiness in the popular mind to be a Christian construction.[6]

Neusner's work on holiness suffers because he insists on treating rabbinic sources in isolation from each other. While his translations of many rabbinic sources are a valuable aid to scholars, he reconstructs the rabbinic concept of holiness primarily from the data provided in the Mishnah. While I agree with him that every document, indeed every writer, will have some agenda or motive, the rabbinic texts of the early centuries CE must be taken together in order to portray, as accurately as possible, "the rabbinic" concept on any major issue. In this case, the early rabbinic commentaries on the Pentateuch, namely, the *Mekhilta* (on Exodus), the *Sifra* (on Leviticus), *Sifrei Numbers* (on Numbers), and *Sifrei Deuteronomy* (on Deuteronomy), contain material of the same provenance and time period as the Mishnah (indeed a fair amount is identical to the Mishnah), quote many of the same sages, and are interested in many of the same matters. Although all of these sources are usually attributed to early third century redactors, the material is largely the work of generations of sages spanning the first two centuries of the common era.

The *Sifra* is interested in many of the same matters of sanctific-ation as the Mishnah, but focuses as well on the ethical dimension to holiness found in Leviticus 18–20. Nevertheless, Neusner does not include this moral aspect in his definition of holiness because he derives his definition almost exclusively from the Mishnah, which does not explore that avenue in terms of holiness. While the Mishnah is the core document of rabbinic literature, its agenda is limited. To truly arrive at a balanced picture of sanctification in rabbinic Judaism, the array of literary evidence must be broadened.

My work fits into this picture of scholarship as an attempt to provide a balanced view of holiness in rabbinic Judaism as it fits into its larger Graeco-Roman context. Many basic components of holiness in rabbinic Judaism are also present in cultures throughout the Roman empire. Notions of separateness, power, and perfection marking off sacred areas and persons are not unusual in the early Christian centuries. Nevertheless, there are certain particulars in the rabbinic presentation of holiness which make it distinctive and even peculiar when placed alongside its pagan neighbors. Other distinctives appear when the rabbinic model is compared with its Christian counterpart. This book aims to present, as accurately and systematically as possible, the concept of holiness as it was understood by the Rabbis. For this I will draw on as many rabbinic sources as prove helpful.

The book is arranged in categories which, although they have many overlapping concerns in the pagan as well as Christian worlds, are truly rabbinic. These categories are upheld in rabbinic literature as, what could be called, pillars of holiness. First, holiness is inherent in and emanates from the Holy One, i.e. God himself. Second, the holy house is central to rabbinic thinking on holiness even though it was only in actual existence until 70 CE. Physical destruction could not erase the importance of the holy house and its cult as a primary means of access to the Holy One. The Rabbis' detailed analysis of the cult is a rich source for uncovering principles of holiness. Third, the land of Israel is the holy land in rabbinic thought, all other lands being considered unholy and the realm of death and impurity. Fourth, although it could have been listed first, is the holy word, which is the medium for any understanding of holiness at all. It is also the primary means by which holiness is maintained in Israel, that is, obedience to the holy commandments. Finally, the notion of Israel as a divinely selected holy people, whether in control of its holy house and land or not, sustained hope that access to God was still possible among Israel. The holy people maintains its holiness in specific ways both in the areas of ritual and ethics.

RABBINIC SOURCES

It might be helpful to survey at the outset the many rabbinic sources cited throughout this book. While I suggest that the variety of rabbinic sources be brought to the examining table in any attempt to outline "the rabbinic concept" of any topic, one should not be blind to differences in date, provenance, and motivation of each text.

We begin with a word about the Hebrew Scriptures, because, while it is technically not a rabbinic construction, it is the foundation source for rabbinic thought. The Rabbis constantly use biblical material to support their claims Very often they assume knowledge of the scriptural text in their writings and do not find it necessary to prove certain notions seeing that they are obvious already in Scripture. They regard their material as supplementary to Scripture, not as something outside of it. Their interpretation of the Bible is nevertheless distinct and does not always coincide with that of other groups, indeed they often differ among themselves. My point is that, in many cases, it is up to the reader often to supply the biblical prooftext that the Rabbis are assuming. Often a biblical concept or particular text is considered self-evident and common knowledge in the academic circle in which the Rabbis studied and they see no reason to elaborate on the obvious. If the reader does not include this underlying scriptural base, at almost every turn, s/he may come to the distorted conclusion that the Rabbis did not believe in some very obvious biblical principles or that they invented new modes of thought when they are many times simply clarifying the old.

Redaction critical methods of the Bible, while important to biblical studies today, are not helpful in tracing rabbinic ideas since the Rabbis viewed the Hebrew Bible as a seamless piece of divine revelation. Thus, in this study, the early provenance of the biblical material and its literary history will not be analyzed.

The Mishnah (m.) is the earliest compendium of rabbinic law on various topics and has served as the legal basis for both of the Talmuds. Of its six divisions, one is devoted to matters of holiness in the cult and another to matters of ritual purity. In these areas, especially, there is a strong dependence on the biblical text although it is not the style of the redactor to quote Scripture directly. The arrangement is much more topical. While the writer expands and clarifies many aspects of biblical law in detail, most principles are securely rooted in a careful, valid reading of Scripture. The vast majority of sages who contributed to the work lived during the first two centuries CE, although a few are said to have lived even before the turn of the era. Rabbi Judah the Prince, who lived in Palestine in about 200 CE is credited with the final editing of the Mishnah.

The Tosefta (t.) has a direct relationship with the Mishnah. Also of Palestinian provenance, it is arranged in the same six divisions and contains much of the same material. However, it supplements the Mishnah with much more data. It is usually understood that the Tosefta was compiled after the redaction of the Mishnah.

The next set of rabbinic sources valuable to our study are the early commentaries on the Pentateuch noted above: *Mekhilta*, *Sifra*, *Sifrei Numbers*, and *Sifrei Deuteronomy*. The sages mentioned in these works are Tannaim, living during the first two centuries CE in Palestine. All of these commentaries qualify as midrash. Reuven Hammer defines the term midrash:

> Midrash is both a process and a product. It is a method of study and interpretation of the Bible and it is the name given to the literary works that emerge from that study. A midrash is both the individual interpretive comment to a work or a verse and also the book into which these individual pericopes have been incorporated. Midrash is exegesis, explanation of a Biblical text and a commentary on it. To qualify as midrash, there must be a connection to a text.[7]

Thus, unlike the Mishnah and Tosefta, the rabbinic comments in these sources are connected explicitly to selected passages of the books of the Torah as exegetical commentary.

The value of these early commentaries cannot be overestimated for anyone seeking information on early rabbinic beliefs. While the Mishnah is largely limited to matters of legal practice, these Tannaitic commentaries to Scripture, which also focus on matters of law, include more philosophical and value-related material. For example, one might find discussion on the value of human life or repentance or the importance of morality or other aspects of religion in these works, whereas the Mishnah does not elaborate on these issues. Thus, these Tannaitic commentaries should be studied in tandem with the Mishnah and Tosefta in order to gain a balanced opinion of rabbinic thought in the earliest Christian centuries.

The Babylonian Talmud, the *"Bavli,"* is the major commentary on the Mishnah. It was produced by Rabbis living in Babylonia from ca. 200–700 CE. It is a passage-by-passage commentary on the Mishnah. Comments from early sages (before 200 CE), called Tannaim, are followed by statements from later sages, called Amoraim, who comment both on the Mishnah and on the statements of the rabbis who preceded them. The general tenor of the document is legal, *"halakha,"* although it does include *"aggada,"* that is, non-legal material, including wise sayings, homilies, anecdotes, and even folklore. During the same time, but redacted sometime in the fifth century, the sages of Palestine produced the Palestinian or Jerusalem Talmud, *"Yerushalmi,"* another extensive commentary on the Mishnah. The Babylonian Talmud has received greater attention since it has been traditionally regarded as the more authoritative of the two. The Talmuds are cited in this book by b. (*Bavli*) or y. (*Yerushalmi*) followed by the appropriate tractate name.

Abot de-Rabbi Nathan is an aggadic text, a commentary to *Pirke Abot*, "Sayings of the Fathers," an ethical tractate of the Mishnah. It has been found in two versions which I will indicate as either *ARN*a or *ARN*b.

There are several other rabbinic works which discuss holiness in varying degrees and enhance our understanding of the concept. The following two stem from the fourth to fifth centuries CE in Palestine and are arranged as commentaries to the biblical text. The first is *Genesis Rabbah (Gen. R.)*, a collection of rabbinic comments on select verses from the book of Genesis. The second commentary, *Leviticus Rabbah (Lev. R.)*, is more loosely connected to the text and indulges in longer, more homiletical passages on selected principles derived from various passages of Leviticus. Both of these texts are considered *midrash aggada* in contrast to the Tannaitic commentaries described above which, since they are more legal in character, are labelled *midrash halakha*.

Other rabbinic works of a later date, most of which are homiletical in nature, are referred to occasionally throughout this book and they are included in the list below. With few exceptions, they are thought to be written in Palestine. Most of these sources are very difficult to date, and the dates given below at best are estimates.[8] Nevertheless, the sages listed within the books, language styles, and the authors' knowledge of related sources and historical data help to catalog them.

Text	Date (approximate)
Mishnah (m.)	third century
Mekhilta de-Rabbi Ishmael (Mekh.)	third century
Sifra (Sifra)	third century
Sifrei Numbers (Sif. Num.)	third century
Sifrei Deuteronomy (Sif. Deut.)	third century
Abot de-Rabbi Nathan (ARN)	third century
Tosefta (t.)	third century
Genesis Rabbah (Gen. R.)	fourth to fifth centuries
Leviticus Rabbah (Lev. R.)	fourth to fifth centuries
Palestinian Talmud (y.)	fifth century
Lamentations Rabbah (Lam. R.)	fifth century
Mekhilta de-Rabbi Shimon ben Yohai (Mekh. ShY)	fifth century
Pesikta de-Rab Kahana (PRK)	sixth century
Tanhuma (Tanh.)	sixth century
Song of Songs Rabbah (Cant. R.)	sixth century
Babylonian Talmud (b.)	sixth to seventh centuries
Sifrei Zuta (Sif. Zut.)	unknown
Seder Eliyahu	eighth to ninth centuries
Pirke de-Rabbi Eliezer (PRE)	eighth to ninth centuries
Pesikta Rabbati (Pesikta R.)	ninth century
Exodus Rabbah (Ex. R.)	tenth century
Numbers Rabbah (Num. R.)	twelfth century
Deuteronomy Rabbah (Deut. R.)	unknown
Midrash ha-Gadol (Mid. ha-Gadol)	thirteenth century
Midrash Tehilim (Mid. Teh.)	fourteenth century

Two Targums, or rabbinic translations of Scripture, should be added to the list although their dates are unknown: Targum Onkelos and Targum Jonathan ben Uzziel (or Pseudo-Jonathan). These Targums contain some quite literal translations of the Bible into Aramaic, while other sections read more like midrash, filling in gaps of the text in typical, rabbinic ways.

By utilizing all of these rabbinic texts, one can gain a multifaceted perspective on holiness in rabbinic Judaism, one which is by-and-large complementary. To reduce the discussion simply to either the halakhic or the aggadic material is to distort the picture entirely.

1

THE HOLY ONE

> There is none holy as the Lord, for there is none besides you;
> neither is there any rock like our God.
>
> (1 Samuel 2:2)

Modern phenomenologists often refer to the transcendent side of holiness as the "Other."[1] The "Other" is defined as that which is out of the ordinary sphere of existence. Most people in the Graeco-Roman world would have agreed. The term *hieros* is the most frequent Greek term for "sacred." *Hieros* marks out items which are in some way associated with the gods, often owned by the gods.[2] The central element in the word is "outside the realm of the ordinary"; it usually refers as well to supernatural power.[3] Similarly, the Latin term, *sacer*, refers to places, objects and people that are distanced from everyday use, either because they are special to the gods or because they are cursed. *Sacer* does not refer to the gods themselves, but rather to items and transactions, e.g. prayer and sacrifices, that relate to the worship of the gods. The terms *hagios* (Gk.) and *sanctus* (Lat.) refer both to gods and people and signify veneration. One finds these terms in descriptions of the majesty of the gods.[4] Thus, the Greek and Latin terms support the argument that sanctity has a lot to do with "otherness."

The rabbinic "Other" is likewise described by the term "sacred" or "holy." In Hebrew this word is *qadosh*, literally, "separated," or "set aside." Throughout rabbinic literature of the early Christian centuries, the most frequent name for God is *Ha-Qodesh Barukh Hu* (Heb.), or in its original Aramaic form, *Qudsha Barikh Hu*. These titles for God literally mean, "Holiness, blessed be he," but are usually translated, "The Holy One, blessed be he."[5] The point is that holiness describes God more closely than any other designation. His very essence is holiness. One could say that holiness is God's

11

"innermost reality" to which all of His attributes are related.[6] "Holy" is another way of saying "God" in rabbinic Judaism.[7] Thus, the Rabbis would have agreed with their gentile neighbors that true holiness is outside of the ordinary realm and exhibits supernatural power. It is a "characteristic of ineffability possessed only by God."[8]

Nevertheless, this cross-cultural definition only partially satisfies the full rabbinic concept of holiness, exhibited most perfectly in the Holy One, blessed be he. As the Holy One, God is not only separated from all imperfection and weakness, but he is also "Other" because he embodies within Himself all goodness, including justice, mercy, and life itself.[9] Ethical goodness is an essential component of the rabbinic definition of holiness and marks it off as unique in the ancient world. The command to Israel to be holy as God is holy (Lev. 19:2) is not simply an instruction to be "other," nor is it a command to be mighty.

Other persons and items can partake of God's inherent holiness only by extension. That is, because of their association with or designation by the Holy One, other persons, animals, places, objects, and times can be called holy. Although they can never be inherently holy, they can mirror, albeit inadequately, the divine holiness in various ways. The numerous items designated "holy" in Scripture, for example, "holy mount," "holy tent," "holy persons," "holy prophet," "holy temple," "holy land," "holy children," are all holy only because of their relationship to God. They are holy in that they belong to the sphere of God's being or activity. The same is the case for the Sabbath, priesthood, and Israel; all are considered God's holy possession by his designation. As holy, these items are privileged and in some way experience or contain divine energy and supernatural power.

The New Testament inherited the concept and categories of holiness established in the Hebrew Bible. According to these writers, Jesus Christ, as divine, shares the inherent holiness of God. Christians derive their holy status from their relationship with Christ and strive to match the ideal he represents. Thus, it is important for a fair understanding of not only rabbinic Judaism, but also the Christian world surrounding it, to begin our discussion of holiness with a chapter which analyzes its divine source and primary components. Only then can we begin to understand holiness as it is reproduced by someone or something in the material world.

The holiness of God can be discussed in two ways. On the one hand, the Holy One is the omnipotent "Other" whose mighty energy is represented by fire. His holiness stands for his distinction from his creation, his limitless perfection and his sovereignty over the universe. On the other hand, God is absolutely and undeniably good. He is worshiped as holy in Israel because he is both supreme and good. This chapter examines these two complementary sides of God's holiness in rabbinic literature. References to holiness will be analyzed both contextually and linguistically. That is to say, in addition to word studies, the following examination of holiness will take seriously the contexts in which holiness appears in the texts.

HOLINESS AS CONSUMING FIRE

According to one side of the rabbinic definition of holiness, the Holy One is an exalted, powerful otherness that brings people to both admire and fear him. Fire, the most common symbol for God in Jewish literature, illustrates this supreme otherness well.[10] The divine *'Esh 'Okhelet*, "Consuming Fire" (literally, an "eating" or "devouring fire," Exod. 24:17; Deut. 5:22; see also Exod. 3:2; 19:18), is a powerful force which causes human beings to fear and worship. It creates the energy and fascination as well as the sense of the numinous and inviolability that make up one side of holiness.[11] One cannot dialog with fire and it is completely "other." The Holy One as fire is: (1) separated from normal, social relations, and discussion in the human realm; (2) absolutely perfect, pure, and fathomless; and (3) omnipotent.

The divine fire is linked directly to holiness on several occasions in Scripture. The divine fire enveloped the thornbush and also the mountain of Sinai making them holy (Exod. 19:18). Both the Tabernacle and the First Temple were consecrated, or made holy, by God's public manifestation by fire. On both occasions the divine fire consumed the inaugural sacrifices (Lev. 9:24; 1 Chron. 7:2–3; *Sifra Millu'im Shemini* 34; see also Philo, *Vit. Mos.* 2.154). Angels, which are sometimes designated "holy ones," *qedoshim*, are referred to by Isaiah as the "fiery ones," or *seraphim*. Their duty was to worship God with the words: "Holy, Holy, Holy, the LORD of hosts! His presence fills all the earth!" (Isa. 6:3). One of the fiery beings touched Isaiah's lips with a coal from the altar in order to purify him and make him a holy channel for God's prophetic word (Isa. 6:6).

Thus, fire is a good symbol of God's exalted, dangerous holiness. Fire separates pure from impure, creating a boundary which cannot be bridged. For that which can stand its heat, fire functions as purifier and perfecter. Fire is powerful, even uncontrollable; if unleashed it represents a dangerous threat which is respected by all. We now turn to these three aspects of holy "Consuming Fire": separation, perfection, and power.

Separation

The Hebrew term for "holy," *qadosh*, is often explained as "separated" or "set aside."[12] This is certainly the core of the rabbinic definition where it is often used to indicate separation and withdrawal from ordinary usage. In Leviticus, God commanded Israel more than once, "Be holy even as I the Lord your God am holy" (Lev. 11:44; 19:2; 20:26). The *Sifra* interprets this order to mean "As I am separated, so be ye separated" (*Sifra* 81a). Jacob Milgrom explains that God's holiness "is his quintessential nature . . . distinguishing him from all beings."[13] John Armstrong calls the fundamental element of holiness "divorce from ordinary human nature and ordinary life."[14] God is God and humanity is humanity and the separating boundary line is indelible (Ps. 8:5; 9:20; Isa. 31:3; Hos. 11:9; see also 1 Sam. 2:2).

The Greeks and Romans conceived of the realm of the gods as the living world of nature.[15] Rivers, stones, and trees were often considered sacred. According to the Rabbis, nature cannot produce what is holy.[16] Even in his manifestation as fire, it is not the fire but the Holy One above it which is worshiped. God, as Creator, is beyond nature, exalted and incomparable with anything in existence (Deut. 4:16ff.; Isa. 57:15). In fact, God is impossible to comprehend. The Rabbis often repeat God's words to Job: "Can you find out the deep things of God? Can you attain unto the purpose of the Almighty? It is high as heaven; what can you do? Deeper than the nether-world; what can you know?" (Job 11:7–8; y. *Ber.* 9:1; *Tanh. Qed.*15; *Mid. Teh.* 106.2; 139:1; *Yalkut* Job 906).[17]

Greeks and Romans often venerated human beings, both living and dead. Sometimes the dead could gain the adoration and veneration of the living, as is the case with hero/ancestor worship and with the cult of the emperor.[18] Caesar was deified after death. Augustus set the pattern for the future by proclaiming that he shared divinity with an official god, in his case, Apollo. Herodian (third century CE) reported: "It is the custom of the Romans to deify those of their emperors who die, leaving successors, and this rite they call *apotheosis*."[19]

The Rabbis objected to any blurring of the line between divinity and humanity. According to their interpretation of Exodus 6:1 and

7:1, Moses is warned against any aspiration to divinity, "Though I made you a god to Pharaoh, you must not become overbearing (and think yourself God); I am the Lord" (*Tanh.* 2, 13a). Pharaoh is a prototype of any Roman emperor, Jewish messiah, or anyone who claims to be divine. Even angels, although they are called "holy," are not to be supplicated: "Let no man in misfortune cry either unto Michael or Gabriel, but pray unto me [God], and I will answer him at once, as it is said 'Whosoever shall call on the name of the Lord shall be delivered' (Joel 2:32a)" (y. *Ber.* 13a; see also *Lev. R.* 24:8).

The name "Heaven" was common among Iranian religions denoting the highest deity who knew all things. Mithra is reported to be the god of heaven as is Ahura Mazda. The Graeco-Roman idea is that Zeus (Gk.) or Jupiter (Ro.) is god of the cosmos. The Rabbis too referred to God as "Heaven," as well as "Height of the World," "High One" and other lofty titles, but their emphasis was on the gulf that separated God's essence from that of human beings and the latter's absolute responsibility to the former (m. *Ab.* 1:3; 4:12; *Mekh. ba-Hodesh*, 5, 219; m. *Ber.* 2:2; t. *Sota* 14:4). More often than not the passages which refer to God as "Heaven" point to Israel's duty to accept the "yoke of the kingdom of Heaven."[20]

The use of "Heaven" to describe Zeus and other gods notwithstanding, the traditional Graeco-Roman pantheon was quite approachable by the common person. Anyone could consult the god at his oracle, and people often put messages in the god's statue. In fact, the Greek gods are seldom described as holy. Thus, it is no accident that the Jewish writers of the Septuagint, for the most part, ignored *hieros* as a designation for holy items. They use it as an adjective only twice: to describe temple vessels (Dan. 1:2), and military ram's horns (Jos. 6:8). Instead, they choose the term *hagios* which emphasizes the majesty of the deity and is rarely used in classical Greek.[2] By using *hagios* to refer to God's holiness, the writers of the Septuagint made an implicit distinction between the nature of the Jewish God and the gods of the pagan world.[22]

The Greek philosophers described God as an absolute, intellectual principle which is completely separate from the world. Terms they use to describe him include the "all-pervading energetic Mind," the "First Cause" of the universe, or simply "Being." Philo applies Greek thought to Judaism's one God: "God is sole and one [*hen*], not composite, a simple nature, while everyone of us, and of all other created things, is many [*polla*]." But for the Rabbis, the Holy One was not a unified abstraction but remained personal, that is, in a relationship with Israel (see below, "Holiness as Goodness").

He could never be the metaphysical "Absolute" or "Unknowable" of the Greek philosophers.

What is the nature of the Holy One's separation, according to the Rabbis? The Levitical command, "Be holy even as I the Lord your God am holy" occurs in two very different contexts (see Chapter 5). One occurrence concerns Israel's diet (Lev. 11:44; 20:26). By the very food she eats Israel is to be distinct from all other people. The other context reveals the reason: Leviticus 18–20 discuss sexual and social vices which are apparent among other nations but have no place among Israel who must rather imitate God's holiness. Here we learn that God's holiness has to do with inherent morality (Lev. 19:2ff.). Israel is enjoined to be separated from the nations of the world and their abominations (*Mekh.* 63a on Exod. 19:1), in particular, with regard to sexual immorality (*Sifra* 93b; *Num. R.* 9:7). Holiness then signifies utter withdrawal from what is morally evil.[23] As one separates from impurity and immorality, one emulates God himself, who by nature is distinguished from all other entities, and who is especially separated from evil.

Separation is a key element of Jesus' holiness according to the writer of Hebrews. Although Jesus lived as a human being, the writer emphasizes that he is also divine: "holy, blameless, undefiled, separate from sinners, and made higher than the heavens" (Heb. 7:26). Again, the moral aspect is prominent. Christians derive their holiness from their relationship with Christ who is their "sanctification" (1 Cor. 1:30). Like the Rabbis, the early Christians inherited much of their theology from the Hebrew Bible but, unlike them, considered Jesus divine and attributed to him the holiness of God.

The separation of the Holy One is closely related to his demand for exclusive worship. It is in this context that Gerhard von Rad argues that holiness is a type of jealousy.[24] Indeed, Joshua associates holiness with jealousy when he tells Israel, "You will not be able to serve the Lord because he is a holy God, a jealous God" (Josh. 24:19). The notion that God will not share Israel's devotion with any other deity is a fundamental premise in rabbinic Judaism. The *Shema* prayer ("Hear O Israel, the Lord our God is one") asserts that God is unique, alone, unchanging, the power of unity within all things. This verse from Deuteronomy (6:6) is recited in evening and morning prayers daily by the Rabbis and is attested in the Second Temple period (m. *Ber.* 1:3; Mark 12:29).

The Rabbis regarded idolatry as the quintessential enemy of holiness and often took drastic measures to curb its attraction. R.

Nahum b. Simlai was called holy because he never looked at the emperor's image on a coin (y. *AZ* 3:1, 42c). The Rabbis ruled that anyone who transgresses the command against idolatry "breaks off the yoke, annuls the covenant between God and Israel, and misrepresents the Torah" (*Mekh. de-Pisha* 5, Lauterbach, 37). One Rabbi said that the mere presence of idols in a city made it unfit to receive the word of God.[25]

The ultimate act of holiness is to lay down one's life rather than succumb to idolatry (b. *Ber.* 61b).[26] This rabbinic rejection of any other god to the point of martyrdom is referred to by the Rabbis as *qiddush ha-Shem*, that is, "the sanctification of the Name," or "the sanctification of God." How does one sanctify God? The Rabbis ask and answer this question by pointing out that the way a Jew lives will either cause others to acknowledge God's holiness or to denigrate it. Loyalty to the law in the face of public insult is one way of proclaiming God as the primary authority in a Jew's life. *Qiddush ha-Shem* is a public avowal that God has a claim on a Jew that the latter is willing to honor even though it cost him his life. Rejecting the law brings dishonor to God and misrepresents him in the world, thus bringing *hillul ha-Shem*, or "desecration of the Name."

The rebellion under Hadrian was met with a ban in Palestine on Judaism, and Jews were apparently asked in some cases to perform an idolatrous rite to prove their compliance. Many did not comply because of *qiddush ha-Shem* (*PRK*, Buber, 87a). The situation deteriorated to such a degree that the rabbinic council at Lod decided that only to avoid idolatry, various sexual sins, and homicide should a Jew give up his life. Nevertheless, some Rabbis continued to resist on all accounts (b. *San.* 74a; y. *San.* 21b; y. *Sheb.* 35a; see also b. *AZ* 27b).

Qiddush ha-Shem is also accomplished by oral proclamation. In the synagogue, the *Qaddish* or *Kaddish*, a special prayer of holiness, is publicly recited several times a day and is considered a corporate way of accomplishing *qiddush ha-Shem*.[27] A quorum of ten men was needed in order to recite the *Kaddish*, making it a formal service and public proclamation of fidelity to God. The *Kaddish* begins with the words, "Magnifed and sanctified [*yitgadel v'yitqadesh*] be his great Name in the world which he has created according to his will. And may he establish his kingdom during your life and during your days . . . ." The prayer that God's Name would be made holy, or sanctified, in the world is a request that his supremacy would be recognized by everyone. The *hitpa'el* verb form, *yitqadesh*, is translated in the passive voice but also as a jussive, "may it [God's name] be made holy." As a prayer to God, the *Kaddish* is a plea that God will cause himself to be made holy, that is, that he will bring the whole world to recognize his exclusive sovereignty. The same thought is expressed in the Lord's Prayer (Matt. 6:9ff.) where Jesus prays to the Father saying, "May your Name be hallowed . . . your kingdom come, your will be done on earth as it is in Heaven." The concept is Jewish.

Perfection

There is a perfection in God's holiness which adds to his aura as completely "other," than anything in the physical world. As fire tolerates no imperfection, so the divine holiness is perfect. It is not just separation from the natural world. Holiness denotes an ideal, a perfection which is beyond human grasp.

> In the text, "For he is a holy God" (Josh. 24:19), the adjective has a plural form, which the Rabbis interpret as follows, "He is holy with all kinds of holiness," i.e. He is the perfection of holiness (y. *Ber.* 13a). On the words, "Ye shall be holy" (Lev. 19:2) the comment is made: "It is possible to imagine that man can be as holy as God; therefore Scripture adds, 'for I am holy' – My holiness is higher than any degree of holiness you can reach."
>
> (*Lev. R.* 24:9; cf. Isa. 55:8–9)[28]

Thus, divine holiness is perfection itself.

God's holy perfection is mirrored, to some degree, in those people he designates to be holy. For example, the priests who officiate in the temple are, like the angels, sometimes called *qedoshim*, "holy ones," because they represent God and reflect his holiness so closely. As such, they must be without any blemish or physical imperfection in order to officiate in the sanctuary (Lev. 21:17–23). On account of holiness, the Dead Sea sectarians forbade Jews with defects to live in any part of the Temple city (11Q19 45:12–14). The Rabbis offer praise to God that holy men of impeccable quality were found to serve him, "Blessed be the Omnipresent that no disqualification was found in the seed of Aaron" (m. *Mid.* 5:4). Even the Nazirite, because he was devoted to God, had to be perfect. R. Judah says concerning Nazirites, "the Omnipresent did not permit any inadvertent error to be made by them" (t. *Ned.* 1:5).

Other holy items, e.g. sacrifices, were also unacceptable unless they were perfect (see Chapter 2). According to the Torah, holiness requires even various seeds and fabrics to remain perfect as to kind; they may not be mixed (Lev. 19:19; Deut. 22:9–11). Mary Douglas explains, "We can conclude that holiness is exemplified by completeness. Holiness requires that individuals should conform to the class to which they belong. And holiness requires that different classes of things shall not be confused."[29] God himself models this type of perfect separation for he is not a mixture of physical and metaphysical essences. Interestingly enough, even the use of the word, *qadosh*, in Leviticus illustrates the perfection principle. When it is spelled out in its full Hebrew form in the Massoretic text it refers to God and when it is spelled defectively, i.e. without the full "o" vowel, it refers to others.[30]

God's perfection is moral and it must be reflected in human, social relationships as well as in cultic ritual. Leviticus 19, which exhorts Israel to imitate God's holiness, clarifies this command in terms of ethical integrity. Individuals must be perfectly honest in their dealings with each other. Holiness is central to life and must be operative in both ritual and social contexts. Douglas concludes, "To be holy is to be whole, to be one; holiness is unity, integrity, perfection of the individual and of the kind."[31]

Josephus, an erstwhile Pharisee, used Greek thought to set forth the perfection of God compared to the limitations of human beings: "Uncreated and immutable to all eternity, in beauty surpassing all mortal thought, made known to us by his power, although the nature of his real being passes knowledge" (*Ag. Ap.* 2.17). He is

> perfect and blessed, self-sufficing and sufficing for all, he is the beginning, the middle and the end of all things. In his works and bounties he is plainly seen, indeed more manifest than aught else; but his form and magnitude surpass our powers of description. No materials, however costly, are fit to make an image of him; no art has skill to conceive and represent it. The like of him we have never seen, we do not imagine, and it is impious to conjecture.
>
> (*Ag. Ap.* 2.23)

Josephus contrasts this divine perfection with the immorality of the Homeric gods, which, he says, have been criticized by their own Greek poets and lawmakers for being a bad influence on society (*Ag. Ap.* 2.32–40).[32] Philo's description of God is even more Hellenistic.

For Philo, like the Greek philosophers, God is "pure being [*hen*] . . . abstract static Unity [*monas*] . . . pure immaterial intellect."[33] He is perfect because he is transcendent and above human comprehension.

In contrast to Greek philosophy, the Hebrew notion of holy perfection was not Platonic, i.e. the Rabbis did not ascribe perfection only to an ideal world that was incomprehensible, imageless and intangible. For the Rabbis, God has a will which translates into action in the imperfect, human sphere (see below, "Holiness as Goodness"). Isaiah's vision of the angels offering praise with the chant, "*Qadosh, qadosh, qadosh*," emphasized to him the contrast between divine holiness and his own imperfection (Isa. 6:5). Yet when his lips are purified with a coal of fire from the altar, he is sent to work among a very imperfect, calloused group of people.[34]

Several New Testament writers associate holiness with perfection. As the divine creator, Christ is able to perfect human souls: "It was fitting that he, for whom and by whom all things exist, in bringing many sons to glory, should make the pioneer of their salvation perfect through suffering. For he who makes holy and those who are made holy have all one origin" (Heb. 2:10–11). In this passage, bringing believers to "glory" is parallel to making their salvation "perfect" and causing them to become "holy." Another example of the identification of holiness and perfection is implicit in Matthew's version of the Levitical command, "Be ye holy, for I the Lord your God am holy" (Lev. 19:2). Matthew substitutes the word "perfect" for the word "holy": "Be ye therefore perfect, even as your Father which is in heaven is perfect" (Matt. 5:48; see also Matt. 19:21; Col. 1:28; Phil. 3:12). Paul equates holiness with perfection explicitly: "Since we have these promises, beloved, let us cleanse ourselves from every defilement of body and spirit, and make holiness perfect in the fear of God" (2 Cor. 7:1). The Church's perfection rests on her sinlessness. She is to be "without spot or wrinkle or any such thing, that she might be holy and without blemish" (Eph. 5:27).

Power

John Armstrong said, "Holiness is before all else a sovereign power, which has no need to consult other powers in man, or lowlier creatures and natural forms, and one located in a special centre. . . . Before such an apotheosis of holiness, the only proper human reaction is to shrink in awe and dread."[35] The Greeks and Romans connect holiness with power, probably more than with any other concept. The sacred power felt at a shrine or exhibited by a sacred oracle was expected. The gods were feared and worshiped for their power. Indeed Agamemnon sacrificed his daughter to Poseidon because of the god's sacred power.

The Rabbis too connected holiness and power. The title, "The Holy One, blessed be he," is an abbreviation for a much longer designation for God which connects the Supreme King with the Holy One: "The Supreme King of Kings, the Holy One, blessed be he" (e.g. m. *San.* 4:5; m. *Ab.* 3:1). In the same vein, the writer of 3 Maccabees associates God's holiness with his power: "Lord, Lord, king of the heavens and ruler of all the creation, holy among the holy, monarch, all-powerful ruler" (3 Macc. 2:2).

To say that God is holy is to claim that he is powerful. The angels' exaltation of God, "Holy, holy, holy!" continues with: "The LORD of Hosts! His presence fills all the earth!" (Isa. 6:3). This verse reveals that God's cosmic power is extolled by the praise of his holiness. The angels' praise is recited in the daily *Amidah*, the congregational prayer recited in the synagogue while standing. It is called the *Qedushah*, "Holiness," and forms the third section of the Prayer of Benedictions. The congregation is invited to affirm God's sovereignty by joining in on the "Holy, holy, holy."[36] The version of the trisagion of the heavenly creatures found in the New Testament also emphasizes God's might: "Holy, holy, holy, is the Lord God Almighty, who was and is to come!" (Rev. 4:8).

The holiness of God is a compelling force that brings people to fear and obey him. The High Holy Day liturgy celebrates God as *Qadosh ve-Nora'*, "Holy and Awesome [literally 'feared']." Similarly, the Jewish author of Revelation attests to God's terrifying holiness, "Who shall not fear thee, O Lord, and glorify thy name? For you alone are holy. All nations shall come and worship thee for thy judgements have been revealed" (Rev. 15:4).

Against the Greek notion that the divine spirit is immanent in nature, both the Rabbis and the early Christians claim that the breath of life is a holy force originating outside the physical world with the powerful God who created all things.[37] Israel's God was not the power of the sun or the storm. He was separate from these natural elements even though he could manifest himself in them. Thorkild Jacobsen compares Roman and Jewish concepts of holiness: if a Mesopotamian had heard God speak out of the burning bush, "He too would have seen and heard numinous power, but power of, not just in, the bush, power at the center of its being, the vital force causing it to be and making it thrive and flourish. He would have experienced the numinous as immanent."[38] Israel, by contrast, separated God from animism and dynamism. While pagans often tried to live in accordance with the order apparent in nature, Jews and Christians sought to understand the intentions of a Creator who was responsible for and controlled the entire universe.[39]

The Holy One is more than the transcendent, Perfect One, withdrawn from human nature and comprehension. He is a dangerous fire: "Who is able to stand before the Lord, the holy God?" (1 Sam. 6:20). The Psalmist warns of God's dangerous holiness, referring to him as "holy and awesome" (Ps. 111:9). The Psalmist exhorts the earth to tremble before the Holy One (Ps. 96:9). His holiness always brings him victory (Ps. 98:1). The earth should praise God by declaring: "Holy is he! Mighty king! (Ps. 99:3–5; 89:7). The Torah writer exclaims: "Who is like unto you, O Lord, among the gods? who is like you, glorious in holiness, fearful in praises, doing wonders?" (Exod. 15:11; see also Ps. 77:13 [Heb. 14]; Isa. 40:18–20, 25f.). The all-consuming fire burns when and where it pleases. Hosea declares God's powerful prerogatives: "I will not execute my fierce anger, I will not again destroy Ephraim; for I am God and not man, the Holy One in your midst, and I will not come to destroy" (Hos. 11:9). Holiness is not an automatic, predictable power. The Holy One has his own will and rationality and retains his prerogatives to do as he wishes.

Scripture warns Israel not to encounter God's holiness directly on account of its dangerous power. For example, the ark and vessels of the sanctuary , which are "holy of holies," are lethal to the encroacher. The men of Beth Shemesh are smitten for even looking at the ark of God. Israel is also forbidden to gaze directly upon the sacred vessels (Exod. 33:20; Num. 4:20; 18:3; Judg. 13:22; 1 Kings 19:13). Punishments for sacrilege, that is, violation of God's holiness, are severe; even if they are unintentional, the offender may be put to death. Holiness has been aptly defined as "that which is unapproachable except through divinely imposed restrictions."[40]

Fire is an appropriate representation of holiness mainly because of its power. People must keep their distance from the fire which signals and protects holy ground (Exod. 3:5; 19:12–13, 23; Josh. 5:15). Moses cannot come near the burning bush until he removes his shoes. The divine revelation at Mt. Sinai is a good example of God's holiness as a devouring fire. Both the people and the mountain had to be "made holy" before God could come among them (Exod. 19:10, 23). That is to say, they had to be separated: the people had to be separated from all impurity and the mountain had to be secured by boundaries from all trespassers. As fire consumed the mountain, the earth quaked, thunder and lightning ensued, and an ominous trumpet was sounded. Out of this terrifying situation came the voice of God to Israel. The people were so frightened that they fell backward and pleaded with Moses to find out what God required rather than to risk their lives further in the presence of God's overpowering, direct revelation to them (Exod. 20:15–18). According to the Rabbis, the smoking cloud which covered the mountain, and afterward rested upon the Tabernacle, was there to conceal God's holiness because of its dangerous power (b. *Yoma* 53a; see also t. *Yoma* 1:8; *Cant. R.* 3:7). Early Christians found in the account of Jesus' mountain transfiguration an event which paralleled the revelation at Mt. Sinai (Matt. 17:1–8).

God's holiness is revealed in his ability to fill the universe with his glory or to withdraw from it completely. Sometimes the titles "Holy One, blessed be he" and "The Omnipresent" (*Maqom*) are interchanged in rabbinic sources.[41] As quoted above, the celestial host praises God for his omnipresent holiness, "Holy, holy, holy is the Lord of Hosts; the whole earth is full of his glory" (Isa. 6:3). "At times the universe and its fullness are insufficient to contain the glory of God; at other times he speaks with man between the hairs of his head" (*Gen. R.* 4:4).

Paul claimed the power of God for Jesus and called it holiness: "The son of God with power according to the spirit of holiness" (Rom. 1:3–4; see also 1 Cor. 1:24). *Mi-pi-ha-Gevurah*, "from the mouth of the Almighty," is a phrase used to emphasize God's authority. The same phrase is used of Jesus by the Gospel writers (Mark 1:22; Matt. 26:64). The idea is that the person has direct power from Heaven. The crowd was astonished that Jesus taught "as one who speaks from the mouth of the *Gevurah* [the Almighty]."[42] Jesus himself is said to have prophesied that the people would see him sitting on the right hand of the *Gevurah* (Matt. 26:64).

It is a favorite pastime of the Rabbis to compare the omnipotence of the God of Israel with the limitations of pagan gods. Celestial bodies, for example sun and moon, and human heroes were often deified, but to the Rabbis these items were merely the servants of the true God. Consequently, they challenge the idolater: "Have you ever heard of the sun being ill and unable to dawn and function? To God's servants [e.g. the sun] we cannot ascribe ailments which induce weakness, so how can we ascribe such to Him?" In contrast to human warriors who, although usually victorious, had on occasion failed to defend a certain city, the Rabbis extol God's constancy, "With the Holy One, blessed be he, it is not so, 'behold,

the Lord's hand is not shortened that it cannot save' (Isa. 59:1)"
(*Lam. R.* 1:2, sec. 23).

Although the Greeks and Romans feared their gods as super-
naturally powerful and capable of fierce anger and destruction, they
did not claim that the gods were omnipotent. Rather, each of them
was ascribed its own sphere of dominion. Some were subject to
death and all were subject to Fate.[43] The Romans believed in many
spirits, or *numina*, "powers, involved in or presiding over a limited
but necessary operation, and having no existence apart from that
operation."[44] These powers might be associated with, for example,
ploughing, sowing, uprooting, pruning or watering. The worshiper
would approach whichever Roman god was in charge of the need he
desired. The Greeks and Romans had no commitment to a
particular belief system or even to any particular one of the gods.[45]
Multiple shrines could be attended by the same individual. Even
the mystery cults allowed continuing devotion to one or another of
the other cults. As described above, it was common belief that many
powers existed in the world.

The rabbinic claim that God was the sole power in the universe
(m. *Ber.* 4:2) was difficult to support in the face of the magical arts
prevalent in the Graeco-Roman world (see Chapter 6). It was
difficult to define the difference between miracles performed by holy
power and those performed by magic. Miracles were clearly part of
legitimate Israelite experience from the beginning, but magic was
categorically prohibited.

What is the difference between holy power and magical power?
The Rabbis handle the difficulty of magic in various ways. If it
heals, say R. Samuel and R. Abbahu, it is not superstition (y. *Shab.*
6:10, p. 8c; b. *Shab.* 67a). A similar view is attributed to God in
this next text: "'Sacrificed unto demons' (Deut. 32:17). If they had
worshiped the sun, moon, stars, and planets, which are needed by
the world and benefit the same, I would not mind it so much, but
they worship things like the demons which not only do not benefit
but do harm to the world" (*Sif. Deut.*, sec. 318). The point is that
there is a clear risk of danger in tampering with magic and
interacting with demons. The exorcisms performed by Jesus'
disciples were considered dangerous by the Rabbis for another
reason: they led people into idolatry (b. *San.* 107b; b. *Sota* 47b; see
also Just., *Dial.* 1,2, 85). Other Rabbis explained acts of exorcism
and miracles not ascribed to the God of Judaism by saying that God
ordained all miracles at creation. Thus, they are all within the
expected natural order, even if they are activated by illicit means.

The fight against magic and divination notwithstanding, there is ample evidence of magical practices among Jews, even among some of the Rabbis (m. *San.* 6:4; y. *Hag.* 2:2, 77d; y. *San.* 6:9, 23c). The difficulty is exemplified by Honi ha-Me'aggel, "the Circle-Maker." Honi was a great miracleworker, but his practice of drawing circles, stepping into them and praying for rain caused Simeon b. Shetah to say, "Were you not Honi ha-Me'aggel, I would pronounce a ban against you" (m. *Ta'anit* 3:8; cf. b. *Ber.* 6b). At all costs, the Rabbis continue to assert that there was no other omnipotent, holy power in the world but that of the Holy One.

The Rabbis faced a further dilemma with regard to holy power. If God was so mighty and so fearsome, why did the Jewish Temple lay in ruins? Why were Jews often persecuted and some of their greatest sages martyred? Indeed, they raised questions such as these among themselves: "Is it fitting to give the name 'Might' to One who sees the destruction of his house and remains silent . . . whose children are in chains – where is his might?" (y. *Ber.* 7:11c; see also b. *Yoma* 69b). The Rabbis answer their own question by saying that God's power remains even when he is silent (*Mekh. de-Shira* 8, p. 142). In fact, his restraint is a sign of power: "You are mighty in that you hear the blasphemy and reviling and insults of that wicked man [Titus] and remain silent" (*ARNb*, vii, marginal note by Tanna Abba Hanan). They declare, "This is the greatest manifestation of his might that he subdues his anger and shows long-suffering with the wicked; and it is likewise the manifestation of his terrible acts, without which how could a single nation be allowed to continue in existence?" (b. *Yoma* 69b). Thus, the Rabbis, who will not renege on one iota of God's omnipotence, suggest that his power is revealed in his ability to restrain himself from destroying the wicked.

The Name of God was considered especially holy and powerful.[46] It is referred to as *Shem ha-Qodesh*, "the Holy Name." Because of its holiness, pronunciation of the Tetragrammaton, i.e. the four letters which make up his personal name, YHWH, was banned except to the priests in the sanctuary.[47] "And when the priests and the people that stood in the Court heard the glorious and revered Name pronounced freely out of the mouth of the High Priest in holiness and purity, they knelt and prostrated themselves, falling on their faces, and exclaiming: Blessed be his glorious, sovereign Name for ever and ever" (b. *Yoma* 66a).[48] For a time using the name in greeting was advocated (m. *Ber.* 9:5), but it was discontinued out of reverence, and the Talmud says, "He who pronounces the name according to its letters" is excluded from the World To Come (b. *San.* 10:1; see also *PRK* 148a). The Rabbis are emphatic that any theurgic use of the Tetragrammaton was a capital crime. Ironically, since it became a secret, the Tetragrammaton came to be regarded as more powerful than ever and was illicitly used by many Jews and Gentiles in magical arts.[49]

Above we discussed the concept of *qiddush ha-Shem*, Israel's obligation to maintain the holiness of God's Name in the world. However, God often hallows His own Name. He does this by performing public miracles which judge the wicked and show mercy to the righteous (Ezek. 38:16). The Rabbis say: "Our fathers went down to Egypt only in order that the Holy One, blessed be he, might work miracles and do mighty works for the purpose of hallowing his holy Name in the world" (*Sif. Deut.*, sec. 306, Friedman 132b). The miracles at the Red Sea, Jordan River and the valley of the Arnon were all in order to hallow God's name by striking terror into the enemies of Israel (see *Mekh., Beshallah* 3 near the end). Daniel's preservation in the lions' den hallowed God's name because it forced the king to acknowledge the God of Israel (Dan. 6:26–28). Ezekiel promises that God's holiness will eventually be acknowledged worldwide, "So I will show my greatness and my holiness and make myself known in the eyes of many nations; then they will know that I am the LORD" (Ezek. 38:23; see also Zeph. 3:19; *Tanh. Noah*, sec. 19; Mic. 4:1–2; Zech. 14:9–20).

A variation of the *Kaddish*, discussed above, is the Sabbath prayer before the reading of the Torah. It attributes power to God's holy name and links his holiness with his role as supreme king and creator: "Magnified and hallowed . . . be the name of the King of Kings, the Holy One, blessed be he, in the worlds which he has created, this world and the world to come."[50] As noted above, the early Christian "Lord's Prayer" likewise affirms the holy power of God's Name (Matt. 9:6ff.).

The New Testament also records numerous praises of the power of Jesus' name (see Luke 24:47; John 14:13; 20:31; Acts 3:6, 16; 16:18). One of the most striking is found in Philippians 2:9–11 where Jesus has "a name which is above every name: That at the name of Jesus every knee should bow . . . and every tongue confess that Jesus Christ is Lord, to the glory of God the Father" (see also Rev. 19:16, "King of Kings and Lord of Lords"). The superiority of the name of Jesus which causes the world to acknowledge him as sovereign is an implicit sign of his holiness.

HOLINESS AS GOODNESS

It should be clear from the above that separation, perfection, and power are all part of divine holiness, according to the Rabbis of the early Christian centuries. However, holiness is not simply an exclusive, unapproachable fire which purifies or destroys everything in its path. The Hebrew God is always personal and as such has a clear will which further defines his holiness. One cannot define his essence simply as sheer power and transcendent perfection. Indeed, if holiness were wholly "other" and completely divorced from human affairs, it could not be experienced by human beings at all. Rather, there is an umbilical cord between the divine Creator and his human creations. "Though he was necessarily apart from his creatures by reason of his infinite majesty and absolute perfection, there was a firm and secure connecting link between them, because man had been created in his image."[51]

According to the Rabbis, holiness, the divine energy, is activated on behalf of the community. Holiness without an active goodness, or righteousness, is not holiness. In other words, God does not use his power like some kind of omnipotent tyrant, but always has in mind a "supremely good end."[52] Holy power supplies daily needs. This constant provision, the Rabbis say, is just as much a miracle as the opening of the Red Sea (*Gen. R.* 20:9). The Rabbis echo the sentiments of the Psalmist, "O, taste and see that the LORD is good; blessed is the man who trusts in him" (Ps. 34:8) by saying that even the Holy One's judgment is always true and just (*Mekh. Beshallah* 6, Friedman, 33a). For the Rabbis, God is holy, not just because he is superior, but because he is good. The "Holy (One)," by definition, is also the "Good (One)" (*PRK* 161a).

Jacob Milgrom says of God, "Holiness is the extension of his nature; it is the agency of his will."[53] In other words, holiness is not just a divine state of being but it is the extension of the divine nature into the human realm. Holiness, as the agency of the divine will, is neither a mere exhibition of power nor an abstract condition of "otherness" or "perfection," but a means to effect righteousness in the earth, and especially in Israel. "Extol ye him who rides upon the *Araboth*. . . . A father of the fatherless and a judge of the widows, is God in his holy habitation" (Ps. 68:4–5; b. *Meg.* 31a; see also y. *Ber.* 13a). Thus God's holiness is intrinsically linked to his will to do good, especially to those in need.

The link of holiness and good deeds in God's behavior is set forth as a model for Israel (see Chapter 5). Living in a time long after the destruction of the Temple, the Rabbis apply the holiness of the sanctuary to Israel's good deeds:

> Help and support are from Zion: "May he send you help from the sanctuary and give you support from Zion" (Ps. 20:2). "From the sanctuary": from the sanctifying power of deeds that are to your credit. "And give you support from Zion" (*siyyun*) (Ps. 20:2): on account of the distinction (*siyyun*) of the deeds that are to your credit. Said the Holy One, blessed be he, to Moses, Go, say to the children of Israel, My children, just as I am separate, so must you be separate. Just as I am holy, so must you be holy. "You shall be holy" (Lev. 19:2).
>
> (*Lev. R.* 24:4)[54]

Thus, by doing good deeds, Israel can reactualize the holiness of the destroyed Temple cult and fulfill the divine command to be holy. Holiness is simply not holiness without goodness. Israel's good deeds are holy, an extension of God's holiness into the human sphere. Idolatry, on the other hand, "holds back the coming of goodness into the world" (*Mekh.* on Exod. 20).[55] Disavowal of the Holy One not only brings his wrath (see above), but obstructs his goodness to humanity.

God's goodness, in a variety of forms, is undeniably the aspect of holiness most emphasized by the Rabbis. The daily prayer of the Rabbis illustrates the centrality of goodness in the mind of the Creator: "Through His goodness, He renews each day the work of creation."[56]

Holiness is not mere separation from the world but a separation or dedication to perform the divine will in the world. The divine pathos is not passion operating blindly as an uncontrollable fire, but it is directed by intentionality and will to benefit humanity. Abraham Heschel said about the divine pathos:

> It is also not a self-contained, self-centered state (reflexive concern) but a transitive concern. While the emotions of the gods of mythology are determined by their own interests and pleasures, the divine pathos is motivated by its regard for man's dignity, nobility, and the quest for human righteousness. It is, therefore, inextricably involved in human history and human affairs.[57]

In describing the divine pathos, Heschel has put his finger on the controlling motive and goal of holy power in rabbinic Judasim: the benefit of human beings.

The Greek philosophers did create a concept of the divine that was essentially good and refer to "the Good" as the divine principle (see pp. 188–90). In Philo's effort to translate Judaism into Greek terms he points to the centrality of goodness, a concept he knows will go over well with both Jews and Greeks: "If anyone were to ask me what was the cause of the creation of the world, having learned from Moses, I should answer that the goodness of the living God, being the most important of his graces, is in itself the cause" (Philo, "On the Changeableness of God," 23).[58]

Nevertheless, the Hellenistic "Good" was more of a condition than a personal force. For the Stoics, the divine reason "fixed" the universe at its inception, and then, like many philosophers themselves, remained detached from human affairs.[59] The Stoics' "Good" did not intervene among or empower the community, neither did it promise a future life.[60] The Stoic deity is often described as pure goodness or pure reason with little or no personalization. Epicurean philosophers regarded the gods as completely unconcerned with the world.[61]

Both the Rabbis and early Christians stress the universality of God's goodness: "For there is no distinction between Jew and Greek: for the same Lord is Lord of all, and is rich unto all that call upon him (Rom. 10:12)." Psalm 145:9, "God is good to all", is explained by the Rabbis: R. Levi says that God is good unto all, and He has mercy upon all who partake of his attributes (*Gen. R.* 33:3).

Divine presence

Paradoxically, the term, *Qadosh*, takes in both the transcendence, or separation, of God from his creatures as well as his undeniable nearness, or presence among them.[62] The rabbinic titles for God, "Heaven," *Shamayim*, and "Omnipresent," *Maqom* (literally "Place," see *PRE* 35, 82a), express God's exaltation and his nearness, respectively, but *Qadosh* refers to both. The prophet Isaiah is aware of this. On the one hand, he says, "Yea, thou hast lifted up thine eyes on high, even against the *Qadosh* of Israel!" (Isa. 37:23) and "The High and Lofty One, that inhabits eternity, whose name is *Qadosh*" (Isa. 57:15). On the other hand, the prophet says, "For great is the *Qadosh* of Israel in the midst of you" (Isa. 12:6). Thus, the Holy One is both the transcendent Other separated from his creation as well as the immanent Presence in the midst of Israel. Holiness is at the same time both near and far.

Some Rabbis explain the paradox by saying, "At times the universe and its fullness are insufficient to contain the glory of God's Divinity; at other times He speaks with man between the hairs of his head" (*Gen. R.* 4:4). However, in keeping with the general rabbinic tendency to emphasize God's nearness over his transcendence, other rabbis suggest: "The Holy One, blessed be he, appears to be afar off, but in reality there is nothing closer than he. . . . However high he be above His world, let a man but enter a synagogue, stand behind a pillar and pray in a whisper, and the Holy One, blessed be he, hearkens to his prayer. Can there be a God nearer than this, Who is close to his creatures as the mouth is to the ear?" (y. *Ber.* 13a; see also *Tanh. Naso*, 12, "Primarily the Divine Presence dwells among the inhabitants of the earth").

Thus, a good starting point in a discussion of holiness as goodness is the fact that although God is the exclusive "Other," he desires to bring holiness into the congregation of Israel. This is attested by the many times in Scripture where God visited his people. Each time, God's presence meant that the area had become holy and restrictions applied. Nevertheless, it also meant that God wanted to disclose himself to Israel. In being present among them, God did not change from his holy state, but rather his holiness penetrated into the community of Israel in an effort, not to hide but, to reveal himself to them.

Perfection, a quality of God's holiness discussed above, is apparent in his immanence as well as his transcendence. On Deuteronomy 4:7, "For what great nation is there that has God so nigh unto them as the Lord our God," the Rabbis comment, "The adjective 'nigh' is in the plural. This is explained as implying 'every kind of nearness,' which means nearness in the closest degree" (y. *Ber.* 13a). In fact, the Rabbis claim, "In every place where you find the imprint of men's feet there am I" (*Mekh.* on Exod. 17:6; 52b).

The Rabbis often reflect on God's presence within Israel as revealed holiness, or *kabod*, "glory, effulgence of light."[63] Glory, in a sense, is holiness made visible.[64] When Moses descended from the holy mountain, after having been in contact with God for forty days, his skin shone with God's glory (Exod. 34:29). People were afraid to look at him; it was as if God had become visible. The glory of the Lord at the temple dedication was evidence that the place was filled with the divine presence (2 Chron. 5:14). Glory was also visible as the cloud over the tabernacle which guided the Israelites' journey in the wilderness. This glory, according to the Psalmist, is the same glory which is above the heavens and the earth, but God has made it visible to human eyes (Ps. 148:13; see also Hab. 3:3).[65] In Isaiah's vision, the meaning of the angels' "Holy, holy, holy" was that the whole earth was full of God's glory (*kabod*) (Isa. 6:3). Glory then is a visible manifestation of holiness.

The revelation of holiness is always veiled. God cannot be fully manifested because he would incinerate the community altogether. The Rabbis point out that if the brilliance of the sun blinds our eyes, how can we expect to apprehend the glory of God (b. *Hul.* 59b; see also; *Mid. Teh.* to Ps. 103:1; *Lev. R.* 4:3). He hid Moses in a cave to shield him from the full sight of the divine glory. Holiness is necessarily elusive. It cannot be captured or manipulated. God lives in the thick darkness of the Holy of Holies (1 Kings 8:12–13; Exod. 20:21); he must be hidden, especially when he is near.[66]

The Rabbis consider viewing God's glory like viewing his periphery. They illustrate this by a story of a man who wanted to see the glory of the king. However, he swooned just looking at the curtain of precious stones spread out at the king's gate. He is told, "How much the more so had you entered the city and beheld the glory of the king!" (*Sif. Deut.*, 355).[67] Jesus is also covered with this glory while being transfigured, according to the Gospel writers, on a high mountain. At this event the voice of God endorses him in the presence of Moses and Elijah as a few disciples look on (Matt. 17:2; Mark 9:2).

A favorite term of the Rabbis for expressing God's holy presence is *Shekhinah*, or "dwelling," often rendered "Divine Presence." *Shekhinah* expresses God's holy nearness in a way that the Rabbis felt was too explicit to say directly of God.[68] Physical activities and terms when applied directly to God seemed also to ascribe to him the limitations of humans beings, thus other terms are often substituted. A good example is the claim that the *Shekhinah* was enslaved and went into exile with Israel (*Sif. Deut.* on 30:3). There is a reluctance to speak explicitly of God's features, for example his face shining upon someone.[69] R. Nathan explains the well-known blessing, "The Lord make his face to shine upon you" (Num. 6:25): "This means the brightness of the *Shekhinah* (*Sif. Num*, no. 41, p. 44). The concept of the *Shekhinah* provides a mechanism for expressing God's felt presence among Israel. The *Shekhinah* was the light or brightness of God's holiness that filled the Temple. It is called, "The light of the Holy One, blessed be he", and "the fire from on high" (*Num. R.* 15:6; *Lev. R.* 31:8). In fact, the *Shekhinah* is dazzling in its brightness (*Num. R.* 12:8). The Rabbis claim that the divine presence fills their homes (*Mekh. BaHodesh*, 2, Lauterbach, 220) just as it filled the Temple. It is also present wherever ten men gather for prayer (b. *Ber.* 6a; b. *San.* 39a). Thus, the term *Shekhinah* denotes the divine presence which holiness brought near to humanity.

The phrase *Ruakh ha-Qodesh*, "the Holy Spirit," too, denotes the holy presence of God as reflected in the parallelism of the psalmist, "Cast me not away from your presence; and take not your holy spirit from me" (Ps. 51:13). Sometimes *Ruakh ha-Qodesh* is interchanged with *Shekhinah* in rabbinic texts.[70] Like the *Shekhinah*, the Holy Spirit is described as fire or light[71]. For instance, the Holy Spirit on Phinehas' face "burned like a torch" (*Lev. R.* 1:1l; see also Acts 2:3). New Testament texts often claim that the Holy Spirit can reside not only with but within believers (see Rom. 8:9–11; John 14:17). Rabbinic literature often uses the term *Ru'akh ha-Qodesh* rather than *Shekhinah* when referring to the gift of prophecy and esoteric visions. The prophets of old received divine revelation by the agency of the Holy Spirit (see pp. 130–42 for the link between holiness and revelation).[72]

Kabod, *Shekhinah* and *Ru'akh ha-Qodesh* all describe the Holy One as near and good. God wants his holiness to be revealed to his people. When Moses asks to see God's glory, God agrees and lets his "goodness" pass by. Goodness and glory are used interchangeably in the passage (Exod. 33:19–22). In God's goodness, he manifests his glory among his people in order for them to know he is present and pleased. Likewise, the Rabbis claim that the fire of the lampstand in the Temple represented the *Shekhinah* and was a testimony not only to God's presence but also to his goodness toward Israel (b. *Shab.* 22b).

Scripture equates the Holy Spirit's presence with goodness: "I will pour my spirit upon your seed and my blessing upon your offspring" (Isa. 44:3). The Targum inserts the word "holy" in front of "spirit," making it clear that the divine holiness is the source of this blessing. Psalms 143:10 reads, "you are my God; your spirit is good; lead me into the land of uprightness" (see John 16:13; Rom. 8:14). The Targum translates the verse, "Your Holy Spirit shall lead me. . . ."[73] The Holy Spirit is equated with goodness as it enhances the life of Israel. The Rabbis do not refer overly much to the Holy Spirit and some say that the Holy Spirit has ceased. This is probably due to the spirit's strong personification as a separate divine being in early Christianity.[74] Nevertheless, the designation "Holy Spirit" in rabbinic literature is often simply a way of referring to God indirectly as a living presence and active goodness among Israel.[75] Similarly, early Christians associated goodness with the Holy Spirit: "How God anointed Jesus of Nazareth with the Holy Ghost and with power, who went about doing good and healing all that were oppressed of the devil, for God was with him" (Acts 10:38).

We have seen above that God's holy Name often indicates his great power in the world. At the same time, it signals divine goodness and access given to Israel. The term, *Shem ha-Qodesh*, or *ha-Shem*, became an accepted way of describing God's nearness. At the building of the Temple, God said he was placing his name on his dwelling place signifying that Israel, and even Gentiles, who came to his house could be assured of access to him there (2 Chron. 7:16). The "Name" emphasizes God's desire for humanity to reach him.[76] In fact, God promises to do good everywhere his name is honored: "In every place where I cause my Name to be remembered I will come unto you and will bless you" (Exod. 20:24; b. *Ber.* 6a). The element of power is certainly prominent here but that power is focused on acts of goodness.

Like *Shekhinah* and *Ru'akh ha-Qodesh*, "the Name" is a more personal way of referring to God's holy goodness without being guilty of irreverence or reducing God to human terms.[77] The Rabbis say that God's works for Israel are done not bodily but by his Name.[78] Thus, the use of the term *"Ha-Shem"* gave the Rabbis more lattitude in describing God's love of Israel and immanent presence among them without diminishing his power and the reverence due to him. Similarly, Jesus promises to do whatever his disciples ask in his name in order to bring glory to the Father (John 14:13).

Jesus' holiness is described in the New Testament as immanent presence, of which the incarnation is the supreme demonstration (see Phil. 2:6–7). He is referred to as "holy child" (Acts 4:27). At birth, he was given a name, Immanuel, which means, "God is with us." Similar to rabbinic assurances regarding the divine presence, Jesus promises his followers: "I am with you always," and "Where two or three are gathered in my name, I am there in the midst of them" (Matt. 18:20).

Although holiness is by definition antithetical to impurity (see below), the conviction that the Holy One was always present among Israel was so strong that some Rabbis claimed that he was present even in Israel's impurity: "So beloved is Israel that even though they may become impure, the Presence of God remains among them" (*Sif. Num.* on Num. 5:1–2). Texts are brought in support of this claim from Leviticus: God is the one "who dwells with them in the midst of their uncleanness" (Lev. 16:16) and who rebukes Israel's defilement of his sanctuary but nevertheless still allows it to remain among them (Lev. 15:31; *Sif. Num.* on Num. 5:1–4). The point is that holiness, according to the Rabbis, is more immanent among Israel than it is transcendent. Without diminishing its aspects of supremacy, perfection and power, the Rabbis insist that holiness is actually more apparent in God's goodness to his people.

Justice and mercy

Holiness is a force within the world which acts morally because it is an extension of God himself. Its inner law is the moral law; there is ethos inherent in the divine pathos.[79] The Rabbis notice that the biblical command, "Be holy because I, the LORD your God, am holy" (Lev. 19:2), precedes a list of mostly ethical obligations, from respecting one's parents (19:3) to paying employee wages on time (19:13). They conclude that holiness is intrinsically bound up with divine justice. For support they quote Isaiah and other biblical texts:

> "You shall be holy [for I the Lord your God am Holy]" (Lev. 19:2). "But the Lord of hosts is exalted in justice, [and the Holy God hows himself holy in righteousness]" (Isa. 5:16). It has been taught: Said R. Simeon b. Yohai, When is the name of the Holy One, blessed be he, magnified in his world? When he applies the attribute of justice to the wicked. And there are many verses of Scripture [that prove that point]. "Thus I shall magnify myself and sanctify myself and make myself known [in the eyes of many nations]" (Ezek. 38:23). "The Lord has made himself known, he has executed judgment" (Ps. 9:7).
>
> (*Lev. R.* 24:1)[80]

The point is that God's holiness is a powerful force for morality. His judgments are the natural outgrowth of the contact of holiness with evil. They are the divine signature that holiness is present, forcing the wicked to acknowledge him. In other words, God is declared holy in the world when he repays wickedness with judgment. The righteous praise him for his justice and the wicked come to realize that God is moral and will not let the guilty escape retribution. Holiness here has a strong moral character. Its power acts to preserve the righteous and punish the wicked. And, as the last line of the quote above makes clear, this includes the wicked among Israel as well as other nations. Holiness means to purge injustice no matter where it is found.

The Hebrew definition of holiness has a strong moral component in contrast to other religions in the Graeco-Roman world where sanctity centers primarily around proper rules of ritual purity. The Hebrew definition forges an unbreakable bond between ethics and holiness.[81] The Rabbis expect the Holy One to establish justice in the world. As Abraham said when challenging God's plan to destroy Sodom even though some righteous persons lived there, "Far be it from you! Shall not the judge of all the earth deal justly?" (Gen. 18:25). A holy God is expected to be fair.

What is God's justice? It is not "inexorable law." He is all wise and does not seek his own vindication or majesty but "the best interest of the individual, the people, the race, and the fulfilment of his great purpose in the universal reign of God."[82] According to the Rabbis, he constantly weighs each situation in terms of justice and mercy. The Holy One says, "If I create the world in my merciful character [alone], sins will abound; if in my just character [alone], how can the world endure? I will create it in both the just and the merciful character, and may it endure!" (*Gen. R.* 33:1; see also 39:6). Thus, God is never forced to exercise judgment or mercy. As the holy sovereign, he can be persuaded but not manipulated. Moses asks to be shown how God rules the world: "God answers, 'I will cause all my goodness to pass before you' (Exod. 33:19). "I am under no obligation to the creature at all; but I give to them gratuitously, as it is written 'I will be gracious to whom I will be gracious'" (*ibid.*) (*Tanh.*, ed. Buber, *Ethannan,* sec 3; see also *Mekh.* on Exod. 12:22b). Thus, no matter whether Holiness reveals himself in justice or mercy, he is always regarded as good.

The Rabbis had difficulty proving the justice of God when Jews were coming under severe persecution in the early Christian centuries from the Roman government and later from Christian emperors. Nevertheless, they were convinced that God was inherently good. The following is an attempt to harmonize the Torah with the reality of the persecution of righteous individuals: When God brings judgment on the world, "he does not distinguish between the righteous and the wicked; what is more – he begins with the righteous first. R. Joseph wept: Are the righteous as nothing? Abayyi said to him: They are the first for their own good; as it is said: 'That the righteous is taken away from the evil to come' (Isa. 57:1)" (b. *BQ* 60a). Nevertheless, the equation of justice and goodness was unshakeable. The Talmud states unequivocally, "All that the Merciful One does is for the Good" (b. *Ber.* 60b). Nahum Ish Gamzu, whose name means "this too is for the best," was known for his conviction that even trouble is somehow for the good (b. *San.* 108b). Paul expresses the same belief to the Roman church, "We know that in everything God works for good with those who love him, who are called according to his purpose" (Rom. 8:28).

One does not often equate holiness with mercy or love, but in rabbinic Hebrew, the term *hesed*, "grace, love, and kindness," can also imply holiness. Throughout the literature, *hasid*, which is from the same root as *hesed*, and *qadosh* are interchanged as synonyms. *Hasid* is usually translated "holy man." It has been suggested that the word in rabbinic texts means "beautiful soul" emphasizing the graciousness or beauty of holiness.[83] God's gracious love for Israel in the Song of Songs led R. Akiba to proclaim this book the "Holy of Holies of the Temple of Song."[84] The Rabbis claim that the various names of the Holy One describe his different attributes, but the most sacred, i.e. his personal name, the holy tetragrammaton, is equated with mercy, as it is said, "O YHWH, YHWH, God, merciful and gracious, slow to anger, abounding in kindness [*hesed*] and faithfulness" (Exod. 34:6; *Exod. R.* 3:6; *Tanh.*, *Shemot*, sec. 20).

In its aspect of mercy the power of holiness is not diminished in any way. It was noted that strength is required to exhibit mercy to the wicked. Thus, as one ancient writer said of God, "You have compassion upon all men because you can do all things and overlook the sins of men unto repentance" (Wis. Sol. 11:23). Paul too shares the belief that God's mercy is a sign of his power and that this should be appreciated not disparaged: "Do not despise the goodness of God for it is his goodness that leads you to repentance" (Rom. 2:4).

The humble and repentant can be assured of God's holy presence which grants mercy: "'Everyone that is proud in heart is an abomination to the Lord' (Prov. 16:5) – broken, he says: This is mine; as it is said: 'The Lord is nigh unto them that are of a broken heart' (Ps. 34:19)" (*Mid. ha-Gadol* on Gen. 38:1). Whoever is humble invites the *Shekhinah* to dwell on earth but the haughty bring about defilement and the departure of the *Shekhinah* (*Mekh.*, *ba-Hodesh*, 6).

Holiness is accomplished in the world by deeds of mercy. The concept of *qiddush ha-Shem*, "hallowing the Name," discussed above, is not only accomplished by the risk of one's life for the sake of honoring God. A Jew can also cause God's name to be acknowledged as holy by deeds of righteousness. God's name is hallowed by any special deed of mercy, as in this rabbinic story. A Gentile claimed Isaac was really Hagar's child, not Sarah's, and so God dried up the breasts of the pagan women. They kissed the dust at Sarah's feet and Abraham said to Sarah, "This is no time for modesty; sanctify the name of the Holy One, blessed be he, and sit in the market place and nurse their sons" (PRK 146b; *Gen. R.* 53:9).

On the other hand, R. Ishmael was rebuked by R. Akiba for the opposite action, desecrating God's Name. In judging a case involving both a gentile and a Jew, Ishmael was switching back and forth from Jewish to Roman law, whichever was more favorable to the Jewish contender (b. *BQ* 113a). Akiba's point is that this devious behavior brought shame on God's reputation and so caused a desecration of the Name, *hillul ha-Shem*. Likewise, "To rob a Gentile is worse than to rob an Israelite on account of *hillul ha-Shem*" (t. *BQ* 10:15). According to the Mishnah, *hillul ha-Shem* is worse than a crime requiring the death sentence. Neither repentance nor *Yom Kippur* can atone fully for it, but it also requires the day of death (m. *Ab.* 4:4).[85] Just as justice exhibits God's holiness, obstruction of justice desecrates it.

Thus, God is sanctified in the world through Israel (Isa. 43:3) when she acts in accordance with the Torah with respect to her gentile neighbors by both deeds of justice and deeds of mercy. The expectation was that gentiles would praise the people of Israel for their ethical conduct and good deeds, and recognize God's name as holy, a powerful force motivating his people to do good in the world. However, when Israel acts unethically, she desecrates God's Name bringing reproach upon him (b. *Yoma* 86a; *Mekh.*, *de-Shira*, 3, p. 128; see further, Chapter 5).

New Testament writers draw from Christianity's Jewish heritage in linking holiness and righteousness. Peter rebukes the Jews that they "denied the Holy and Righteous One" and chose Barrabas instead of Jesus to be released by Pilate (Acts 3:14). Here "holy" and "righteous" are closely identified. Holiness and justice are part of the same fabric of Revelation 15:4: "Who shall not fear and glorify your name, O Lord? For you alone are holy. All nations shall come and worship you, for thy judgments have been revealed." Like Isaiah (5:16), discussed above, the Revelator sees God's holiness manifested through his acts of justice.

Life

In some respects holiness is life itself. When God swears by his holiness (e.g. Amos 4:2), he is really swearing by his life.[86] Even in modern parlance, we often speak of "the sanctity of life." Is there really a link between holiness and life?

The place to begin the rabbinic discussion is in the priestly texts of the Bible, the base upon which rabbinic law is set. The command to be holy is more pronounced in these texts than in any other, and surprisingly, it is prominent in the food laws (see also pp. 169–73). The ultimate goal of Leviticus 11, a chapter devoted to clean and unclean animals and food, is Israel's holiness, and the chapter concludes: "For I the LORD am your God: you shall sanctify yourselves and be holy, for I am holy. You shall not make yourselves unclean through any swarming thing that moves upon the earth. For I the LORD am He who brought you up from the land of Egypt to be your God: you shall be holy, for I am holy. These are the instructions concerning animals, birds, all living creatures that move in water, and all creatures that swarm on earth, for distinguishing between the unclean and the clean, between the living things that may be eaten and the living things that may not be eaten."

The food laws are helpful to our discussion because they reveal what is incompatible with holiness. Leviticus 11 lists various animals which may not be eaten and emphasizes the impurity of carcasses. Is there any common thread in these laws which gives a clue to what is antithetic to holiness? It appears so. First, the eating of animal flesh is restricted to just a few kinds of animals, which could be raised for human consumption. All creatures permitted for food are non-carrion eaters (Lev. 11:1–19). Thus, causing death by taking innocent life is curtailed and those animals which feed on dead meat are forbidden for human consumption. Second, carcasses bring impurity to those who touch them. Carcasses found in food vessels will contaminate both food and container (Lev. 11:52–55). The Rabbis explain that a carcass is an animal that has not been slaughtered properly by humane rabbinic methods and from which the blood has not been drained (m. *Hul*. 2:4; see also 1:2; Lev. 17:11–13). The point is again a reverence for life and for blood which represents it (Lev. 17:11). Both principles reveal a strong emphasis on avoiding contact with death and animals which thrive on death, on the one hand, and respecting life, on the other.

The hypothesis that impurity and death are antonyms of holiness is corroborated by the rest of the impurities mentioned in Leviticus (Lev. 12–15). The impurity system is clearly trying to teach something implicit about holiness on a symbolic level; it is too selective to be a manual for disease. Rather, these laws regulate a number of impure conditions which point to the abhorrent but powerful force of death. The most impure and ritually contagious item in the system is the corpse itself. Next in line is the leper (a person affected with any of a variety of scale diseases), a visibly decaying individual. The other conditions revolve around the loss of life-giving fluids, semen and blood (see pp. 173–80 for further discussion).

Jacob Milgrom has done a fine study of the dynamics of this impurity system.[87] He looks at the possible stages between holiness and impurity in which an Israelite might find himself. There are four: *qadosh*, "holy;" *tahor*, "pure;" *hol*, "common;" *tame'*, "impure" (see Figure 1.1). The middle two stages are inactive, that is to say, they are simply states of being. *Hol* simply refers to a non-holy state, i.e. a layperson's condition as opposed to the priest. *Tahor* refers to the state of being free from any impurity. In contrast to these two middle states, the outer categories, "holy" and "impure" are both contagious forces which act upon those in common and/or pure conditions.

What is holy must be kept away on pain of death from what is impure. Contact between these two categories brings disastrous results. For example, anyone who eats a holy offering which has come into contact with impurity is to be cut off from Israel (Lev. 7:20). On the other hand, holy items can legitimately be reduced to a pure status, and pure items may become holy. Pure items may also legitimately become impure. For example, a person becomes impure when he buries his parents, certainly an honorable and necessary act.

Thus, Milgrom argues that the true antonyms in the biblical impurity system are those items designated "holy" and those which are "impure."[88] While in a sense "pure" and "impure" are opposite terms, "holy" and "impure" are more extreme antonyms since they are both antagonistic forces which stand at opposing poles of the entire system.

What do these categories and symbols suggest in terms of our definition of holiness? It should be clear from the foregoing pages that, according to the Rabbis, only God is inherently holy. Thus, he is the epitome of the first category, *Qadosh*. According to the above dynamics, the direct opposite of holiness in the system is impurity. In all of its forms, impurity represents death, therefore we can claim that holiness represents life. As God represents holiness, he is also antonymic to the forces of impurity, other gods and death itself. Reciprocally, divine holiness is equated with life at its finest. Is this equation, in fact, borne out by Scripture?

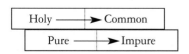

Figure 1.1   The dynamics of holiness and purity.
Source: Jacob Milgrom, *Leviticus 1–16*, Anchor Bible, Garden City, NY: Doubleday, 1991, 732.

The answer is, yes. In the second half of Leviticus, the call to holiness is again sounded, but this time the Israelites are told that the ethical life, girded by God's moral law, is the way to holiness (Lev. 19:2ff.). The two categories of holiness, fire and goodness, are treated in Leviticus. The first half presents God as holy represented by not only the firecloud above the tabernacle but also by the offerings by fire from the people. He is thus dangerous and unapproachable except through explicit, cultic means. However, the Holiness Code, comprising mostly Leviticus 17–26, "focuses exclusively on the beneficial aspects of divine holiness. It generates blessing and life; it is the antonym and ultimate conqueror of impurity, the symbol of death."[89] The first half of the book is largely about the way to the Holy One through the sacrificial cult, but the latter half exhorts Israel to emulate the divine holiness through a life of ethical goodness (see Lev. 19:2; 20:26). Transgression of any part of God's holy law was sin which, without repentance, brought death.

Now a full equation of the priestly teaching on holiness through its synonyms and antonyms begins to emerge:

Synonym	Antonym
Qadosh	*Tame'*
Holiness	Impurity
God	False gods
Life	Death
Obedience	Sin

Let us see if rabbinic literature supports these biblical equations. For the Rabbis, the polarity of God and false gods as well as their respective equation with life and death were fundamental principles. God is, of course, omnipotent. However, of the various other forces within the world, death is the strongest (b. *BB* 10a). All other gods were lifeless. "'The Lord is the true God; he is the living God and an everlasting king' (Jer. 10:10); but the gods of the idolaters are lifeless things. Shall we then forsake him who lives forever and worship dead objects?" (*Lev. R.* 6:6). There are many such references which emphasize God as living as opposed to the nonexistence of pagan gods (see b. *Ber.* 33a).[90] God is life itself: "Everything decays but You do not decay" (*Lev. R.* 19:2; see also b. *Meg.* 14a). Inherent holiness belongs only to God, who is the only source of life. He is referred to as the "fountain of life" already in Scripture (Ps. 36:9; see also Rev. 21:6). Indeed God breathes life into human beings at birth (Gen. 2:7). Likewise, Jesus was claimed by early Christians to be the "Resurrection and the Life" (John 11:25; see also 14:6; 2 Tim. 1:10; 1 John 5:12).

The antonymic dynamics between holiness and impurity is also supported in rabbinic literature. The Mishnah divides the biblical impurity system into several categories or degrees of impurity ranging from extreme impurity to extreme holiness. These categories in order of increasing holiness are charted in Figure 1.2. The most impure category is *Ab Abot ha-Tum'ah*, "Father of Fathers of Impurity" and the most holy items on earth are *Qodesh Qodashim*, "Holy of Holies." The more holy an item is, the more susceptible it is to impurity, even second or third hand, in some cases, and for sancta – even from four removes, or degrees, away. For example, persons who have touched a corpse, and so are Fathers of Impurity, will render the food they touch impure in the first degree; if the

---

Father of Fathers of Impurity
Ab Abot ha-Tum'ah
(Corpse only)
⇩
Father of Impurity
Ab Tum'ah
(Primary Items: Corpse-contaminated person, Leper, Person with
Sexual Flow, Carcass)
⇩
First Degree
(Susceptible Items: Persons, Food, Liquid, Earthenware, Rinsable Vessels)
⇩
Second Degree
(Susceptible Items: Food, Liquid,* Hands)
⇩
Third Degree
(Susceptible Items: *Terumah*=Priestly Agricultural Gifts)
⇩
Fourth Degree
(Susceptible Items: *Qodashim*=Sacrifices)
⇩
Holy of Holies
Qodesh Qodashim
(Also susceptible to fourth degree impurity)

---

*At two degrees away from the impurity bearer, liquid still receives the more intense first degree level of impurity. Refs.: m. Toh. 2:3–7; m. Zab. 5:1, 10; m. Yad. 3:1; b. BQ2b.

Figure 1.2 Rabbinic levels of impurity and holiness.

latter comes into contact with a priestly food gift the latter will receive third degree impurity (and become invalid). The entire system with its ramifications has been treated elsewhere.[91] Here it is sufficient to point out the overall spectrum of the system with its two opposing poles, impurity and holiness.

The Rabbis follow the biblical lead in associating death and sin (see Ezek. 3:20; 18:23, 30–32; 33:11, 19). The Talmud states clearly, "There is no death without sin" (b. *Shab.* 55a). Everyone has sinned and so everyone must eventually die (b. *San.* 101a; b. *Ber.* 28b).

Obedience to the law, however, associates the Jew with God and with life: "Therefore if a man keeps the law and does the will of his Father who is in heaven, he is like the creatures above, as it is written, 'I said ye are divine beings, and sons of the Most High, all of you'; but if he does not keep the law and do the will of his Father who is in heaven, he is like the creatures below, as it is written 'Surely like man ye shall die'" (Ps. 82:6–7; *Sif. Deut.*, sec. 306 on Deut. 32:2). The law is the only way to life. Scripture teaches, "You shall walk in all the way which the Lord your God has commanded you that you may live, and that it may go well with you" (Deut. 5:33; see also 4:1; 8:1; 30:15–20; Prov. 15:27; y. *Pe'a* 1, p. 15d; y. *Qid.* 61b).

Keeping the law puts a Jew on the side of holiness. The Rabbis interpret Numbers 15:40, ". . . Remember and do all my commandments and be holy unto your God" as follows:

> The matter is to be compared to a man drowning in water, to whom the shipmaster threw out a cord, saying unto him, Cling to this rope and do not let go of it; if you loosen your hold upon it, there is no life for you. Likewise the Holy One, blessed be he, said to Israel, "As long as you cling to my laws, you cleave unto the Lord your God which means life. Be holy for as long as you fulfill my commandments you are rendered holy, but if you neglect them, you will become profaned."
>
> (*Num. R.* 17:6; cf. John 6:63)

Israel is enjoined to live a life of holiness in imitation of God's holiness; in this way the forces of impurity and death are overcome.[92] Thus, Israel lives between the two poles of (1) holiness/life, i.e. a blessed, ordered and significant existence which leads to eternal bliss, and (2) evil/death, i.e. a cursed, chaotic and meaningless life which will end in destruction.[93] She is challenged to choose between obedience to God, which promises life, and rebellion against God, which leads to death (Deut. 30:15–20).

The divine breath, or Holy Spirit, is not just the giver of physical life but that which activates goodness among Israel. Scripture uses the phrase, "the living God" to refer to the Holy One in contexts which emphasize his presence among his people (e.g. Josh. 3:10) or his intervention on their behalf (Hos. 1:10 [Heb. 2:1]). This holy force also motivates Israel to do good. "The adjective 'holy' . . . suggests that God's spirit is a force that moves his people Israel, both individually and collectively, to obey the will of God as revealed through the Torah and the prophets."[94] Holiness is the additional strength needed by all life to implement God's goodness on earth. The spirit of the Holy One is the vital source which animates human beings to resist evil and do good.[95] Ezekiel promises spiritual aid to Israel in her efforts to please God, "And I will put my Spirit within you, and cause you to walk in my statutes, and ye shall keep my judgments, and do them" (Ezek. 36:27).

The Holy Spirit gives life according to the New Testament as well. Salvation comes "by the washing of regeneration, and renewing of the Holy Ghost" (Titus 3:5). The Holy Spirit raised Jesus from the dead and promises to do the same for all believers (Rom. 8:11; see Gal. 6:8). In John's gospel, Jesus explains, "It is the Spirit that gives life, the flesh is of no avail; the words that I have spoken to you are spirit and life" (John 6:63). Paul disparages justification through the law and claims that "the Spirit gives life" (2 Cor. 3:6).

The Rabbis recognize, however, that God's people did not always obtain "the good life" in this world, but that pain and persecution were often their fate. Their definition of real life is one that is blessed by God's approval and carries with it the promise of a future, better life in the hereafter.[96] The Talmud states: The souls of the righteous rest in peace; they shall be "bound up in the bundle of life" (b. *Shab.* 152b), and in another place, "The righteous whom the Holy One, blessed be he, will restore to life will never return to their dust" (b. *San.* 92a). Eternal life for the righteous is a strong tenet of both rabbinic Judaism and early Christianity (John 3:16).

The paradox of holiness continues. On the one hand, holiness is "other," withdrawn, exclusive, perfect, and powerful. And yet, many texts reveal another side to holiness, one which is active in the community and gives it life and quality. Isaiah states this paradox well: "For thus says the high and lofty One who inhabits eternity, whose name is Holy: I dwell in the high and holy place and also with him who is of a contrite and humble spirit, *lehahiyot*, 'to give life to,' the spirit of the humble and the heart of the contrite" (Isa. 57:15).

CONCLUSION

From the above discussion the rabbinic picture of divine holiness comes into relief out of its Graeco-Roman context. In contrast to the vague picture sketched by the Graeco-Roman terms for holiness, *qadosh* indicates both an awesome power as well as an infinite goodness. Someone said, "The primary quality of God according to Jewish teachings – ethical personalism – was not considered by the Greek writers. This idea of God's ethical will, which is beyond the universe and beyond nature and has absolute dominion over nature and over man, was far from the Greek model of thought."[97] This appears to be the case.

The Holy One is a Consuming Fire which, if unleashed, could easily incinerate the universe. The Holy One is a separate entity from his creation; he exhibits a perfection humanity cannot experience and his power is formidable. At the same time, the Holy Fire turns out to be a person with a clearly defined will bent on the welfare of his people. Goodness, in terms of a present, beneficent power which can exercise justice and mercy with wisdom and equity, is characteristic of holiness. The Holy One demonstrates ethos in his pathos. Morality stems from the divine model. Most of all, holiness guarantees life, both in this world and in the future. Early Christianity adopted the Jewish concept of divine holiness and applied it to the person of Jesus.

To conclude this analysis of the Holy One, we are left with a logical crux. On the one hand, God is a powerful fire, seemingly unapproachable since he transcends human categories and forms of discourse. On the other hand, he is passionately involved in the affairs of his people. The exalted "Other" is at the same time an active Goodness within the community. He is the giver of life, but he is also the most dangerous force in the world. The questions raised earlier still remain in tension. How is it possible for the Holy One to be both withdrawn from and active among the community? How can the powerful, moral "Other" tolerate contact with frail, often immoral humanity? As Joshua said, "[Israel] will not be able to serve the Lord because he is a holy God" (Josh. 24:19). How can God be active in any but a destructive manner? How can perfection co-exist with imperfection? How can the Devouring Fire be immanent without becoming explosive? The answers to these and other questions are taken up in detail in the chapters below.

2

THE HOLY HOUSE

Temples were considered bonds between heaven and earth in ancient cultures. Mount Olympus in Greece was considered to be both the meeting place of the gods and the meeting place of heaven and earth. The Mespotamians built their temples in the shape of the sacred mountain. Likewise, several rabbinic legends depict the Temple Mount as a sort of "cosmic capstone" that keeps the world together.[1] Mt. Sinai, where God spoke to Israel out of a holy fire, was a sacred meeting place between the two. Later, this fire hovered over and took up residence within the sanctuary, making God's presence a permanent, visible reality among the people. The frequent phrase from Leviticus, *Ohel Mo'ed*, "Tent of Meeting," indicates the purpose of the sanctuary: a meeting place between God and his people.[2] Moses went into the Tent to communicate with God, who would speak from between the two cherubim on the ark (Exod. 25:22).

At the dedication of the first Temple, Solomon acknowledges the absurdity of thinking that the new house can really contain the omnipresent God of all the earth (2 Chron. 6:18). Nevertheless, God affirms that he is pleased with the new, earthly house and will both reside and accept petitions there: "Now my eyes will be open and my ears attentive to the prayers from this place. And now I have chosen and consecrated this House that my Name be there forever. My eyes and my heart shall always be there" (2 Chron. 7:12–16). Baruch Levine explains, "God's power is produced in heaven, but it is distributed from the temple. . . . Although God never ceases to answer prayers from his heavenly abode, the literature of supplications seems to indicate that it was primarily the temple from whence came the divine assistance requested in prayer and sacrifice."[3] The opposite scenario, the removal of God's earthly dwelling-place, was also experienced by Israel. According to Ezekiel, the divine firecloud left its position between the cherubim of the Holy of Holies and consigned the place to ruin (Ezek. 10:4–5). Nevertheless, the prophets promise a future revival of holiness extending outward from the Temple and engulfing its surroundings (Ezek. 43:12; Isa. 27:13; Joel 2:1; Zech. 14:21).

The fiery holiness discussed above in Chapter 1 was formally mediated to Israel via a carefully prescribed system of holy space, personnel, and ritual. According to this system a certain area was set aside for God and his holy representatives, and well-defined rituals were established in order to allow the safe visitation of the Holy One among Israel. The divine holiness must be carefully mediated along strict guidelines, otherwise it will be fatal for the community. Anthropologists have described the holiness present at sanctuaries as a dangerous living entity with which human beings interfere at their own peril, a sort of electricity.[4] Nowhere in Scripture do we have such a concrete manifestation of what holiness is as in the cultic system of the Temple, and nowhere in ancient texts do we find such a detailed analysis of this cult as in rabbinic literature.

The Rabbis outline the Temple system in great detail. They classify levels of holiness in terms of space, persons, and rituals. Sacred personnel, furniture, food, and vessels, along with a host of various items donated to the sanctuary, form a category of *qodesh*, "holy things." These items can include: ornaments (necklaces, rings, bracelets, earrings), implements (golden cups, sacred vessels), dress (shirts, cloaks), houses, land, produce, nonofferable animals, building material, and money.[5] Some of these items, however, are *qodesh qodashim*, "Holy of Holies." All sancta function in necessary ways for access to the Holy One, but those items which are *qodesh qodashim* are the nearest to the Holy One and therefore the most potent. These classifications are brought into relief by well-clarified restrictions. Holiness at every level is defined by prohibitions.[6] The holier the item, the tighter the restrictions governing it. As we examine the hierarchy of holiness in the Temple system, other key principles about holiness will emerge.[7]

HOLY SPACE

To better understand the way in which God's holiness is mediated to Israel, we must analyze the hierarchy which exists in terms of restricted space. In the biblical accounts where God revealed himself, the place was marked as holy ground and protected by explicit restrictions. For example, when the Israelites prepared for the divine revelation at Mt. Sinai they were ordered to set a boundary for the mountain, to abstain from sexual intercourse, and to wash their clothes (Exod. 19:10–12). Similarly, Moses and Joshua were both ordered to remove their sandals when approached by heavenly visitors (Exod. 3:5; Josh. 5:15).

For the Greeks and Romans too, holy space was understood as restricted area. The Greek word *temenos* (literally, "an area cut off") refers to a marked-off area or enclosure which was considered sacred and included an item considered holy, e.g. a building, altar, grove, spring, or cave.[8] *Hieron* too marks off an area where divine power is felt but is a more general term and can be used of a sacred place, object, or ritual. The Latin word *templum* is similar in meaning to the Greek word *temenos* and originally indicated a marked-off open space for observing the sky and making predictions.[9] Some Graeco-Roman temples were open to everyone while others were restricted by gender or social status.

The Mishnah outlines ten gradations of holy area and the defining restrictions (m. *Kel.* 1:6–9) (Table 2.1). At the most holy level is the Holy of Holies, *qodesh qodashim*, the room in the sanctuary which is God's own. He alone is allowed to enter this room, except for an annual visit from his most holy representative, the high priest. Similarly, Graeco-Roman temples housed the god's statue in the *naos* (Gk., sanctuary, or *cella*, a special room in the *naos*) or *aedes* (Lat.) while the worshipers paid homage outside. At the lowest level of holiness is the entire land of Israel, which is still holy, *qodesh*, separated from all other lands by divine designation (see Chapter 3).

Table 2.1 Ten degrees of holiness according to the Mishnah

Area	Restrictions/qualifications for Entry
Holy of Holies	Only the high priest on the Day of Atonement
Sanctuary	Only officiating, purified priests
Area between Porch and Altar	Only unblemished, properly groomed priests
Court of Israel	Only purified, Jewish men
Court of Women	No partially purified persons
Rampart	No Gentiles or corpse-contaminated persons
Temple Mount	No menstruant, parturient, or person with a flux
Jerusalem	Lesser holy offerings and second tithe are eaten within
Walled Cities	No lepers or corpses
Land of Israel	Produces holy agricultural gifts

Sources: m. *Kel.* 1:6–9; see also t. *Kel. BQ* 1:6–8; *Sif. Zuta* on Num. 5:2.

The Jewish sanctuary complex in Jerusalem in the late second Temple period was magnificent. The Rabbis unequivocally state, "No one has seen a truly beautiful building unless he has seen the Temple" (b. *Suk.* 51b). One Jew described the "wonder" and "holy quality" of the sight inspired the spectator, "so as to make him think that he has come close to another man from outside the world" (Arist. 9). Josephus says the building was covered with plates of gold which reflected the sun and fairly blinded the observer (*War* 5:222–223).

The complete compound, which Herod built on the Temple Mount, including the Court of the Gentiles and the huge retaining walls below it covered an area well over 172,000 square yards, creating the largest site of its kind in the Graeco-Roman world (Figures 2.1, 2.2). For comparison, "The entire holy area was twice as large as the monumental Forum Romanum built by Trajan, and three and a half times more extensive than the combined temples of Jupiter and Astarte-Venus at Baalbek."[10] Remains of these retaining walls, which originally towered well over 80 feet and sunk down over 50 feet below street level, can be seen in Jerusalem today.[11] Some of these stones are over 40 feet long and weigh over 100 tons. To guard the holiness of the site, these stones could not be hewn on the Temple Mount itself but had to be hewn outside and carried in (*Mekh.* on Exod. 11, p. 288; b. *Sota.* 48b).

Holiness in Israel in Temple times then is channeled from the Holy One to the holy people at the particular site of the sanctuary. Nevertheless, this does not mean all had equal access. The site contains a labyrinth of rooms and courts which mark off areas of greater and lesser holiness and thus various levels of access to the Holy One. Clues to the hierarchy of the Temple complex lay in the personnel admitted to each area and the materials of the furniture and utensils used in it.

The Sanctuary proper housed two rooms: the Holy of Holies and the Holy Place. The former was the private room of the Holy One. No one could enter it except the high priest and he only one time annually to procure atonement for Israel by a special blood ritual and prayer. The Holy of Holies of the first Temple housed the holy ark of the covenant which contained the law, but the ark was missing from the second Temple. The Holy Place could be entered only by the officiating priests. Unlike the objects in the Temple courts, all of the furniture and utensils inside the sanctuary were *qodesh qodashim*, most holy, and made with gold (Exod. 30:26–29).

The rituals performed inside the sanctuary proper illustrate various truths about holiness in Israel. "Most holy," fragrant incense

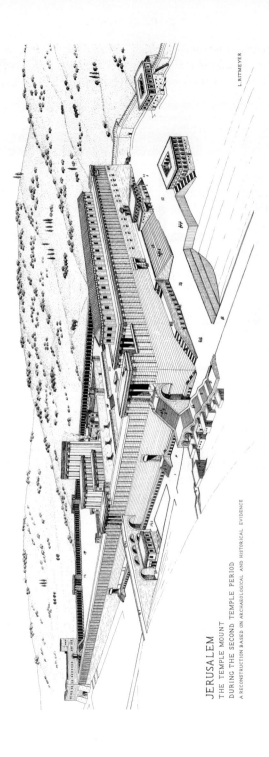

JERUSALEM
THE TEMPLE MOUNT
DURING THE SECOND TEMPLE PERIOD
A RECONSTRUCTION BASED ON ARCHAEOLOGICAL AND HISTORICAL EVIDENCE

L. RITMEYER

Figure 2.1 Jerusalem, The Temple Mount during the Second Temple period.
Source: A reconstruction by Dr Leen Ritmeyer.

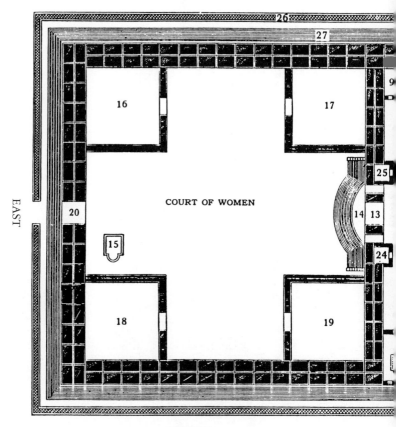

SCALE IN CUBITS
1 cubit app. 18 inches

Figure 2.2 Ground plan of the sanctuary (Temple and courts) according to
Maimonides.

1. Ark
2. Candlestick
3. Table
4. Altar of Incense
5. House of the Hearth
6. Chamber of Hewn Stone
7. Chamber of the Bowl
8. Wood Chamber
9. Salt Chamber
10. Parwa Chamber

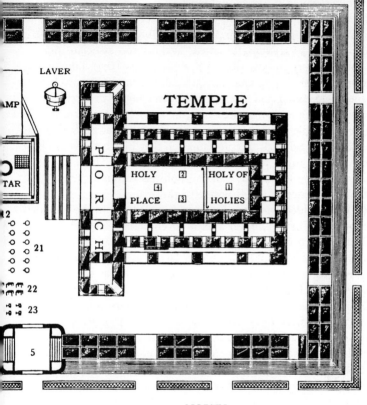

SOUTH

NORTH

EAST

TEMPLE

LAVER

HOLY PLACE [2] [4] [3]

HOLY OF HOLIES [1]

P O R C H

21

22

23

5

Source: Adapted from a drawing in *Tiferet Israel*, a commentary to Mishnah Middot (Vilna: ROM Press, 1937).

11. Rinsing Chamber
12. "North side"
13. Gate of Nicanor
14. Fifteen Steps to the Temple Court
15. Chamber of the Law Court (not mentioned in the text)
16. Chamber of the Nazirites
17. Chamber of the House of Oil
18. Chamber of the Woodshed
19. Chamber of the Lepers
20. East Gate to the Court of Women
21. Rings of the Slaughtering Place
22. Tables of the Slaughtering Place
23. Place of Flaying
24. Chamber of Vestments
25. Chamber of Baked Cakes
26. Latticed Railing
27. Rampart

was offered twice daily on the gold-plated altar (b. *Ker.* 6b; b. *Zeb.* 59a; b. *Men.* 26b). No other type of incense was allowed on pain of flogging (Exod. 30:34–35). This incense could not be used for any function other than the cult (Exod. 30:37). What is most holy is completely devoted to the Holy One.

The Rabbis often compare studying the Torah and prayer to offering incense up to God (b. *Men.* 110a; *Targ. Jon.* on Exod. 40:5; see also Ps. 141:2). New Testament authors too associate prayers with the sanctuary incense (Rev. 5:8; 8:3–4; Acts 10:4). Like prayer, the offering of incense to God is relational; the smoke rises to him as human thanksgiving and the priestly offerer hopes to receive some divine wisdom in exchange (see Philo, *Sp. Laws* 1:171). According to Luke, it was while offering incense in the Temple that Zechariah was visited by an angel with the proclamation that Elizabeth would bear a son who was to be named John (Luke 1:9–23). Thus, from the incense ritual we learn that realizing holiness through the cult is a habitual experience and well-protected process.

The holy, golden lampstand gave perpetual light in the window-less sanctuary. The design was a set of seven branches which support small bowls into which oil was poured. The fire had to be tended regularly so that it would not go out. Hecateus of Abdera says that the eternal lights are never extinguished; service was by night and day (*Ag. Ap.* 1.199). This is confirmed by the Rabbis who under-stood that at least one lamp of the seven had to burn continually (m. *Tam.* 3:9; 6:1; *Sifra Emor. par.* 13:7, *Sif. Num.* 59). Josephus says three lamps burned by day and seven by night (*Ant.* 3:199). The principle is clear: in order for the presence of God to remain in his house, the holy fire must be tended. The continued presence of divine holiness requires human maintenance.

As discussed in Chapter 1, holiness is about divine goodness as well as divine supremacy. The light of the lampstand as well as the holy Bread of Presence (the weekly loaves for the officiating priests) illustrate the divine goodness which is essential to holiness (Exod. 25:23–24; b. *Men.* 97a). Every Sabbath the bread from the previous Sabbath was taken outside and divided between the high priest and the two divisions (incoming and outgoing), and fresh bread was laid out. Both the holy bread and the holy light demon-strate the beneficial side of holiness. They provided nourishment and illumination for holy men on duty. Early Christians liked to use these terms, "light" and "bread," to refer to Christ (John 6:35; 8:12).

The Court of the Priests, which surrounded the Sanctuary, was of a higher grade of holiness than all of the other courts. Along with the sanctuary, it was called the "Camp of the Divine Presence" (m. *Kel.* 1:9; *Sif. Zuta* on Num. 5:2). Laity and disqualified priests had no access to it. (t. *Kel. BQ* 1:6) and defilement of it brought more severe consequences to the offender than defilement of the other courts (m. *Erub.* 10:15). The *hoi polloi* were likewise restricted from the temples of the gods in Greece and Rome, but not always. On occasion people were allowed to come into Graeco-Roman sanctuaries and even to place petitions in their statues.[12]

Holiness is mediated to Israel via animal sacrifices (see below). The Court of the Priests is devoted to this activity. It included areas for slaughtering, flaying, and rinsing the offerings. The most important item in the Court of the Priests was the stone altar. Approximately 36 feet square at its top and, including its horns, 15 feet high, this altar was considered *qodesh qodashim* (m. *Mid.* 3:1; *Ant.* 8:88; Exod. 27:1; but see also *War* 5:225, 75 feet square by 22 and a half feet high). Reflecting its holy character, its stones were perfect, taken from virgin soil and untouched by iron tools (m. *Mid.* 3:4). Priests ascended the altar via a stone ramp since it was considered disrespectful for them to climb altar stairs and thus reveal their legs (m. *Tam.* 1:4; m. *Yoma* 2:1–2; Exod. 20:26). Similarly, at Greek temples worship took place outdoors at an altar near the *naos*.

The altar's fire is holy. What makes it so? According to Leviticus, the fire of the first altar came from Heaven and miraculously consumed a host of animals laid upon it (Lev. 9; so also at the First Temple's dedication, 2 Chron. 7:2–3). The Rabbis explain that because the altar fire is of divine origin it must be perpetuated as holy fire (*Sifra Nedaba* 5:10). Fire from any other source was illegitimate for sacred use, and brought severe repercussions from God (Lev. 10:1ff.; see *Sifra Mil. Shem.* 22). Even the space over the altar, where the smoke ascends to God, was regarded as holy as the altar itself (b. *Zeb.* 83b; 87b). If an inappropriate or unclean offering was accidentally placed on the altar, the fire was so powerful that it incinerated the impurity and sanctified the item. What was placed on the altar fire, if damaged, could not be taken down again (unless it was a completely inappropriate item), because it had become holy (m. *Zeb.* 9:1; see Exod. 29:37). The process of holiness is dynamic, almost chemical in that the very nature of the offering is transformed by contact with holy power.

Approaching sancta was dangerous; unworthy encroachers risked their lives (Exod. 19:13; Lev. 10:1–5). Items which had been in contact with the altar could be dangerous to those who handled them (Exod. 19:13; Lev. 10:1–5). An unclean person who ate any of the sacred offerings was subject to *karet* (Lev. 7:20). According to the Rabbis, the term *karet* means death by divine agency, no descendants in this world and/or no life in the next.[13] The foreigner who approaches the altar unworthily, however, *yumat*, "will die" (by human agency). The Rabbis make every effort to alleviate the potential danger of this system. Desecration of *qodesh qodashim* is unforgivable, but unintentional desecration of *qodesh* is pardonable (Lev. 22:14).

Altar vessels had to be perfect and new, never used before for any common purpose. Like the most holy incense, once used in the Temple Service, the vessels could never be used in any other manner. Even the prohibited firepans of the evil Levites of Numbers 16–17 became holy by being in God's presence and could never again enter the profane sphere; they were hammered into plating for the altar. Their original consecration for God's service was irreversible, and they could not be used for ordinary purposes.[14] Holiness is meant to be irrevocable.

Holiness requires purity. In the Court of the Priests stood the sacred laver, a basin of brass in which priests washed before and after officiating or handling sancta. The laver rested on twelve huge lions and was emptied and refilled daily by a clever piece of machinery which lowered it into a pool or fountain of waters called the "Sea" (m. *Yoma* 3:10). Apparently, twelve priests could wash at the Laver at the same time. Both rabbinic and early Christian writers often use the purity of the cult to symbolize the moral purity required for the acquisition of holiness by each member of Israel (see Chapter 5)

Holiness and impurity are diametrically opposed. Impurity had to be kept away from the sanctuary at all costs (see the graded system outlined in Table 2.1). Underneath the Temple Mount, arched chambers were built to serve as a receptacle for ritual impurity. A corridor leading to the Chamber of Immersion ran under the length of the Sanctuary; a fire and toilet room were also found there. Persons impure with corpse or other impurities (e.g. sexual intercourse, menstruation) were forbidden to enter the Temple compound. A person could be extirpated from Israel by entering the sanctuary courts while impure. According to the Rabbis, defilement of the sanctuary was the uppermost concern in the late second Temple:

> More grievous is imparting pollution to the sanctuary and
> its sancta than all other transgressions in the Torah. All
> other transgressions that are listed in the Torah are atoned

for with a single goat, but imparting pollution to the sanctuary and its sancta is atoned for through 32 goats (Lev. 23:19; Num. 28–29). All other transgressions in the Torah are atoned for one time in the year (Day of Atonement), but imparting pollution to the sanctuary and its sancta is atoned for every month (Num. 28:15), as it is written: "Surely because you have polluted my sanctuary with all your detestable things and with all your abominations, therefore I will cut you down; my eye will not spare and I will have no pity" (Ezek. 5:11). While grievous were the detestable things and abominations that you did, more grievous than all of them was imparting impurity to the sanctuary.

(t. *Sebu.* 1:3; see also 2 Chron. 23:19; Num. 28:13).[15]

To ensure the purity of the Temple a complex system of winding tunnels and channels to nearby reservoirs was constructed. Water had to be readily available for the use of the priests for rinsing sacrifices, hands, feet, and floors. On the occasions of the pilgrimage festivals, the large number of people in Jerusalem required an enormous amount of water for purification and drinking. Already in the early centuries BCE, Aristeas comments on the "endless supply of water" from "marvelous and indescribable reservoirs underground" for five *stades* around the Temple foundation (Arist., 89). In the Herodian period, a series of aqueducts were constructed in order to bring additional water into Jerusalem The water from Solomon's Pools, southwest of Bethlehem, and the springs surrounding them were led 21 kilometers along the Lower Aqueduct into the city and then directly onto the Temple Mount via Wilson's Arch, supplying the Temple's extensive cistern system.

Ritual purity is necessary to approach a sacred site throughout the Graeco-Roman world. The impurity resulting from birth, death, disease, or sexual intercourse had to be kept away from the divine realm. Herodotus reports, "Birth, sexual intercourse, and death were not allowed in sanctuaries."[16] Even certain clothes, foods, weapons, or types of metal might restrict access to a sanctuary. In Rome, the celebrant had to purify at least his hands and feet and wear clean clothes.[17] All Greeks were expected to know what was sacred and the rules involved. People could not enter the *agora* at Athens unless they had been symbolically purified at the lustral basins provided at the entrances.[18] Pollution could prevent one from participating in political life since it prohibited entry into the *agora*. Sometimes local rules regarding sacred areas were recorded on inscriptions.

Figure 2.3 Arch of Titus, Rome, depicting captured Jews with the Temple Menorah.
Source: Bill Harrington.

At a lesser degree of holiness than the Court of the Priests, the Court of Israel was for Jewish men only, and women were further restricted to the Court of the Women. While restricted from active participation in the service, women were nevertheless allowed to observe it from a distance. A balcony was built above the Court of the Women so that women could observe the full service from above without mingling with the men (m. *Mid.* 2:5). Large Graeco-Roman sanctuaries sometimes had various buildings attached for observing areas, dining facilities and storage rooms. Many were much more accommodating than the Jewish Temple by providing *stoas* for relaxation, overnight facilities, a theater, and even a stadium.[19] Holiness in the Jewish version, while it included times of fellowship (see Chapter 3), was much less entertaining.

The *hel*, a rampart 15 feet wide, encircled all three sanctuary courts which were further surrounded and protected by the *soreg*, a stone latticed railing about 5 feet high (m. *Mid.* 2:3; see *War* 5:193). When Antiochus III conquered Palestine (ca. 198 BCE), he issued the following edict: "It is unlawful for a non-Jew to enter the enclosure of the sanctuary which is [also] forbidden to the Jews, except to those of them [Jews] who are accustomed to enter after purifying themselves in accordance with the law of the country" (*Ant*. 12.3.4). In the Roman period, slabs were placed at the Temple entrance in Greek and Latin stating that no non-Jew was allowed to enter the area of the Sanctuary courts beyond the Rampart under penalty of death (*War* 5.5.2). Gentiles and lightly impure persons were allowed to gather outside the *soreg* in the Court of the Gentiles (m. *Kel*. 1; see Ezek. 44:9).[20] Jesus' protest against the corrupt moneychangers took place in this court (Mark 11:15–17; Matt. 21:12f.; Luke 19:45f.).[21]

Thus, holiness of space is maintained by partitions and exclusions. Separation is necessary to keep lesser holy items from contaminating those with more potent holiness. Separating the Court of the Priests from that of Israel was a stone partition, about one and a half feet high (*War* 5:226). Thus, the laity could watch the service and still be kept a safe distance from it. Staircases and gates reinforced the graded sanctity of the courts. The women's court was separated by a wall and a gated staircase (m. *Mid*. 2:5). A further set of stairs led down to the Court of the Gentiles.

Various other restrictions ensured the sanctity of the Temple courts: No one was allowed to enter the Temple courts with a staff, sandals, with only an undergarment, with dusty feet, or carrying coins wrapped in a kerchief (b. *Ber*. 9:5). No sitting or spitting was allowed in the sacred complex. The area could not be used for a shortcut, in fact, no entry was allowed except to perform a religious duty. After completion of a service in the Sanctuary, one had to back out slowly and walk sideways through the court. Maimonides says, "Whenever anyone entered the Court he had to walk quietly to the place where he was permitted to go and regard himself as standing in the presence of the Lord, as it is said: 'And my eyes and my heart shall be there perpetually' (1 Kings 9:3). He would have to walk with awe and fear and trembling, as it is said: 'In the house of God we walked with quivering' (Ps. 55:15)."

Holiness travels along lines of vision. Outside the Jerusalem Temple, as far as one could see the Sanctuary, one had to maintain deportment. Maimonides explains, "When the Sanctuary was standing, acting irreverently was forbidden [all the way] from [Mount] Scopus, which is outside Jerusalem, and inward. It was forbidden only if one could see the Sanctuary and there was no fence intervening between him and the Sanctuary."[22] For the same reason, Jewish high priests, as well as some of their Hellenistic counterparts, were forbidden to look at a corpse (m. *San*. 2:1; Luc. *De Syria Dea* 2.62; Servius, *ad Aeneid* 6.176). It seems that holiness takes into account the spatial relationship of the worshiper. If a person can see the sanctuary s/he comes into some kind of relationship with it. The high priest who looks at a corpse brings about a negative reaction since the chief representative of the living God is forbidden to come into contact, albeit only visually, with death, the realm of idolatry.

Early Christians expressed their new faith by reinterpreting symbols from their Judaic heritage. Several New Testament authors regard the new Christian community as a superior replacement for the Temple (1 Cor. 3:9, 16f.; see also 6:19f.; 2 Cor. 6:16f.; Eph. 2:19–22; Rev. 3:12). According to 1 Peter, Christ is the foundation "living stone" upon which Christians, also as "living stones," build up "a spiritual house, an holy priesthood, to offer up spiritual sacrifices, acceptable to God by Jesus Christ" (1 Pet. 2:4–9). The *Oikos Theou*, "house of God," becomes the "household of God" in 1 Timothy 3:15 (see also 1 Pet. 4:17; Heb. 3:6; 10:21; 1 Clem. 59:2).[23]

With Christ's death on the cross, the veil separating the Holy of Holies from the Holy place is said to have been torn (Matt. 27:51; see also Heb. 6:19–20), indicating the demise of its usefulness.

The idea that a community of believers could replace the Temple Service was already put forward by the Jews of Qumran, largely a community of ex-priests who had rejected the Jerusalem Temple in its corrupted state. Like the Rabbis, however, the Qumranites fully expected the Temple to one day be purified and restored. In the meantime, they believed that God resided among them bonding them into a spiritual "Temple of Men" (4QFlor l. 6; 1QS 8:8; 9:6).

HOLY PERSONNEL

The Holy House has its own holy personnel; the *hieron* has its *hiereus* [Gk., "priest"]. The priest was a sort of "walking temple" who took on the inviolability of the shrine.[24] A Greek or Roman priest was devoted to the cult of one god/goddess at a particular shrine and responsible for the upkeep of that deity's sanctuary and statue. Since Graeco-Roman religion had no sacred text defining its rules, it depended on the expertise and knowledge of its priests.[25] The ancient priest was not, at least officially, a moral leader but a ritual expert commonly represented by the picture of a sacrificer.[26] Priests were mediators between humanity and the gods, but divine access was through correct rituals, not emotional piety.[27]

In Rome the *pontifex* (Lat., "pontiff, priest"), literally, "bridge-builder," spans the gap between this world and that of the gods.

The two main sacerdotal colleges were the Pontiffs and the Augurs. These priesthoods were tied to the state. The Roman senate controlled the colleges, like committees, but this was a two-way street since most collegial priests were also members of the Senate.[28] The biggest attestation to the Roman marriage of "church" and state was the fact that Julius Caesar became *Pontifex Maximus*, "Chief Priest," by public election.[29]

The oldest method of acquiring the priesthood in Greece was via inheritance. Nevertheless, other means of acquiring the priesthood were available, including, purchase (common for the eastern provinces), election (rare), and lot (mostly on the mainland).[30] Greeks apparently saw no sacrilege in purchasing a priestly office.

The primary qualification for being a priest was a good family background. Often a wealthy family would try to marry a son or daughter into the priesthood for prestige. Other regulations varied with regard to age, sexual experience or lack of it, wealth, and/or prominence. "Diodorus Siculus (16.26) says that originally Apollo's oracle at Delphi was a young virgin girl, but later a change required her to be an elderly woman."[31]

In Israel, the priesthood was supposed to be by inheritance only (but in Second Temple times no fewer than eighty-five high priests were appointed by the political authorities). Of the Levites, only those who descended from Aaron, the brother of Moses and the first high priest, were legitimate priests. The eldest direct male descendant from Aaron (and in Second Temple times via Zadok) became the high priest. According to one's rank, access was granted to sacred areas and objects. The hierarchy of the Levites is more clearly presented by a word pyramid; each category is part of what lies underneath it:

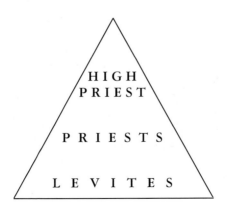

High priest

The high priest is "most holy" (1 Chron. 23:13; b. *Git.* 59b). In his capacity as the head of the Temple Service, the high priest represents Israel and brings them to remembrance before God (Exod. 28:12; 28:29; 39:7). He is the only one allowed into the immediate presence of God, that is, the Holy of Holies, and that only once a year. On this occasion, the Day of Atonement, the high priest is the sole mediator between God and Israel. He symbolically takes all Israel into God's presence because he bears the tribal names on his breastplate and shoulders. The high priest could officiate at the altar on any occasion throughout the year, whenever he wished. When he entered the Temple, he was escorted by three persons, one walking on each side and one walking behind him (m. *Tam.* 7:1).

The great honor and effectiveness which accompanied the high priest because of his holiness came at a price. He had to maintain dignity in his deportment and reflect the perfection of God as far as possible. According to the Rabbis, he could not appear naked, even in the bath or the toilet, nor could he be publicly visible while his hair was being cut (t. *San.* 4:1). He could eat the mourners' bread, but he was not allowed to tear his clothes as was the custom (Lev. 21:10). The high priest does not follow the bier for corpse impurity is transmissible by sight as well as by touch (m. *San.* 2:1). He clipped his hair every Sabbath eve with a pair of shears; he was not allowed to use a razor (m. *San.* 2:1; m. *Hor.* 3:5; b. *San.* 22b). The high priest remained in the Sanctuary (where he was given a special room, m. *Mid.* 5:4) most of the day; he was allowed to go home only at night and for one to two hours during the day (t. *San.* 4:10); his home had to always be in Jerusalem. He could only marry a virgin, and he could not marry more than one wife (m. *San.* 2:1; b. *Yoma* 13a). If he did marry a prohibited wife, his offspring, if sons, were disqualified as priests, and if daughters, were not marriageable to priests.[32] The bride of the high priest could not be a proselyte nor the child of an illegitimate marriage; she could not have ever suffered as a captive in war. Some say she must be an Israelite of unblemished descent between the ages of 12 and 12 and a half.[33]

The notion that the holiest person in the group should be distinguished by many restrictions was not unique in the ancient world. The *flamen dialis*, the chief priest of Jupiter, also was circumscribed by strict taboos, some of which were shared by Israel's high priest:[34] no riding a horse, no seeing the army mustered, no taking an oath, no rings, no knots, no touching a she-goat, raw flesh, ivy or beans, no walking in the open air without a hat, no touching bread fermented with yeast, no passing under a vine arbor, no taking off the inner tunic except indoors, no touching or viewing the dead and no haircut by a slave. Hair and nail clippings of the *flamen dialis* must be buried under a fruitful tree. The feet of his bed must be smeared with clay, no one else may sleep in it, and he may not be more than three nights away from it. For the *flamen dialis*, as for the Jewish high priest, every day was a holy day. In addition to the *flamen dialis*, there were fourteen other *flamines*, each devoted to a specific deity and easily distinguished by a headdress: a close-fitting skullcap with a spike of olive wood attached.

The Vestal Virgins were the most important female priests in Rome. They began their service full-time as pre-teenagers and served for a minimum of thirty years tending the sacred fire of the goddess Vesta.[35] They had to remain virgins for the entire time of service; punishment for unchastity was burial alive. Nevertheless, most of the Vestal Virgins chose to remain in the priesthood for life. Vestals wore the dress of a married woman and a special hairstyle normally restricted to a bride.[36] In addition to tending the fire, the Vestal Virgins made the sacred salt, guarded Vesta's store, performed her rituals, and fetched water from the sacred spring.

In Second Temple times the Jewish high priest was consecrated solely by putting on the sacred vestments. This investiture removed him from the lower sanctity of the priestly realm and empowered him to operate in the most sacred realm.[37] There were four outer garments and four under garments (Figure 2.4). The outer garments included: ephod, breastplate, robe, and gold frontplate. Of less value and worn by all priests were: turban, tunic, sash, and breeches.[38] Wool and linen were used to make these clothes, a combination forbidden in all but sacred garments (Exod. 28:4–42; Lev. 19:19).

Access to the Holy One is, in a sense, written all over these garments. The ephod, an apron-style linen garment made of fine threads (Exod. 39:2–7) was connected to shoulder pieces, precious stones with the names of the twelve tribes engraved on them. These shoulder stones were a constant reminder to God of Israel (Exod. 39:6). The breastplate of the ephod displayed twelve precious stones, each with one of the names of the tribes of Israel engraved upon it. The breastplate, like the shoulder stones, was a continual reminder of the tribes of Israel before God (m. *Sot.* 9:12; b. *Sot.* 48b; see also Philo, *Heres*, 176; *LAB* 26:12).[39]

Figure 2.4 The garments of the high priest.
Source: Jacob Milgrom, *Leviticus 1–16*, Anchor Bible, Garden City, NY:
    Doubleday, 1991, 506.

The gold frontplate on Aaron's turban with the inscription, Holy
to YHWH, was undoubtedly the most important article of the high
priest's clothing. Even the ordinary Roman priest, who did not
usually wear any distinctive clothing, wore a special wreath on the
head when officiating. Aristeas describes the priest's headdress:
"And on his head he had the so-called turban, and above this the
inimitable mitre, the consecrated royal diadem with the Name of

God in holy letters set in relief on a golden plate in the middle of his forehead, gloriously completed" (Arist., 98). Ben Sira's grandson calls it "an engraving of a seal of holiness" (Gk. Ben Sira 45:12).

By bearing the name of God on his head, the high priest was visible evidence that God's name and therefore His presence was in his house and on his chief representative. Josephus describes the blue turban and its gold plate emphasizing the written name of God upon it as "an ornament upon the crown, and this of gold, because of the brilliant rays of light in which God most rejoices" (*Ant.* 3:184–187). This radiant light from the high priest's forehead reminded the people of God's glory which was present with them (Arist., 98; see also Lev. 9:4, 6, 23; Num. 14:10).

For the Rabbis, the gold frontplate guaranteed acceptance for inadvertently defective offerings. Because of its inscription "Holy to YHWH," it had the power to remove the sin of the holy things that the Israelites consecrated from any of their sacred donations (t. *Pes.* 6:5; see also m. *Pes.* 7:7, Exod. 28:36–38; t. *Men.* 1:6). In other words, if the sacrifices were inadvertently defiled, after they had been placed on the altar when nothing could be done about it, the frontplate would make them acceptable to God (m. *Zeb.* 8:12; m. *Men.* 3:3). As the "most holy" mediator, the high priest could by his diadem correct cultic mistakes.

Early Christian writers associate the high priesthood with Christ. In an effort to show Jesus as superior to the levitical priesthood, the author of Hebrews refers to him as a high priest after the order of Melchizedek, to whom even Abraham submitted (Heb. 7:11f., 24). As the supreme high priest, Christ represents the people before God by not only entering the Holy of Holies to make atonement for them but by giving them direct access to God without the aid of animal victims (Heb. 10:12–22; see also 4:16; 6:19–20; 7:19, 26f.). While the human high priest represented God in his clothing and service, Jesus is the full embodiment and revelation of God "better than the angels" (1:3–4). Unlike the human high priest, Jesus is truly holy, perfectly sinless (7:26–27). He is not a decaying mortal but the eternal and powerful creator (1:10–11). Impurity and death have no control over him (7:23–25). This does not make him unapproachable, but he remains compassionate and accessible (4:15). Also early church fathers often emphasize the intercessory role of Christ as a holy high priest who offers the prayers of Christians to God (*Mart. Pol.*, 14:3). The imagery of the priestly service and garments is reinterpreted in light of the Christian faith (see Just., *Dial.* 42:1).

Priests

After the high priest, the ordinary priests, the *kohanim*, form the next holiest group of Israel's cultic personnel, those in the category of *qodesh*. The priest (1) serves as God's representative at his house. This includes offering sacrifices and incense to him as well as maintaining other aspects of the cult (1 Sam. 2:28a). In addition, these priests must (2) teach Israel the divine law so she can please God (Deut. 23:10). "The Lord's commandments compose the curriculum of the priest-teachers, so to speak, in Israel's schoolhouse. Its purpose is to reduce the incidence of impurity in Israel so that holiness, the sphere of God, can expand beyond the sanctuary."[40] Thus, important functions of holy personnel are both cultic maintenance and religious education.

From the priests we learn that holiness means nearness to God. Priests are sometimes referred to in Scripture as *qerobim*, "those who are near." "*Qarob* is a technical term, designating an official who can have access [*qarab*] to his sovereign directly, without resorting to an intermediary (Ezek. 23:12; Esther 1:14). Biblical *qarab* describes the inner circle of the royal court (e.g. 1 Kings 2:7:5:7)."[41]

Because of their nearness to God, holy persons partake of divine power and goodness to a greater extent than others. However, this holy status entails greater responsibility and thus it can be detrimental as well as beneficial. God said he punished Moses and Aaron because they were near to him but "sanctified me not." The Rabbis explain the meaning of this phrase as "you caused (the people) not to sanctify [i.e. honor] me" (*Sif. Deut.* 340; see also Lev. 10:3; b. *Zeb.* 115b). Those who are holiest then are at the same time most honored and most at risk.

Perfection was of the essence in God's holy agents. Priests were initiated into the Temple service at age 20 by a two-fold test: they had to prove genealogy in the priestly line and they had to be without any visible physical defect (b. *Hul.* 24b; b. *Ar.* 13b).[42] If they were disqualified on account of a defect but were pure in lineage, priests could not officiate in the public service but were given menial tasks in the Temple courts; those who passed the test on both counts were inscribed in the record and given the white priestly garments described above (m. *Mid.* 2:5; 5:4).

The priests were ranked in holiness and so in priority.[43] One could not be demoted, only promoted (b. *Yoma* 72b; m. *Men.* 11:7). If flogged, he was afterward returned to office. In the supervision of the Temple, a variety of tasks had to be undertaken by the priests, including superintending all dedications of items to the Temple, maintaining the holy vessels and vestments, answering questions of procedure, inspecting sacred gifts, summoning Levites to respective duties, overseeing the guarding of the Temple, ensuring proper water supply and drainage, overseeing the preparation of incense, veils and garments. Below are the twelve priestly ranks, according to the Talmud (b. *Hor.* 13b):

1   Anointed high priest
2   High priest consecrated by vestments
3   Anointed high priest who was impure
4   Anointed high priest who was blemished
5   Priest anointed for battle
6   Adjutant
7   Controller
8   Supervisor
9   Treasurer
10 Chief of division
11 Chief of subdivision
12 Ordinary priest

Most of these duties were common fare for a priest in the Graeco-Roman world. Across the empire priestly duties included: administration and regulation of the cult, assessing fines, keeping the treasury, making loans, maintenance of buildings, festivals, and housing. On occasion the priest might be asked to perform a purification for a home after birth or death, officiate at weddings/funerals, administer oaths, or perform rites for new brides.

Perfect purity had to be maintained by the Israelite priest. If the priestly garments were soiled in any way, they were not washed, but replaced; the old garments were used to make wicks for the Temple lamps (b. *Zeb.* 88b; m. *Suk.* 5:3; b. *Yoma* 24a). Ministering priests were to cleanse hands and feet and prostrate themselves prior to ministering. If they did so in the morning, they could minister all day provided they did not leave the Sanctuary, fall asleep, pass water or become distracted in mind. If one of these conditions occurred, the priest had to cleanse himself before ministering again. No one could enter the Court of the Priests to minister, even if clean, until he had immersed. No blemished priests were allowed to enter the Sanctuary or the Court of the Priests (Lev. 21:23). Impure priests or non-priests who ministered in the Sanctuary were punishable with death by the hand of Heaven (see b. *Ta'an.* 17b). Four violations of procedure would result in sure danger to the offending priest: improper washing, a physical blemish, improper dress, and drunkenness.[44] Physical purity was necessary for officiating or entering at a Graeco-Roman shrine as well, and contact with death always served as at least a temporary disqualification.[45]

Becoming a Greek or Roman priest was a distinct honor. Priests were allowed to take hides and other parts of the sacrifices as a reward for their service. They were given a salary and housing, free meals, as well as freedom from certain public service obligations. They had the right to erect a statue of themselves; they were given honorific decrees and seats at the theater. Like the Jewish system, some, but not all, cults allowed only priests to enter the temple (Eileithyia at Olympia and Aphrodite at Sikyon), and those priesthoods which were hereditary or purchased were usually lifelong.[46]

A priest commanded upper-class social status. In Rome, a place in one of the priestly colleges could give access to the emperor, who was an honorary member of all of them.[47] Priests were also often soldiers, politicians, administrators, and lawyers, clearly they were members of the elite. Since the priesthood was often not based on inheritance, it was very competitive.[48] The priest was expected to provide the public with various Roman cultural activities, such as games and feasts. Initiates into the priesthoods were required to give sumptuous banquets. This showed their generosity and made the public grateful recipients who recognized the social and political gulf in status between them. As the priest donated to various causes, he would receive in exchange "symbolic capital," that is, the obligation, gratitude, and loyalty of the lower classes.[49]

The Israelite priest too wielded considerable power in the community. He was given precedence in all sacred matters: first in reading law, first in pronouncing benedictions, and first in selecting a fine sacrificial portion.[50] Priests were supported by prescribed donations from the Israelites – certain prime portions of the sacrifices along with the hides, an agricultural tithe, firstfruits of the crops, a percentage of dough offerings, first fleece of the herds, redemption money for firstborn sons, devoted items (which often included animals or land), and firstborn animals (treated as sacrifices from which priestly portions were taken). Priestly portions of the sacrifices belonged entirely to the men of the subdivision who were assigned to minister on that day. In the same vein, Paul exhorts his Corinthian followers to provide for him as the priests are provided for by portions of the Temple sacrifices:

"Do you not know that they which minister about holy things live by the things of the temple? and those which wait at the altar are partakers with the altar?" (1 Cor. 9:13). After the 70 CE destruction of the Temple, priests continued to be honored by Jews. They received firstfruits, imparted blessings and took part in the reading of Scripture.[51] Nevertheless, the expert in the Law eventually took precedence over the priest.

Holiness comes at a price. A priest's daughter who became a prostitute was to be burned (Lev. 21:9). Priests were only allowed to mourn certain close relatives and they were also restricted as to whom they were allowed to marry. Below is a table of marriage and mourning restrictions incumbent on the high priest and the ordinary priest for easy comparison (Table 2.2).[52]

Nevertheless, the priesthood is holy by divine election and is therefore powerful against impurity (Lev. 22:9; Num. 25:12–15; Jer. 33:17–22). The officiating priest who purges the sanctuary of its impurities is immune to its contagion. Impurity pollutes the sanctuary, but it does not pollute the priest as long as he serves God in the sanctuary. As Jacob Milgrom says, "Through their uninterrupted service, the remaining priests exemplify the principle that

Table 2.2 Priestly restrictions

Marriage rites	High priest	Priest
Widow	no	no
Priestly widow	no	yes?
Divorced	no	no
Prostitute	no	no
*Mourning customs**		
Disheveled hair	no	yes
Torn clothes	no	yes
Bald/beard	no	no
Shaved flesh	no	no
Lacerated	no	no
Corpse impure for wife	no	no
Corpse impure for other family members	no	yes

Sources: m. *San.* 2:1; m. *Hor.* 3:5; b. *Yoma* 13a; b. *San.* 22b; Lev. 21:1–4, 7, 10–21.

*No priest in mourning is allowed to officiate in the Temple Courts.

holiness is more powerful than impurity, that life can conquer death."[53] Through their constant instruction of Israel and maintenance of the cult, the priests ensure that holiness is maintained in Israel. According to Exodus 19, the goal is to make all of Israel into a "royalty of priests and a holy nation" (Exod. 19 :6).

Unlike the Jewish system, some Graeco-Roman cults allowed women to serve in the priesthood. The legal status of a woman could be greatly enhanced by being a priestess. Priestesses usually served goddesses; priests served gods. Some married deities required married priests. "Similarities in gender, age, sex experience . . . may result from ancient belief that the priest or priestess during performance of rituals actually embodied the spirit of the deity."[54] Sometimes husbands and wives served as collegial priests/priestesses. Some may ask why women were not included in the Jewish priesthood as well. The answer probably lies in the area of ritual purity. The more extended nature of female impurity, and the complete expulsion of women from the sanctuary at these times, would have made it difficult for any woman to serve as an Israelite priestess. The physical demands of slaughter as well as flaying, hoisting and tossing large animal limbs onto the altar, in addition to the demanding role of motherhood, may have also been prohibiting factors.

It should be noted that permission to serve in the priesthood does not necessarily indicate a liberated Graeco-Roman attitude toward women. Take the Vestal Virgins, for example. According to Deborah Sawyer: "The Vestal Virgins are an example of a male-defined idealized womanhood, which disempowers women according to their nature and empowers them according to male social values."[55] Sawyer points out that the Vestal Virgins were taken out of society before they were women, as early as age 6, and they had to remain sexually inactive lest they be buried alive. She continues: "As 'de-sexed' women they are then 'safe' to be granted some powers, that only men, the first gender in Roman society, can properly expect to exercise." Sawyer claims that it was the virginal status of these women which was the primary feature which marked them as holy from the rest of society because it was for violation in sexual matters that they could be killed.[56] Judaism stops short of such a claim. Marriage and sexual activity is necessary for the continuation of the priestly line.

The methods of the Graeco-Roman priests were incompatible with holiness by the Jewish definition. Robert Garland emphasizes three major aspects of the Roman priest's work: rituals, augury and prodigies.[57] The pagan priest is constantly asked to look for and interpret omens in the phenomenna around him. In sacrificial rituals the Etruscan diviners (*haruspices*) interpreted the entrails of the victims (see below). Augury was originally based on the flight patterns of birds. By the first century BCE auspices were usually taken by offering food to sacred fowl; if they took it the answer was favorable. Prodigies were unusual or abnormal phenomena, for example birth of monsters, lightning, or rain as blood. These events were taken as warnings of danger, and the priestly duty was to try to avert the harm before it happened.[58] All of these methods were outlawed in Israel (Exod. 22:18; Lev. 19:36; Deut. 18:10–14).

Using language familiar to his readers from Exodus, 1 Peter regards all Christians as a "holy priesthood" and a "holy nation." These terms remind the reader of the Sinai experience when God declared that Israel was a "royal priesthood" and subsequently revealed himself to them on the holy mountain (1 Pet. 1:15–16; 2:9; see also Exod. 19:5–6). So also, according to the Revelator, Christ has made his followers "kings and priests unto God" (Rev. 1:6; 5:10). Especially interesting is the notice in Ephesians that the "holy ones are called to a life without blemish," comparing ethical perfection to the physical perfection required of the priests of the Temple (Eph. 1:4; 2:21; 5:27; see also Col. 1:22). Indeed, among the Rabbis too all Israel is considered holy to some degree and subject to a life of moral purity (see Chapter 5).

Some of the early Church Fathers refer to all Christians as priests in the sense that all of their prayers are effective (Orig., *Ag. Cels.* III: 73–74). Each one is capable of bridging the gap between this world and Heaven. As "priests," Christians must keep themselves especially pure; some Fathers extend this notion to complete sexual abstinence (Orig., *Ag. Cels.* VII:48).

Levites

Levites include all the descendants of Aaron. They form a classific-ation of holiness in between the priests and the other Israelites. The Torah explains that Levites take the place of the holy firstborn of Israel. That is, instead of requiring all firstborn boys to be inducted into God's service, the tribe of Levi fulfills this task (Num. 8:16). Levites were assigned to the priests as attendants (Num. 8:19), but they could not handle sancta. Many were gatekeepers, musicians, bearers of burdens, and janitors for the sanctuary (Num. 4:19; *Sif. Num.* 18:3).

Holiness is precious. It must be guarded and maintained. The main role of the Levites was to guard the Sanctuary. This task was continual, day and night, and was shared with the priests (Num. 18:2). The priests guarded from within the Court of the Priests and the Levites from without, since those who were not priests were not allowed access to the holy things on pain of death. The officer over all the companies of the guards was the Master of the Temple Mount. According to the Mishnah, he would walk around and check on all the guards, and he would hit anyone who had fallen asleep on the watch and burn his clothes (m. *Mid.* 1:2). The personnel at Greek temples too were responsible for guarding the *hieron*. A citizen of Apollonius was blinded by fellow citizens because he fell asleep on the watch and wolves devoured the sacred cattle of the sun.[59]

Holiness is also beautiful. This is demonstrated by another distinct function of the Levites, namely, their obligation to provide music for the Temple service. Scripture refers to the music of the Temple as the *hadarat qodesh*, "beauty of holiness": "And when he [Jehoshaphat] had consulted with the people, he appointed singers unto the Lord to praise the beauty of holiness, as they went out before the army, and say, Praise the Lord for his mercy endures forever" (2 Chron. 20:21). The term, *hadarah* means "adornment," and thus *hadarat qodesh* literally means "holy adornment." The phrase always refers to public worship (see 1 Chron. 16:29; Ps. 29:2; 96:9). In their musical capacity, the Levites enhanced the worship of the Holy One.

The Levites sang at all obligatory burnt offerings of the community and peace offerings of Pentecost. According to the Rabbis, there were never less than twelve Levites on the platform between the Court of Israel and the Court of the Women to chant (without instruments for the essential Temple service song). Other Levites played musical instruments, including lyres, flutes, harps, trumpets, and cymbals (m. *Ar.* 2:5). Each trumpet was made of a silver bar, and there were at least twenty-one trumpet blasts in the Temple daily (m. *Suk.* 5:5; m. *Ar.* 2:3). Flutes were made of reeds, and, according to the Mishnah, a song would end with a lone flute for a pleasant finale (b. *Men.* 28a; m. *Ar.* 2:3).

Because of their status, Levites were relieved of military and agricultural duties and supported by the tithes of Israel. Of the 10 percent of the harvest which the Levites received from the Jews, the Levites gave a portion to the priests (Num. 18:25–29). The following chart illustrates the difference between duties and restrictions for priests and those for Levites, and thus the difference in status:

Priests	Levites
offer sacrifices	perform music accompanying sacrifices
disqualified by impurity and blemish	disqualified by impurity but not blemish
serve God directly	serve the priests
guard the Court of the Priests	guard non-priestly courts
superintend maintenance of Temple complex	maintain the Temple complex
may not marry widow or divorcee	may marry widow or divorcee
may only mourn close relatives	may mourn anyone

The classification of Levites reinforces the notion that holiness must be protected. The priests must be aided as well as guarded. Additionally, worship of the Holy One is enhanced by the accompaniment of the Levite musicians. Holiness is beautiful. The Levites, while technically not "holy" like the priests, are nevertheless distinguished by well-defined restrictions and significant benefits. They have a role to play in the mediation of holiness to Israel.

HOLY RITUAL

People often find it difficult to think of holiness as in any way connected to the sacrifice of animals on an altar and the seemingly endless rules concerning the process. For example, Otto's definition of holiness, described above as "numinous," seems to have no place for the slaughter of animals at a shrine. Nevertheless, the Bible refers to the altar of burnt offerings and certain sacrifices as "Holy of Holies." Holiness in Israel depends upon the proper implementation of the sacrificial system.

Graeco-Roman ritual

Religion in the Graeco-Roman world was primarily a matter of cult and ritual action not of creed and belief. The Latin for religion is not *religio*, but *cultus deorum*, the cult of the gods.[60] Rituals had to be exact, prayers word-perfect, gestures without variance. Of these rituals the single most important act was animal sacrifice.[61] The Greek term for sacrifice, *thusia*, could be used for "cult" in general.[62]

The centrality and significance of sacrifice in Greek and Rome is hard to overestimate. The visual impact of observing the slaughter of a bull or goat is stronger than most people in the modern world realize. *Sphagia* (Gk., "slaughterings") were powerful actions which carried serious weight in the attempt to secure the gods' favor. Even the Greek philosophers, who often criticized sacrifices, still acknowledged them as the proper way to approach the gods: "to show them honor, to give them thanks, or to express our need" (Theophrastus, Porphyry, *On Abstinence* 2.24). The Neoplatonic philosopher Sallustius said: "We offer first fruits of our possessions in the form of votive offerings, of our bodies in the form of hair, of our life in the form of sacrifices."[63]

Homer (ca. 700 BC) outlines the sacrificial rite in terms which could apply to most religions in the Graeco-Roman world. According to the *Iliad*, the general purpose of sacrifice is to gain the attention and good will of the gods.[64] Both blood and bloodless offerings were presented. Some offerings were burned and some simply laid out on altars or tables and then removed after a time. The preferred animals for sacrifices were: cattle, goats, sheep, and (unlike the Jews) pigs. Animal victims were dressed in ribbons, wreaths, draped robes and sometimes gilt horns. Inscriptions take for granted that everyone knew regular procedures and concentrate on details like what victims were to be offered to which god and who received the meat.

Jewish ritual

The Jewish Temple ritual defines and undergirds the rabbinic understanding of holiness. Holiness is not abstractly envisioned as in a theological treatise but is well-defined by prescribed, concrete actions. Every aspect of the Temple ritual reflects truth about God's holiness and its relationship to Israel. The ritual is not symbolical only; its goal is to gain access to the Holy One. There is a dynamic quality to the cult; it is an institutionalized activity which occurs systematically and habitually.

In Hebrew, *qorban*, "sacrifice," literally means "that which is brought near," from the same root as *qerobim*, "the near ones," or priests. *'Isseh* is sometimes translated "offering by fire," but most probably means "(food) gift."[65] The offerer brings his gift near to God when he approaches the altar. The Holy One is represented in the ritual by the sacred altar fire, that symbol of powerful and dangerous divine energy discussed above (Chapter 1). Holiness is effected by giving. A sacrifice is fundamentally a gift to God. Even those offerings from which the offerers eat the majority, God always receives the first portion via the altar fire.[66] Eli's sons sinned by taking their sacrificial portions before God received his portion.[67]

From earliest Greek times the relationship between gods and their worshipers has been through the exchange of gifts.[68] Scholars often refer to this as the *do ut des* principle: "I give in order that you shall give"; even Plato defines prayer and sacrifice as "to ask and to give."[69] Often Greeks dedicated their tools, weapons, discus, or weights to the gods and then promised them part of the rewards of success as a firstfruit or tithe, for example, "Having prayed my prayer with sacrifices I dedicated my gift." One musician even petitioned the gods, "give graciously delightful life in exchange for my song." Ferguson outlines two stages in Roman sacrifice: the *nuncupatio*: "promise of a sacrifice in requital of favours received"; and the *solutio*: the vow of "fulfilment of the promise if the god did his part."[70]

The goal of holiness is access to God. The sacrificial altar is not hidden in God's room, the Holy of Holies, and yet it is Holy of Holies. It is in a transitory zone between God's house, and the Court of Israel.[71] The point is that it is accessible to the offerer and visible to all of the worshipers in the Court of Israel and in the women's balconies. God's holiness comes into the midst of Israel when Israel invites it by her gifts.

Purity is required of any Jew who would offer a gift to God. Ritual purity is necessary to enter almost any shrine in the ancient world. According to Hesiod, one has to wash hands before pouring a libation or performing a sacrifice. In the classical period, metal and stone vessels, which were insusceptible to impurity, were used. The reason for this washing was clearly symbolic not sanitary. Hesiod says to wash hands and feet before crossing a stream![72]

But the Jew must be pure in terms of moral purity as well (see Chapter 5). Any kind of impurity will prevent the mediation of holiness. Ascent of the holy hill required righteousness. The Psalmist asks God, "Who shall ascend the hill of YHWH? And who shall stand in his holy place? The one who has clean hands and a pure heart, who does not lift up his soul to what is false, and does not swear deceitfully" (Ps. 24:3–4); see also "Who will dwell on your holy hill? The one who walks with integrity and does justly . . . speaks the truth . . . does no harm . . . does not magnify the shame of the one nearby, keeps his promises, takes no bribe" (Ps. 15:1–5). Knowing that entry to the holy house requires ethical integrity,

Jesus is outraged at unethical business conducted in the Temple courts and drives out the offenders (Mark 11:15–17).

Holiness includes separation, designation, and perfection. The unblemished, sacrificial victim must be set apart from all other animals and purposes and devoted completely to the Temple, while it is still at home with the owner. As soon as the owner separates it from the flock or herd and designates it holy, it is treated as such. "One's word of mouth [dedication of an object] to the Most High is equivalent to one's act of delivery to an ordinary person" (m. Qidd. 1:6; see also Judg. 17:3; see also Lev. 6:18; Exod. 29:27). Human intention and designation is powerful in creating holiness in this world. Improper intention can render an offering unfit.[73] The necessary perfection of holy offerings can be marred by not only blemished sacrifices but also by as subtle a matter as wrongful intention.

The animal had to be consecrated by its owner; people cannot make holy what they do not own. The gift must be a true gift. Holiness cannot be effected by proxy. As David says to Araunah, who offered to provide a sacrifice for him: "I cannot sacrifice to the LORD my God burnt offerings which have cost me nothing" (2 Sam. 24:24).[74] The owner, not an agent, presents the animal to the priest and before its slaughter (the animal must be alive) lays both hands on the animal's head, identifying it as his own (Lev. 1:3; 3:2, 8; *Sifra Nedaba* 4:2; m. *Men.* 9:8–9; t. *Men.* 10:9–10; b. *Men.* 92b).[75] If the owner was not present, the sacrifice could not be offered. For congregational offerings, the Men of the Post, who stood by the altar, were adequate representatives.

In order to be holy, the ritual must be directed to the Holy One. According to the prayers in Homer, the sacrificer addressed the deity standing and raising the hand to signal for god's attention. There was no prescribed liturgy for the prayer, but the ritual had three parts: invocation, i.e. "identifying the god," argument, and petition.[76] The Roman offerer veiled his head and proper prayer was formulated by the *pontifices*. In Israel, the owner declares the type of offering he is presenting and the name of God is pronounced over it (e.g. "This is a burnt offering unto YHWH") (*Sif. Deut.*, Hammer, 306–308). The offerer then verbalizes praise, petition, or confession (see Maimonides, VIII, 3:15).

When the priest raises his hands and expresses the fully spelled out Name of God, the Holy Name is in fact audibly placed upon Israel. God accepts the gift and in return grants his holy presence among Israel. This presence can only mean goodness to his people.

The full priestly benediction links God's goodness with the bestowal of His name upon Israel: "The Lord bless you and protect you! The Lord deal kindly and graciously with you! The Lord bestow his favor upon you and grant you peace! Thus they shall place my Name upon the people of Israel, and I will bless them" (Num. 6:24–27; m. *Tam.* 7:2). The acquisition of holiness guarantees God's blessing.

The most holy element in the sacrificial ritual is blood. According to Leviticus, blood is the only element which can ensure atonement for Israel because it represents life (Lev. 17:11). Holiness is the divine gift of life, and thus it requires the lifeblood of necessarily sacrificed animals to be handled with reverence. In every blood sacrifice, whether for atonement or not, the tradition is very strict about the handling of blood from the moment of slaughter to its sprinkling on the altar. The four principal acts of service are all blood-rites: (1) slaughtering the animal and removing sacrificial portions; (2) catching the blood in holy vessels; (3) conveying the blood to the altar; and (4) tossing the blood on the altar and into the drains below (m. *Zeb.* 1:4).

Holiness increases the quality of life in Israel and is never associated with human death. By contrast, Greeks often offered food to their dead ancestors: "The dead were given meals and the living might eat with them."[77] Part of the animal was burned for the dead hero so that he would not become angry and dangerous to the living. Holiness in Israel, by contrast, could not involve any dead or mourning human being (Deut. 26:12–14).

One of the most salient differences between Jewish and Graeco-Roman sacrificial ritual is in the matter of divination. For the Greeks and Romans extispicy, i.e. the examination of entrails (*exta*) for signs, was the central focus of the sacrifice. Divination was probably part of every sacrifice. In fact, the word *kalliereisthai* (Gk., "to look for good sacrificial signs") simply means "to sacrifice."[78] Offerers prayed to the deity and the deity replied by the results of the extispicy. There are two stages: (1) at the time of butchery when innards, including the liver, were inspected for abnormality; (2) when parts of animal were set on fire and the behavior of the parts while burning was analyzed. If the inspectors found any unfavorable signs in their examination, the offering was unacceptable. No such parallel to extispicy is found in the Jewish cult.

Nevertheless, some elements of the cultic ritual of the Temple did seem to have a correspondence to Graeco-Roman magical practice and this was discussed by the Rabbis. For example, hyssop is dipped into a mixture of water and the ashes of a red cow and then used to sprinkle a person contaminated by a corpse, thereby expunging his impurity (Num. 19:17–19; m. *Par.* 3:3; 12:1). The Rabbis tell of a pagan who noticed the similarity between this ritual and his own magical practices and asked Rabban Yohanan ben Zakkai about the reason for this ritual.

> Rabban Yohanan asked the heathen: "Has the spirit of madness ever possessed you?" He replied, "No." "Have you ever seen a man whom the spirit of madness has possessed?" The heathen replied: "Yes." "And what do you do for such a man?" "Roots are brought, the smoke of their burning is made to rise about him, and water is sprinkled upon him until the spirit of madness flees."
>
> Rabban Yohanan then said, "Do not your ears hear what your mouth is saying? It is the same with a man who is defiled by contact with a corpse – he, too, is possessed by a spirit, the spirit of uncleanness, and Scripture says, I will cause [false] prophets as well as the spirit of uncleanness to flee the land" (Zech. 13:2).
>
> Now when the heathen left, Rabban Yohanan's disciples said: "Our master, you put off that heathen with a mere reed of an answer [literally, 'you shoved aside that heathen with a reed'], but what answer will you give us?"
>
> Rabban Yohanan answered: "By your lives, I swear: the corpse does not have the power by itself to defile, nor does the mixture of ash and water have the power by itself to cleanse. The truth is that the purifying power of the Red Cow is a decree of the Holy One. The Holy One said: I have set it down as a statute, I have issued it as a decree. You are not permitted to transgress my decree. 'This is the statute of the Torah' " (Num. 19:1).
>
> (PRK 4:7)[79]

From the inclusion of this story among rabbinic texts, we learn that the Rabbis recognize practices among their own ritual which seemed magical, but took great pains to explain that they were, in fact, not exorcisms. Indeed the Rabbi's disciples do not believe that the ash mixture is in any way efficacious of itself. This is confirmed by Rabban Yohanan who gives the official explanation that he does not know why this strange ritual was commanded but like all divine decrees, it must be obeyed. Thus, possible traces of magic or divination among the cultic ritual were clarified so that they would not be misinterpreted by anyone as a mixture of magical practice in Judaism.[80]

The mystery cults, which became very popular during the imperial period as a more emotional, personal alternative to the state cults, encouraged a different type of ritual from the Graeco-Roman model. These cults often included such rituals as shaving the head, ecstatic dancing, fasting, self-flagellation, and even castration. These activities were an effort to afflict the body in order to transcend it and gain a higher reality. The notion was repulsive both to Jews and to traditional Greeks and Romans; Graeco-Roman sources often mock these cults as "barbaric."[81] Nevertheless, many people participated in both traditional sacrifices as well as mystery rituals.

Sacrifice, the central religious element in the Graeco-Roman world, soon came to be understood by early Christianity as a thing of the past.[82] Philosophers had belittled it, but their rhetoric was usually accompanied by the sacrificial and other rituals required by the imperial cults. Among early Christian writers, however, particular sacrifices and other offerings are reinterpreted in light of the new Christian faith. The death of Christ was considered the supreme sacrifice which ended all further need for atoning sacrifices (Eph. 5:2). Yet, the Jewish sacrificial system remained valuable to Christians as a source of ethical and spiritual teaching.

Sacrificial offerings

The Rabbis noted two categories of sacrifices in Scripture: "most holy" offerings and "lesser holy" offerings. The primary "most holy" offerings were: sin, guilt, burnt, and meal. Of the lesser holy offerings, the most common was the individual well-being offering. Most holy offerings were eaten by priests only in the Court of the Priests; lesser holy offerings could be eaten anywhere in Jerusalem. Each of these sacrifices had its own function and symbolism, and each defines a different aspect of holiness. Early Christians found it necessary to reinterpret these offerings in light of their new faith. The rituals have much in common with Graeco-Roman sacrifices, and yet they are unique.

Sin offering[83]

Holiness is both powerful perfection and merciful goodness. It is never simply absolute power, but it seeks ways to enable human access even after frail human beings have provoked it. A person who violates the commands of the Holy One deserves to die (Num. 15:31). If the sinner is repentant, however, the death sentence can be commuted to payment with the life of an animal. This sacrificial animal, an innocent victim which is taking the place of the life of the guilty, is "most holy" (Lev. 6:18[25]). Leviticus teaches: "If any person from among the populace sins inadvertently by violating any of the Lord's prohibitive commandments, and he realizes his guilt or he is informed of the wrong he committed, he shall bring a female goat without blemish for the sin of which he is guilty" (Lev. 4:27–28).[84] If the sinner is not conscious of wrongdoing, the Rabbis teach that no liability for an offering is incurred; the offender must be fully informed (Sifra Hobah 7:7 on Lev. 4:23; b. BQ 26b).

The Rabbis describe the *hatta't* as an appeasement to God. "R. Simeon asks: why does the sin offering precede the burnt offering (Lev. 5:8)? It is comparable to an attorney who comes to appease. Having made his (plea of) appeasement (*hatta't*), the gift (of appeasement) (*'ola*) follows" (b. Zeb. 7b). Gifts to the gods were often for appeasement cross-culturally. The idea is that the god accepts the offender's sacrifice as a substitute for his life. The animal becomes the victim instead of the human being.[85]

There are two types of sin offerings in Israel. The sin offering for a priest or the full congregation, the most serious type, was completely incinerated and no one ate of it (Lev. 4:12, 21; 6:23). The sin offering for an individual Israelite was less serious. Its meat became food for the priests (Lev. 4:30; 6:19). The Rabbis insist that the priests must eat the *hatta't* in order for the offerers to be expiated (Sifra Shem. 2:4; b. Pes. 59b; b. Yoma 68b; b. Yeb. 40a, 90a). "When the priest consumes the *hatta't* he is making a profound theological statement: holiness has swallowed impurity; life can defeat death."[86]

Confession and repentance are preconditions for an effective sin offering (Sif. Zut. on Num. 4:4; t. Men. 10:12; m. Yoma 8:8; b. Shebu. 13a; t. Yoma 4:9). A sinner must verbalize his guilt to God and also to anyone he has injured (m. Yoma 8:9; t. Ta'an. 1:8; Lev. 5:5; Philo, Sp. Laws 1.235). This confession from the Mishnah seems likely: "I have sinned, I have committed iniquity, I have transgressed, and I have done thus and thus; but I have now returned in penitence before you and may this be my atonement" (Maimonides, VIII, "Manner of Offering" 3:15; see also m. Yoma 3:8). The Holy One is not indiscriminately good; the recipient of his mercy must be truly remorseful and turn away from wrongdoing.

Sin offerings are most prominent on the most holy day of the year, *Yom ha-Kippurim* (bib.) or *Yom Kippur*, "Day of Atonement," a time of national repentance from moral as well as ritual violations of the people of Israel. The central role of the high priest as intercessor between Israel and the Holy One is evident for it is only on this day that he enters the Holy of Holies and sprinkles atoning blood from a communal goat sin offering in the presence of God. A second goat is released to the wilderness symbolizing the exit of the sins of Israel outside of the community. The holy people mourn, confess their sins, make reconciliation among themselves and are finally assured of God's forgiveness. The prohibitions on this day are numerous and further reinforce its holiness. Israel must abstain from eating, drinking, bathing, anointing, wearing leather shoes, and having marital relations (m. *Yoma* 8:1). The point here is that the sin offering requires the humility, repentance and confession of its offerer in order to truly effect holiness.

Since the *hatta't* only covers inadvertent violations, one may legitimately ask how various biblical characters received forgiveness for obviously deliberate sins. The Rabbis answer that the death sentence incurred by deliberate sins (Num. 15:30) is reduced by confession and repentance. R. Simeon b. Lakish explains: "Great is repentance, which converts intentional sins into unintentional ones" (b. *Yoma* 86b). Likewise, "How is the high priest's deliberate sins atoned by the bull? Because he has confessed his brazen and rebellious deeds it is as if they become as unintentional ones before him" (*Sifra Ahare par* 2:4, 6; see also t. *Yoma* 2:1; Lev. 5:20–26 [Heb]).

The sin offering was a powerful means of atonement and thus early Christians and Rabbis found it necessary to reinterpret it in light of a Temple-less religion. Paul refers to Jesus as a sin offering: "He [God] made him to be sin who knew no sin" (2 Cor. 5:21). Christ's blood was the atoning blood of the supreme sin offering (Matt. 26:28). Later Rabbis regarded repentance, Torah study, and/or death as atonement for sins (m. *Yoma* 8:8f.; *Lev. R.* on 6:9; b. *Men.* 110a).

Guilt offering

Holiness in Israel cannot be effected without proper recognition and restitution of wrong done to others, whether it is to God or to one's fellow human beings. The *asham*, or guilt offering, is brought for five specific trasngressions: intercourse with a betrothed girl, wrongful gain, sacrilege, impure Nazirite, and leprosy. As with the sin offering, confession and repentance are necessary to rectify any of these violations. An individual must make restitution plus a 20 percent fine to the wronged party and bring a ram for a guilt offering to the sanctuary (Lev. 5:16 [6:5]). This law stands behind the words of Jesus: "Therefore if you bring your gift to the altar, and there remember that your brother has ought against you; Leave there your gift before the altar, and go your way; first be reconciled to your brother, and then come and offer your gift" (Matt. 5:23f.). The notion is that God will not accept a guilt offering if restitution and reconciliation have not been made between the human parties involved.

The most serious of all of the trespasses for which a guilt offering atones is *ma'al*, "to commit sacrilege," literally, "to undergo alteration from sacred to profane."[87] The Rabbis said: "He who desecrates the Holy Things . . . even though he has to his credit many religious duties, is worthy of being driven out of the world" (*Sif. Num.*, Neusner, 170; see also b. *Shebu.* 42b). There are two types of sacrilege: (1) against sancta; (2) involving oaths. Sacrilege for the Rabbis only applies to *qodesh qodashim*, not to all sancta.[88] An item still in an individual's possession at home is subject to sacrilege if it has been designated to God as "most holy." Even sticks, stones, earth, and ashes could become hallowed by words when God's name was invoked upon them, and anyone who comported with them as with a profane thing committed trespass (Maimonides, VIII, "Trespass" 8:8).

There are many biblical examples of sacrilege. Saul's annihilation of the holy priests at Nob (1 Sam. 22:18–19) was a sacrilege because the priests were holy (*Lev. R.* 26:7). King Uzziah had to bring an *asham* because he had committed sacrilege by entering into the sanctuary to burn incense, although he was not a priest; he was still punished with leprosy (*Sifra Hobah par.* 11:1).

Breaking an oath or uttering a false oath was sacrilege because oaths included the holy name of God. A false oath is a desecration of the name of God, *hillel haShem* (*Sifra Qedoshim par.* 2:7; also CD 15:3). Wilful desecration of God's name is so blasphemous that it is the only transgression for which the sinner must die in order for his atonement to be complete. "In desecrating the Name it is the same whether done unintentionally or wantonly" (m. *Abot* 4:4).

In a broad sense, sacrilege applies to the breaking of any of God's holy commandments. Leviticus 5:17–18 warns: "And when a person, without knowing it, sins in regard to any of the LORD's commandments about things not to be done, and then realizes his guilt, he shall be subject to punishment. He shall bring to the priest a ram . . . as a guilt offering." Here not only violations in cultic law governing Israel's relation with God are considered sacrilege, but also wrongful dealings among the people. The concept that a god has inspired a text which carries sacred commands for behavior in society so that social violations, such as breach of property rights, are held on a par with sacrilege and threaten capital penalties is not characteristic of Graeco-Roman religions.

Sacrilege against the deity was feared across the Graeco-Roman world, but to a lesser degree than in Israel. Stealing from temple treasuries or violating temple personnel was, in principle, a heinous crime. As in Israel, perjury among the Greeks and Romans was a capital offense since the names of the gods were invoked in sacred rituals.[89] The family of Glaucus was "obliterated root and branch" because he consulted the Pythia about violating his pledge (Herodotus, 6.86). According to Xenophon, Sparta's military defeats were the result of violating an oath of peace (*Hell.* 5.4.1.; see also Thuc., 7.18.2). When its sacred laws are violated, the shrine must be purified and the offender becomes *enages*, the target of divine anger.[90]

Nevertheless, in fact, sacred property was sometimes used in the profane realm with permission, as long as fees were paid.[91] *Hieros* marks out what belongs to the gods but does not necessarily mean the sacred item is forbidden to humans. Loans were granted to people from temple funds and statues were often plundered.[92] The death penalty for sacrilege at Athens is "in principle," and in practice it was quite exceptional. Usually trespassing on a god's grove and taking his sheep or wood would be treated as a property violation and fined. As early as 440 BCE, wars were financed by borrowing temple money. The danger and fear connected to holiness in the Hebrew tradition is not as sharp in the surrounding cultures.

Burnt offering

The burnt offering, *'ola*, from the root "ascend," is distinctive among the sacrifices in that the animal is completely burned on the altar, except for its hide (all hides of sacrifices were given to the priests). The purpose of the *'ola* was to create an aroma "pleasing to God" (Lev. 1). The aroma is for the maintenance of God's satisfaction, or as the Rabbis translate *nahat ruah*, "pleasure" (*Sif. Num.* 143). The *'ola* is particularly associated with God, rather than Israel, since all of its meat ascends as smoke up to Heaven (*Ant.* 3.225). Similarly, *thuein* (Gk., "to sacrifice") literally means "to make smoke."

The burnt offering in its entirety is a gift to God. It was offered on behalf of the congregation twice daily in the Temple simply to maintain the holy fire, signifying Israel's continuing relationship with the Holy One. Representing the congregation was a delegation of Jews called a *ma'amad*, or "men standing by" the altar since the owner/offerer had to be present to identify with the sacrifice (m. *Ta'an.* 4:1–4). Additionally, an individual might bring a burnt offering for a number of more specific reasons, including celebration of an occasion of happiness, thanksgiving, fulfillment of a vow, or even expiation for neglect of duties (t. *Men.* 10:2; *Sifra Nedaba* 4:8; t. *Par.* 1:1).[93] The burnt offering is not mandatory for individuals, but brought voluntarily. Its main function is to secure the congregation's continuing daily access to God by regular morning and evening sacrifices.

Among the Greeks and Romans an animal's flesh totally burnt on the altar, with no meat assigned to the offerer or the priest, was a rarity and connoted a crisis. Such an offering was the most powerful kind and was only performed in extreme situations to avert disaster, for example war or famine. For example, the Greeks presented Apollo with the "aroma of lambs or goats" so that he would be willing to take a plague away from them (*Iliad* 1.66–67). The *enagismos*, the ritual in which the offering was completely destroyed, was the most powerful of all sacrifices. What was *hieron* was not necessarily dangerous or unavailable for human use; what was *enages*, by contrast, was considered awful and dangerous.[94]

Usually among the Greeks and Romans the offering of the meal to the gods was simply ceremonial with almost 100 percent of the food going to the owner and the invited guests of the feast. The "gift" to the gods turns out to be not much of a gift. According to Walter Burkert, the meal "celebrates the commensality of men in the presence of the sacred, while the gods receive mainly the inedible parts, bones and gall bladder."[95] In Israel, by contrast, the fully burnt offering is a twice daily affair. Jews offered to God regular expensive gifts, from which they derived no benefit, except the continuance of the holy relationship. The devotion of the holy people must be renewed daily at a significant price.

Like the burnt offering which was totally incinerated on the altar, and in imitation of Jesus, Christians are exhorted to offer themselves as "holy offerings," that is, their lives, for the continuance of the faith; life itself is an ongoing sacrifice (Rom. 12:1; see also 15:16; 2 Tim. 4:6). Both Christian and Jewish martyrs too were considered holy sacrifices, their lives totally surrendered for their faith (Rom. 8:36; Ign., *Rom.* 23:2; 4:2; Isa. 53:10; Test. Benj. 3:8; 2 Macc. 7:37; 4 Macc. 6:29).[96] Language of the burnt offering ritual also describes financial gifts of Christians to the church. These are called "sweet-smelling" sacrifices "well-pleasing to God" (Phil. 4:18).

Meal offering

The *minha* is a meal offering to God given in order to secure or retain His favor.[97] It has three principal components: flour, oil, and frankincense. Scripture describes two types of meal offerings: (1) a separate offering; and (2) an accompaniment offering. The Rabbis said the meal offering was the poor man's burnt offering (*Lev. R.* 8:4; m. *Men.* 13:11; b. *Men.* 110a; b. *Men.* 104b). This meal offering was made of flour and water only. Thus, holiness is available to all Israel, not just to those who could afford expensive offerings. The second type of meal offering was a required accompaniment to certain animal offerings (*Sif. Num.* on Num. 15:4–10).[98] This offering consisted of flour and oil and was brought to the priest with a drink offering of wine. The whole accompaniment (flour, oil, and wine) is sometimes called a drink offering.

The procedure for offering a *minha* was as follows. Flour, oil, and frankincense were brought to the altar in a holy vessel. The priest took a handful and burned it on the altar; the rest was for his consumption (Lev. 2:2; b. *Men.* 11a). No leaven was allowed in any meal offering offered on the altar. "Leaven in the dough" was a common metaphor for human evil propensities (e.g. b. *Ber.* 17a; see also 1 Cor. 5:8; Luke 12:1; Mark 8:15).

The perfection of holiness is apparent in the *minha* as well as in the unblemished animal sacrifices. Oil had to be the purest, most finely beaten oil. Flour had to be finely ground from grain sown from clean seeds. Wine had to be covered and unchanged in character.

The pouring of liquids on the altar is prominent in Greek art. The most prominent picture is the pouring of wine on the flaming altar when bones, fat, and parts significant for divination are placed on the fire accompanied by a prayer. Greek art depicts the gods themselves participating in libation ceremonies.[99] Paul uses the metaphor of a libation to describe his own life, in a sense, poured out on the "altar" of Christ (Rom. 8:36).

Well-being offering

Shelamim, well-being offerings, create a holy bond not only between Israel and God but among Jews. They are never described in

Scripture as atoning, but are strictly voluntary. Nevertheless, it was expected that Israel bring God offerings demonstrating their gratitude to Him. *Shelamim* may be brought at the conclusion of a vow or just as a freewill offering of praise (Lev. 7:11–36). *Shelamim* are the only sacrifices which laity can eat. In a sense God and the offerer share in a meal and strengthen the bonds between them. Bruce Malina explains: "Those elements of the sacrifice that are burned symbolise the passage of the donor to God; those elements that are consumed by the offerer and the Temple personnel symbolise the fellowship that exists between a benign and sympathetic patron and his clients."[100] Some portions are given to the priests but the bulk of the animal belongs to the owner.

The Rabbis define this offering in two ways: (1) "peace" offering because it "effects peace among the altar, the priests, and the offerer" (t. *Zeb.* 11:1) (the suet is for the altar, the thigh/breast for the priest and the skin/meat for the offerer); (2) "whole, harmonious" offering because, according to R. Simeon, the offerer feels wholesome (complete, fulfilled) who brings it (*Sifra Nedaba* 16:3; Philo, *Sp. Laws* 1.1.212).[101] The translation "peace offering," without any explanation, is misleading since the offering is not for appeasement.

Holiness in Israel cannot be created in a vacuum. Fellowship with the holy community is essential. The offerer of the well-being offering has a time limit of one to two days, depending on the purpose of the sacrifice, to consume the animal (Lev. 7:15–18). This forces him to invite family and friends to join in the feast, thus creating solidarity among the holy people as well as with the Holy One. Early practice was to eat the sacred meal within the sanctuary precincts (Lev. 7:19–21). However, this was extended to all of Jerusalem to accommodate the large numbers of pilgrims bringing *shelamim* during festivals ("in the camp"=Jerusalem, b. *Zeb.* 55a; m. *Pes.* 3:8–9; m. *Meg.* 1:11; m. *Zeb.* 5:6–8; m. *Kel.* 1:8).[102]

Similarly among the Romans and Greeks, the feast that followed the sacrifice was a much anticipated occasion. "Sacrifice and the flesh feast that followed were so intimately connected that one implied the other."[103] Greek inscriptions state the requirement to eat sacrificial flesh within the holy precincts, as also in Israel. The banquet was a social function which heightened the participants' sense of community. Sometimes there were games, music and drama as well. The group invited to the sacrificial banquet was a closed one depending on the shrine; for example, non-family members, non-club members, women, or foreigners might be excluded.[104] Sacrifices were the primary source of meat, and thus it was not easy for Jews and Christians in Greece at the time of Paul to purchase meat that had not been ritually slaughtered as pagan sacrifice (1 Cor. 8:10).

The gods were the "honorees" of these feasts and they (via their priestly representatives) received the first part of the meal, as among the Jews:

> They were recognized with libations, songs, and prayers, and sometimes, with the laying of couches and setting a share of cooked food on tables, they became participants. . . . The requirements for dining on the spot seem to be an attempt to underline the unity and identity of worshipers joined together in honoring gods or heroes.[105]

The first meat the group ate was *splanchna* (certain of the innards – usually lungs, heart, liver, kidneys, and spleen) skewered and roasted over the altar. The rest of the meat may be taken home for cooking, given to friends, or sold. It was important that the community observe the divination of these innards together and then hold and taste them jointly; in this way a strong bond between them took place at the altar.

Paul recognized the strong bonding power of these communal, sacrificial feasts and warned the church not to participate in them: "But I say that the things which the Gentiles sacrifice, they sacrifice to devils, and not to God: and I would not that you should have fellowship with devils. You cannot drink the cup of the Lord, and the cup of devils, you cannot be partakers of the Lord's table, and of the table of devils" (1 Cor. 10:20–23). On the positive side, Christians were encouraged to participate in the celebration of holy communion, which in its early manifestation was a full meal in which believers ate and worshiped together commemorating the sacrifice of Christ's body and blood. These "love feasts," as they were called, retain the character of holy fellowship present in the Israelite feasts where *shelamim* were shared among priests and Israelites.

The praise of God's people, formerly associated with the well-being offerings of Israel, is considered Christian sacrifice, as is good works (Heb. 13:15–16). The notion that praise, love and doing God's will are spiritual sacrifices, is already attested in the Hebrew Bible (Ps. 40:6ff.; 5:15; 51:17; 119:108; Prov. 16:6; 21:3). These principles are retained in Christianity but their concrete under-pinning, that is, animal sacrifice, is considered obsolete.[106] New

Testament writers often reinterpret the sacrificial system in light of the person and work of Jesus Christ retaining only religious principles applicable to the Christian faith.

The cult after 70 CE

The mediation of holiness via the sacrificial cult remained central in rabbinic thought even after the destruction of the Temple in 70 CE. One of the most important substitutes for observing the Temple laws was studying them: "As you study the laws about sacrifice, that is to me as if you had offered them" (*PRK* 60b; see also *ARNa* 4:1; b. *Meg.* 16b; b. *Men.* 110). The Rabbis continued to study the rituals as still relevant. The Rabbis quote Simon the Just (second to third century BCE) that the world was established on three things: Torah, Temple, and kind deeds (m. *Ab.* 1:2); this was written long after the Temple was destroyed. The Rabbis fully expected the system to be in operation again and they were determined to be prepared for that day. Archaeological evidence too supports this belief that the Jewish Temple would be restored. Of particular interest, mosaic floors in several synagogues from the Byzantine period include depictions of cultic objects used in the Temple, for example incense shovels, menorah, shofar.[107] This artwork shows not only that these items were precious to Jewish memory but also gives evidence of the anticipated renewal of the cult in the future.

In addition to Torah study, the Rabbis acknowledged other temporary substitutes for the Temple Service. Prayer was an important one. In fact, the Rabbis apply the term for the sacrificial service, *abodah*, to prayer, referring to the latter as "*abodah* of the heart" (*Sif. Deut.* 41 on 11:13). Other substitutes for the cult include: repentance (m. *Yoma* 8:8f.; *Lev. R.* 7 on Lev. 6:9), deeds of kindness (b. *Suk.* 49b), and thanksgiving (*PRK* 79a). Indeed, these religious actions often accompanied the offering of sacrifices in the Temple, as discussed above. After 70 CE, the sacrificial system became inoperable, but these religious acts remained as conduits of holiness.

After the Temple's demise in 70 CE, the synagogue began to take first place as the center of Jewish religious life. The synagogue was primarily a place of prayer and Torah instruction, but it also served as a communal, social center. Its roots date back as far as the sixth century BCE when the Babylonians destroyed the first Jewish Temple. Ezekiel, a Jewish prophet in Babylon during this period, promises that God would still be with Israel as a "little sanctuary"

even in the diaspora. The Talmud applies the phrase "little sanctuary" to the synagogue (b. *Meg.* 29a). Thus, to some degree, the
synagogue was seen as a substitute for the Temple. Prayer and Torah
study were conducted there on a regular basis. Although the
synagogue co-existed with the Jerusalem Temple, it gains prominence after 70 CE as it is relied upon to fill the gaping hole in
religious life left by the Temple's destruction.

CONCLUSION

The foregoing analysis of the Temple cult from a rabbinic perspective yields some important conclusions about holiness. Holiness is
mediated at a specified meeting place between earth and heaven.
Continuing long after its destruction, the site of the Temple
remained for rabbinic Judaism the holiest spot in the world. It is
also significant that early Christians could not dismiss this
entrenched system which formed a central part of their Jewish
heritage. As long as the Temple stood it was held in reverence, and,
even after its demise, Christians still felt it necessary to reinterpret
its symbols and retain its principles.

The holy house and its cult spanned the gap between the Holy
One and his imperfect people. It was a place where Israel could
invite the holy presence through gifts and the Holy One promised
to respond with favor through his representatives, the priests. This
belief was shared throughout the Graeco-Roman world. Priests
were mediators and intercessors facilitating access to the gods by
means of prescribed rituals. Holiness is nearness to God and those
who stand in the gap between the divine and the profane are the
holiest.

Holiness is represented in the holy house by many symbols. At
every turn Israel is reminded of the holy presence of God by the
symbolism found throughout the sanctuary. From the magnificence
of the Temple to the bonfire on the altar, the purity of the laver, and
the very name of God printed in gold on the high priest's headpiece,
holy power and perfection was visible to all present. Light, food, and
fire illustrate God's holy goodness as well. Not only is Israel
reminded of divine holiness in the holy house, but God is reminded
of Israel. The high priest entered into the Holy of Holies only in
order to atone for Israel. On his vestments were several constant
reminders to God of Israel's existence. The sight of him was evidence
that Israel was in fact represented in the very presence of God.

Holiness in Israel is a two-way process by which the Holy One comes into the midst of his faithful worshipers. God regards Israel as a partner in holiness. The gift of holiness is met by the gifts of Israel. Holiness is not a one-way street in which God does all of the giving. The sacrifices of Israel which are offered daily illustrate the need of constant gifts which are completely devoted to God in order to maintain his presence among his people. The holy offerings, in effect, invite the Holy One to be present. In addition, other aspects of the cult reveal the regular maintenance that God expects his people to provide him: for example the tending of lights, preparation of food, guarding his house, providing music for worship, conducting regular services, and maintaining purity.

Unlike Graeco-Roman rituals, magic, according to the Rabbis, does not play a part in the Jewish sacrificial ritual. The Temple rituals are not manipulations; God can be persuaded but he cannot be forced to do anything. The Rabbis would have agreed with the statement that God can "never be brought under human control, and never bought or sold. He intervenes, but there is nothing automatic about his action."[108] He remains absolute and sovereign. The way to holiness, which guarantees Israel power and life, is only by obedience to the commands of the Holy One. The Rabbis recognize in magic a source of illegitimate power, one which they insist plays no role within the holy house.

Holiness must be well-protected by a number of restrictions and exclusions. These are common throughout the Roman empire but are especially sharp in Israel. Sacred courts marked off the sanctuary and Levites kept intruders away. Jewish laymen stood a safe distance from the sanctuary separated by the Court of the Priests, and Jewish women kept even farther away. To the Holy of Holies, God's "throne room," access was almost nil. Restrictions applied to the priest, even in his domestic life. The smoke rising from the altar of burnt offering reminded everyone that the Holy One was a consuming fire. Violating any sancta or sacred court was a capital offense. The point was clear: holiness had to be mediated to Israel. It was too dangerous for direct access.

On the other hand, the emphasis of the rabbinic texts is not on fear but on the affirmation Israel receives via the Temple worship. The very fact of the system is evidence that divine holiness includes divine goodness. The goal of the Holy One is always to enhance life in Israel and bestow on it blessing and joy. He has no elitist plans. Other than the priests who are singled out to serve him, Israel is treated equally, whether rich or poor. Women are restricted to a lesser role, but they are not excluded from the sanctuary worship. The system provides a way of relationship between the all-powerful, perfect God and the frail, human community of Israel. For inadvertent violations against the Holy One, the system provides restoration and the possibility of continued relationship. Those who could not afford the prescribed animal offerings could bring a grain substitute.

Holiness is separation and it is meant to be irrevocable. Those persons or items which have been designated holy, for example priests or sacrifices, cannot be retracted without penalty from the sphere of holiness. Sacrificial victims must be separated from the flock or herd and devoted completely to the Temple. No human benefit could be derived from them. Holy incense was never to be used in the common sphere.

Cultic perfection is another strong ingredient of holiness. This is a cross-cultural criterion. The Romans were especially well-known for their insistence on perfectly conducted sacrificial rituals. In Israel, sacrificial animals had to be perfect and meal offerings had to be of the highest quality of wine, oil, and flour. Priests had to be without defect. Perfect purity was required of both officiating priests as well as all worshipers who entered the sacred precincts.

In Israel, even intentions had to be perfect. Sacrificial procedures had to be intentionally directed to God. Also, one could not designate a sacrifice to God while intending to substitute it for a less expensive animal. Purity of thought as well as body was required. The intention of a person could make an animal holy, or it could destroy the effectiveness of a sacrifice altogether. The entire sacrificial system was based on the notion that Israel desired holiness; if she transgressed the commands of the Holy One, she had to declare that it was unintentional and be truly remorseful. Those who sinned defiantly were to be extirpated from Israel (Num. 15:22–31); access to God was never automatic by rituals alone.

Israel is unique in requiring ethical perfection in the acquisition of holiness. Violation of another person's rights is considered on a par with sacrilege. The Rabbis regard restitution of wrongs done to one's fellow Jew as a matter of holiness and it had to be made along with payment of a fine to the injured party. In addition, the Holy One himself was violated by this breach of ethics and he had to be appeased. The standard offering was a sizeable animal, a costly gift, from which the offerer could not benefit. God would not be satisfied with merely the bones of the victim. Ritual was not enough to create holiness in Israel; ethics too was a matter of holiness. Only the Jew with the "pure heart" could "ascend the holy hill."

Holiness brings honor. Throughout the Roman Empire priests were treated with respect. They received special privileges and support from the community. Jewish priests continued to receive the support of the Jewish community even after the Temple was destroyed. Since in Israel all of the people are to some degree holy, the Temple cult affirms the preciousness of the whole nation to God. The gradation between the areas and personnel in the sanctuary compound reinforce the principle that an item closer to God is more precious to him. In turn, Israel brings honor to God by her daily worship through holy offerings at his house. These are made even more beautiful by the costly garments and vessels of the sanctuary as well as the musical enhancement of the Levitical singers.

Holiness is created in community. The feasting and communal bonding associated with sacrifice across the Graeco-Roman world is reflected also in Israel. The well-being offering is a primary example of the fellowship among the people which God expects to occur at his house and within his holy city. The fact that this offering is commanded and a time limit imposed forces the community to feast and fellowship together in order to consume the animals within the prescribed time.

Finally, holiness brings life to Israel. The restrictions on corpse impurity and mourning within the sanctuary emphasizes God's association with life rather than death. This may seem contradictory in light of the sacrificial ritual in which so many animals were slaughtered. Nevertheless, only the blood of a living creature, representing its life, is powerful enough to reverse the decree of death to those who violate God's laws. Those who are penitent are given another chance at life via the temple cult. As the umbilical cord which stretches from earth to heaven, the Temple cult gives ongoing life to Israel.

3

THE HOLY LAND

Holy land is God's Land, the Center of the Universe. The holiness present at the sacred house radiates throughout the land. Separated from all other lands to be an earthly dwelling place for the deity, holy land is the most important of the world's space. For the Rabbis, the land of Israel (Figure 3.1) is owned by the Holy One and therefore subject to numerous restrictions which maintain its holy status. When these requirements are met, God's goodness pours out upon it and its inhabitants, bringing prosperity and protection. When the requirements are not met, the land becomes defiled and in need of purification. Its residents are denied its benefits and expelled.

SACRED CENTER

Mircea Eliade says, "Sacred space is that space which has manifested an irruption of the divine and which alone, therefore, is real or possesses being. The religious man desires to live as near to this sacred space as possible and comes to regard it – the place of his abode, his own land – as the centre of the world. To this belongs cosmos, order: outside it is chaos, where demons and alien spirits rule."[1] Eliade says that this divine irruption results in "detaching a territory from the surrounding cosmic milieu and making it qualitatively different. . . . Something that does not belong to this world has manifested itself. . . ."[2] Thus, sacred space is extraordinary space, extraterrestrial, as it were, and the most valuable place in the world.

The Rabbis echo this sentiment when speaking of the Land of Israel. The Land is the sacred center of the world: "Just as the navel is found at the center of a human being, so the land of Israel is found at the center of the world . . . and it is the foundation of the world. Jerusalem is at the center of the land of Israel, the Temple is at the center of Jerusalem, the Holy of Holies is at the center of the Temple, the Ark is at the center of the Holy of Holies and the Foundation Stone is in front of the Ark, which spot is the foundation of the world" (*Tanh. Qedoshim* 10). The Talmud too states that the foundation stone of the Temple was at the center of the earth (b. *Yoma* 54a-54b; see also b. *San.* 37a; *Tanh. VaYikra* 18:23).[3]

Other cultures reveal this same regard for a sacred center. Brereton describes the Roman version:

> At the founding of cities within the Roman world, for instance, the augur drew a circle quartered by lines running east–west and north–south. This diagram replicated the heavenly order and thereby established it on earth. Through ritual formulas, the diagram was then projected onto the whole tract of land to be encompassed by the city, so that the periphery of the city reproduced the boundary of the universe. The east–west line represented the course of the sun; the north–south line, the axis of the sky. The augur and the city thus stood at the crossing point of these two lines and hence immovably and harmoniously at the center of the universe.[4]

In this way the sacred place transposes the holy order of heaven onto the earth, becoming a sort of "heaven on earth."[5]

The Greeks too shared the concept of the sacred center and regarded the oracle at Delphi as the "navel of the earth." The Homeric Hymn to Apollo reads: "Far-darting Apollo, first went through the earth seeking an oracle-centre for men."[6] *Ge*, the earth goddess, whom Apollo replaced, was associated with an "egg-shaped stone, called navel, *omphalos*, situated in historic times in the innermost sanctuary of the temple."[7] This stone marked the center, or navel, of the earth, a holy place designated by Zeus. The stone was considered holy and therefore powerful.

Jonathan Smith adds that the sacred place is not just the place of divine manifestation but also the place of communication between the divine and the human.[8] This communication is not just a one-time event but can be repeated at the sacred spot. The sacred place becomes a point at which humans can mingle with the divine and conform to the heavenly sphere in some way. The symbols and rituals of the sacred place remind the community of their God and their obligations to Him.[9] The sacred place becomes the "focusing lens," to use Smith's term, for viewing the rest of life. As discussed

Figure 3.1   The holy land during the Roman Empire.
Source: Alex Allan.

above (Chapter 2), the sacred Temple, with its service and symbols, was just such a place of power and communication which provided order and significance for Jewish life. In rabbinic Judaism the sacred nucleus, that is, the Temple, infuses a certain level of holiness throughout the entire land of Israel.

Another reason for the holiness of the land lies in the fact that blood has been shed on account of it. To be sure, the notion of fighting and dying for the land appears both among the classical as well as the Hebrew writers. Pericles placed the first victims of the Peloponnesian War among the immortals. And Virgil's Aeneas saw on the Elysian Plains the spirits of those who had suffered for their homeland, "their brows bound with snowy fillets," equivalents of martyrs' crowns (Virgil, *Aeneid*, VI, 660ff.; see Horace's widely quoted dictum: *"Dulce et decorum est pro patria mori"*). As Smith says, "It is the fighting and, especially, the dying that renders the land uniquely mine."[10] The Bible is, of course, filled with accounts of God leading Israel into battle for conquest of the land. The Psalmist declares: "And he brought them to his holy land [*gebul qodsho*], to the mountain which his right hand had won" (Ps. 78:54, RSV). The fact that it is God leading, commanding, and bringing victory already gives the land a holy character. He owns it and promises it to Israel. At the same time, the land is conquered by Israel's warriors, many of whom will lose their lives for its sake.[11] Unlike the Elysian Plain, however, the land of Israel is not just the far-off home of the honorable dead. It is a tangible, present home also for the living.[12]

In the Graeco-Roman world *polis* and *patria* referred to one's place of origin – the native city or country where one was born and reared and where one's ancestors had lived for generations.[13] These terms usually meant one's native city, not country. When a hero died as a Roman soldier, he was giving his life for Rome and all that it stood for, for example its gods, culture, imperial house, but not for the territory of the empire.[14] Sometimes in Roman poetry the city might include its surroundings, which might even be expanded, as in the case of the *Aeneid*, to the whole of the Italian peninsula. For example, according to Virgil, the land of Italy was promised to the Trojans by the Cumaean Sybil.[15]

The only people in the Graeco-Roman world to actually use the term "holy land" were the Jews. The example in Virgil of the Sybil giving land to mortals is a rare designation. In fact the Jews were known for their unique belief in the holiness of the land of Israel. Tertullian in the second century writes that the Jews consider the "special soil of Judea" to be *terra sancta*.[16] Indeed, the text from Virgil is poetic and certainly did not translate into actual agrarian laws concerning the physical character of the land and its produce. In Israel, on the other hand, the entire country is called "holy," and this status affected it in specific ways, as we shall discuss below.

Christianity in its first centuries adopted the nationalism and fatherland notions of the Romans but, by-and-large, put them into metaphysical language. Virgil is "a central figure in the culture of medieval Christianity" and "figures as a prophet, side by side with

David and Isaiah."[17] The *Aeneid* is held in high regard both by Roman patriots and by Christian believers. Early Christians applied the patriotism of the Romans to Heaven, their celestial city. The Letter to Diognet states, "every place abroad is their fatherland, and in their fatherland they are aliens."[18] Thus, the fidelity of the Romans to their physical city of Rome was transferred in Christian thought to the heavenly city, and physical ties to land are devalued. Origen was one of the main proponents of devaluing the physical holy land and setting Christian sights on Heaven as the Jerusalem promised to God's people. He refutes rabbinic claims on a physical land: "Moses taught that God promised a holy land which was 'good and large, flowing with milk and honey' to those who lived according to his law. And the good land was not, as some think, the earthly land of Judea" (Orig., *Ag. Cels.* 7:28). Saint Augustine, another champion of the heavenly city of God, encourages Christians to be heroic in their love for the "city above": "Why should that man be praised. . . . Because he was a lover of his city? This he could be carnally. . . . But he was not a lover of the City above" (*Contra Gaudentium*, I, 37). Especially in *De Civitate Dei*, Augustine points out the great Roman heroes who performed great acts of heroism for their terrestrial *patria* and urges Christians to do the same and more for their *patria aeterna* (see *Civ. Dei*, V, 18). A potential conflict of loyalties between Rome and the spiritual Jerusalem is apparent. As Ernst Kantorowicsz explains:

> The Christian, according to the teaching of the Fathers had become the citizen of a city in another world. Ethically, death for the carnal fatherland meant little if compared with that for the spiritual *patria*, Jerusalem in Heaven, or with the true models of civic self-sacrifice, the martyrs, confessors, and holy virgins. The saints had given their lives for the invisible community in heaven and the celestial city, the true *patria* of their desires; and a final return to that fatherland in Heaven should be the normal desire of every Christian soul while wandering in exile on earth.[19]

Nevertheless, the Christian insistence that the holy land was only of a spiritual nature was not the only way to interpret the matter. Indeed, Justin, in his Dialogue with the Jew Trypho, makes the first reference to "holy land" in Christian patristic literature, and he regards the physical land of Israel as the inheritance of both Christians and Jews in a future age (Just., *Dial.* 113.3–5).

The notion of a physical Christian holy land began to take hold dramatically in Christian thought during the fourth to fifth centuries with the discovery of the tomb of Jesus. This cave is referred to by Eusebius as the "most blessed place," the "saving cave," and the "most holy cave (*Vit. Const.* 3. 31). Workmen were told to transport the soil of the site elsewhere since it was believed to be contaminated by the idolatry of a Roman temple which had been there previously.[20] Like the rest of the ancient world, Christians too would come to regard their most holy shrine as the "center of the earth."[21]

Other places in Palestine which were important in Christian history soon drew attention as well. The combination of all of these holy places, which could be visited by pilgrims but were, of course, immovable, began to create the notion of a Christian holy land. Many Christians moved to the holy land, populating both urban and desert areas. Jerome settled in Bethlehem because it was the *patria* of the Lord. Others took relics home in the hope that the holiness of the land could be transmitted through them and transported to their native countries. St. Augustine tells of Hesperius who brought a carton of soil from Jerusalem. It was said to frighten away evil spirits and pilgrims began to come to Hesperius' shrine for healing (*Civ. Dei* 22.8). The notion of a Christian holy land remained prominent until the Muslim conquest in the seventh century. At the height of the movement, 3,000 monks lived in the desert of Judea.[22]

Thus, in Christian history as well, there has been a sense of ownership of the "holy land," and that land has been variously understood by Christians. Some have claimed spiritual, others territorial, rights to the "holy land" for the last two millennia. The New Testament itself is a seedbed for both views. According to Matthew, Jesus promises that the meek will "inherit the earth," literally "possess the land" (Matt. 5:5). Does this mean a physical or a spiritual inheritance, or both? Revelation is the best example in the New Testament of early Christian restorationist hopes. The writer claims that the kingdom of Christ will be set up on earth for 1,000 years prior to the descent of the heavenly Jerusalem (Rev. 21).

RABBINIC SYSTEM

Holy land and holy city

Let us set forth the rabbinic system of holy land. All of the area in Palestine was considered holy, but some areas more so than others.

The Mishnah states: "There are ten [degrees of] holiness: The land of Israel is holier than all lands" (m. *Kel.* 1:6). The Mishnah starts with the holiness of the land and then details the greater holiness of various areas within the land. The greater holiness of each area is defined by further restrictions on it. At the very center of the land, the Holy of Holies within the Temple is, of course, the most holy area (Figure 3.2). Rabbi Joseph Soloveitchik emphasizes the land's critical holy character in his comment to this passage: "From this mishna we learn that the Land of Israel is likened to the base of a multi-storied pyramid of sanctity; without that base, the whole pyramid would topple over."[23] The holy cult (see Chapter 2) assumes a larger system of holiness which extends throughout the entire land of Israel. A full list of the Mishnah's graded areas of holiness in the land is found above in Chapter 2, Table 2.1.

From biblical times the city of Jerusalem enjoyed an especially holy status.[24] For Isaiah, while the whole mountain land of Israel was holy, Jerusalem was especially sacred: "O Jerusalem, holy city! for the uncircumcised and the unclean shall never enter you again" (Isa. 52:1). Zechariah regards the whole land holy, but selects Judah with its Jerusalem capital as God's prime territory: "And the Lord will inherit Judah as his portion in the holy land" (Zech. 2:16 [Eng 12]; see also Joel 4:17). Ezekiel too envisions Jerusalem as the most glorious of all lands (Ezek. 20:7) and located in the middle of them (5:5).

Figure 3.2 The Temple Mount in Jerusalem, viewed from the Mount of Olives.
Source: Karen Ensor.

The notion of the holy land, begun at the latest by Zechariah's time, continued throughout the Second Temple period and beyond. 2 Maccabees begins with a letter from Jerusalem to a Jewish community in Egypt relating how Jason and his followers rebelled against the "holy land" (see also 2 Macc. 8:21). Philo, who uses the phrase "holy land" at least eight times, says the Jews of Yavneh tore down a pagan altar erected to the honor of Gaius, the emperor, because it "obliterated the sanctity that was appropriate to the holy land" (*Sp. Laws* 202).[25] In addition, there are many references to Jerusalem as the "holy city" in the New Testament (see Matt. 27:53; Rev. 11:2). Philo says that even Diaspora Jews refer to Jerusalem as the "holy city" (Philo, *Flacc.* 46).

According to the Rabbis, Jerusalem has a companion city in Heaven (b. *Ta'an.* 5a); the supra-terrestrial notion of Jerusalem existed alongside the terrestrial one. Rabban Yohanan ben Zakkai insisted that God would not enter the Jerusalem above until the Jerusalem below was rebuilt (b. *Ta'an.* 5a). The notion that God's delight in the earthly Jerusalem exceeded his pleasure in the heavenly one emphasizes a basic tenet of the Rabbis that God is more interested in his people Israel and their land than in anything else. In contrast to the general Hellenistic notion that the heavenly, or ethereal items are the genuine ones, the Rabbis seem to take the opposite tack. The physical Jerusalem is the important one. Without it, there cannot be a heavenly one. The idea of a heavenly Jerusalem is also apparent in some New Testament writings (Heb. 12:22; Rev. 21:2, 10).

In contradistinction to Yahweh's land, which is holy, other lands are considered impure and the realm of death. The principle discussed earlier that holiness and life are connected applies to the holy land as well (see Josh. 22:19; Amos 7:17). As Jacob Neusner puts it: "Outside the Land, the realm of the holy, lay the domain of death. The lands are unclean. The Land is holy."[26] For the Mishnah: "Israelites who dwell in the land of (unclean) death instead of in the Holy Land simply fall outside of the range of (holy) life." This is certainly the view of the Rabbis in principle and reflects their ideal. In fact, however, many of the Rabbis themselves lived outside of the land.

The Rabbis referred to foreign countries as the lands of "the Worshipers of Stars and Constellations." The fundamental premise here is that the idolatry practiced in other lands rendered them impure. Tacitus complains that converts to Judaism quickly learn to despise their gods, fatherland, and family (*Hist.* V, 5). This is not as farfetched and biased a claim as it may at first appear. Other gods, foreign lands, and idolatrous Gentiles simply were not compatible within the system of holiness the Rabbis envision.

The very soil of the land of Israel was considered inherently different than other soil. In the biblical story, the Syrian general Naaman asks for a few loads of soil from the land of Israel that he can take home to Damascus so he can worship God there (2 Kings 5:17). This notion is taken up by the Rabbis who refer to the soil of gentile lands as impure (b. *Shab.* 15a). Letters were sent from abroad to "the Sons of the High Priests" in Jerusalem and the issue was whether enough foreign earth was on the seals to defile (m. *Oh.* 17:5). All Jews must purify themselves upon their return to the land of Israel (t. *Oh.* 18:1–5; m. *Naz.* 7:3).

Scholars have debated the reason for assigning impurity to foreign soil. Some Tannaitic traditions imply that gentile lands are impure because of corpse impurity (t. *Oh.* 18:1–5; m. *Toh.* 4:5; see also b. *Naz.* 55a). That is to say, because gentiles were not as careful about corpse impurity, their land could not be trusted to be pure. Neverthless, this view cannot account for proclamations that cities in Israel inhabited by gentiles do not defile under this rule nor are pilgrim roads to Israel affected.[27] Furthermore, in other places the Sages make a distinction between earth from a grave area and earth from gentile territory (t. *Kel. BM* 7:1). Gedalyahu Alon argues that probably the impurity of foreign soil is an ancient notion and is linked to idolatry, rather than to corpse impurity.[28] For the Rabbis the land outside of the holy land is confusion, chaos, and impurity, simply because of the worship of other gods. Needless to say, the Rabbis regarded gentile lands devoid of divine revelation: "The *Shekhinah* never reveals itself in foreign lands" (*Mekh. Petihata* 25).[29]

The biggest issue with regard to the holiness of the land was the inescapable fact that in the Graeco-Roman period many gentiles lived within its borders. According to rabbinic law, gentile dwellings, within or outside the land, defile. Even gentile immersion pools within the land are only pure for certain routine impurities (e.g. sex, menstruation) (m. *Miq.* 8:1). For holiness to be maintained both spatial and social categories have to be pure, but the reality was that the land was under Roman jurisdiction.[30]

To deal with this crisis, the Rabbis instituted laws to keep Jews from selling their land to gentiles.[31] Many of these laws prohibit leasing or selling the land to gentiles (m. *AZ* 1:8; t. *AZ* 2:8). The verse, "Give them no quarter *tkhnm*" (Deut. 7:2), is interpreted as forbidding gentiles a place to encamp *khnyh* on the land (b. *AZ*

20a). A Jew is supposed to actively pursue the uprooting of idolatry from the land (m. *Ber.* 9:1; t. *Ber.* 7:2; *Sif. Deut.*12 (127). In order to reclaim Jewish property in the land, the rules were bent. According to the Talmud, one could even buy such a property on the Sabbath (b. *BQ* 80b; b. *Git.* 8b; y. *MQ* 2, 81b). One could also leave the land in order to litigate or arrange purchase of a property in the Land (t. *AZ* 1:8; t. *MQ* 2:1). Landowners were urged to recover Jewish land from gentiles (m. *Dem.* 6:2; y. *Dem.* 25b). Jews were allowed to participate in gentile fairs, usually forbidden due to their idolatrous nature, if they provided a way to purchase property in the land (t. *AZ* 1:8; b. *Erub.* 47a).

At the same time, the Rabbis applied considerable pressure on Jews to live in the holy land. One of the strongest statements to this effect is the following:

> One should rather dwell in the Land of Israel – even in a town in which the majority of the inhabitants are gentiles – than outside the Land – even in a town in which all the inhabitants are Jews. This [ruling] implies that dwelling in the Land of Israel is deemed as important as fulfilling all the commandments in the Torah, and all who are buried in the Land of Israel – it is as if they were buried beneath the altar [of the Temple in Jerusalem] . . . . And [Scripture also] states, "[I am the Lord your God who brought you forth out of the land of Egypt] to give you the land of Canaan, and to be your God" (Lev. 25:38), [which implies] that as long as you in the Land of Canaan, I will be your God, but when you are not dwelling in the Land of Canaan, it is as if I am not your God.
>
> (t. *AZ* 4[5]:3–6)

The text goes on to explain that living outside the land is like idolatry.

Laws were enacted supporting the command to live in the land. According to the Talmud, either spouse could force the other, by appeal to the court, to move from the Diaspora to the holy land, and a woman who refuses to immigrate to Israel with her husband could be divorced without her dowry (b. *Ket.* 110ab). Laws were put into effect which facilitated living in the land.[32] For example, no middlemen were allowed to export foods from the land, reducing the cost of export (b. *BB* 90b, 91a). Servants escaping from Palestine could be pursued and reclaimed, but not those escaping from an owner outside the land (b. *Git.* 43a; b. *Ar.* 49b).

Jewish persecutions in the land for centuries after 70 CE made it hard to insist that Jews had to live there. Indeed, most Jews were soon found in the Diaspora rather than in Palestine. Many moved to Babylon for safety (b. *Pes.* 87a; see also b. *Ket.* 110b), and the rabbinic academy there soon became the major center of Jewish learning in the world. The medievalists excused themselves from living in the land because of the danger to life.[33]

Nevertheless, even after the destruction of the Temple in 70 CE, the holiness of the land continued in importance for the Sages, a special preoccupation. Even though most Jews lived in the Diaspora, there was unanimity among the Rabbis that complete fulfillment of the Law was possible only in the holy land.[34] Living in the land was the ideal; the Diaspora was only an imperfect, temporary situation. In the land, produce was holy, and tithes had to be separated even though there were no functioning priests and Levites to eat them. It seems that after the destruction of the Temple, the holy land and the holy people become even more important than before. As Martin Jaffee says, even though the Rabbis did not have a Temple, still

> the Land retained a holiness in its soil, which distinguished it from any other spot on earth . . . . It is as if, with the destruction of the physical Temple, the Land and the People of Israel had themselves absorbed the invisible essence that constituted its holiness. Laws that once protected the holiness and purity of the Temple and its personnel were now applied to the territory and the people that the Temple had sanctified. . . . The rabbinic world embodied the Temple's sanctity in the surviving realities of the Land and the People of Israel.[35]

Restrictions and requirements

As discussed in earlier chapters, holiness is defined by its restrictions. Since the holiness of the Land derives directly from the presence of the Holy One who owns it and resides within it, restrictions on its human inhabitants are inevitable and unsurprising. There are a number of laws in the Torah which simply cannot be fulfilled outside of the land. These are called, "*mitzvot ha-teluyot ba-'aretz*, commandments which depend upon the Land." Many of these laws center around the Temple, and were discussed in Chapter 2. The rest of the land requirements fall loosely into three categories: (1) agriculture; (2) purity; and (3) government and ethics. Some laws fall into more than one category.

The agricultural restrictions and requirements on Israel maintain the fundamental principle that God owns the land, causes its fertility, and therefore deserves its produce. The people of Israel are his tenants and as such have the right to work and benefit from the land. Recognizing God's ownership and their dependence on him for continuing bounty, they present him, through his priestly representatives, with prescribed portions of the produce and livestock. This activity releases the rest of the crops and animals for normal, Israelite use. The tenants have acknowledged the sovereignty of the Landowner, who promises to guarantee subsequent fertility.[36]

Israel must leave the land fallow every seventh year and refrain from working the land on the Sabbath, that is, every seventh day.[37] Produce growing of itself during the sabbatical year is considered holy and may not be harvested commercially or taken outside of the Land of Israel (m. *Sheb.* 6:5; 7:3). Also, debts were cancelled in the seventh year.[38] According to the Bible, every fiftieth year is a jubilee year in which the land not only rests but all of it must return to its original tribal owners. Defaulting debtors are pardoned and Israelite slaves are released. The jubilee was apparently not observed in rabbinic times (*Sifra*, *Be-Har*, 2:3; y. *Git.* 4:3; b. *Qid.* 69a). Nevertheless, the Rabbis did feel that observance of the sabbatical year was necessary for the continued dwelling of Israel on her land. Exile, poverty, and pestilence were all considered the result of non-observance of this law (b. *Shab.* 33a; b. *Suk.* 40b; m. *Ab.* 5:9).[39] By keeping the sabbatical year, Israel acknowledges God's ownership of the land and her position as a tenant farmer with no right to set aside the divine decrees. She also demonstrates her dependence on God for prosperity. Conversely, when Israel does not observe these laws, she acts as though the land is not God's and "can therefore be organized in alternative ways."[40]

The laws of the Sabbath and the sabbatical and jubilee years reveal an intrinsic connection between holiness and social justice. First, employees cannot be forced to work for days on end. Everyone, even animals, must be given a rest for one full day in the week as well as during other holy times. Second, the laws releasing debts in the seventh year provide a safeguard against enslaving fellow Israelites who, due to unfortunate circumstances, might not be able to repay a large loan. Finally, the reversal of land back to its original, tribal owner during the jubilee year was, at least in theory if not in practice, a preventive measure against the monopoly of wealthy landowners who might otherwise remove a poor farmer from his land. According to the principles of holiness, every Jew has a divine right to a piece of the holy land.

One-third of the Mishnah is about the land and its agriculture. The first of the six sections, or orders, of the Mishnah is *Zera'im*, "Seeds." *Zera'im* discusses the agricultural offerings which Israel must bring to God from his land. Some of these offerings can be eaten only in the holy city of Jerusalem (m. *Zeb.* 14:8).

Let us look briefly at the types of agricultural offerings in Israel. What did the Holy One require from the tenants on his land? Of special importance was the offering of the first of the land's produce, or firstfruits, to God via the priests at his holy house in Jerusalem. The point is obvious. Israel cannot forget to whom the land belongs and who is responsible for its productivity. Holiness, if it is to continue to be present among them must be acknowledged, and this is best done by gifts. In this case, the farmer acknowledges God's sovereignty over the land by taking no benefit from his crop until he has offered the early fruit to the priests.

Giving firstfruits to the deity was an important topic of rabbinic study and early Palestinian practice. That they were a major concern is apparent from the fact that even the Jews of Rome were "contributing sacred sums of money from their first fruits and sending them to Jerusalem by the hands of those who were to conduct the sacrifices."[41] Firstfruit offerings are not just a Jewish phenomenon. In Greek culture too firstfruits were offered to the deity and deposited in a sacred place.[42] Although Christianity eliminated agricultural aspect of holiness, the teaching was retained that "firstfruits," whatever they designated, were holy. For example, the souls under the altar described by the Revelator were "slain" for the word of God; because of the complete dedication of their lives to God, as well as their early martyrdom, they are called holy "firstfruits" (Rev. 14:4). Thus, holiness describes a gift or complete surrender of an item to God.

Terumah refers to a holy, agricultural gift which Israel gives to the priests. The amount is a percentage of the Jewish farmer's produce, between one-fortieth and one-sixtieth of the crop (m. *Ter.* 4:3). Although the term can refer loosely to any agricultural contribution, it is also a technical term denoting a specific offering. The meaning of the word signifies "removal, setting aside, or dedicating." Like sacrifices, *terumah* is an item set aside from its owner's domain and transferred to God's domain. This can be done verbally; an oral dedication is equivalent to transfer (m. *Qid.* 1:6;

t. *Qid. 1:9*). For the Rabbis, holiness can be created by the declaration of human will and intention. *Terumah* is not placed on the altar; it is a gift of agricultural produce to the priests. As with *shelamim* portions, agricultural contributions to the priests may be eaten anywhere in Jerusalem.

Another holy agricultural gift to the priests is *hallah*. From every batch of dough, *hallah*, a "dough offering" must be set aside for the priests. From the moment the dough is rolled out (wheat) or even formed into a solid mass (barley), the priestly dues must be set aside (m. *Hal.* 3:1). Eating dough before the offering is taken out (but after the rolling and forming described above) incurs the death penalty (*Sif. Num.*, vol. 2, 157).

Cattle are tithed in the year they are born (Neusner, vol. 6, 235). Firstlings and cattle tithe are taken from normal animals. According to the Rabbis, both of these are to be offered as sacrifices, the priests receiving special portions and the owners enjoying the rest. Giving firstlings as priestly gifts is a concept known also to the Greeks.[43]

Tithes of produce are required as well. Israel gives 10 percent of all major crops to the Levites, who in turn give 10 percent of this gift, the holy portion, to the priests (Num. 18:26–29). A second tithe was required as well, following the laws of Deuteronomy 14 and 26. This tithe was considered holy and consumed by the owner in Jerusalem during the festivals. It could be first converted to money in the owner's hometown and then spent in Jerusalem during the festival. On years three and six, however, the second tithe was not brought to Jerusalem but given to the Levite and the poor in one's hometown.

Like the second tithe, the fruit of a vine or tree in its fourth year was brought to Jerusalem and eaten within its borders (m. *Ma'as. Sheni* 5:2). It was considered "holy, an offering of praise to the Lord" (Lev. 19:24). For its first three years, the fruit of a vine or tree in Israel was not to be eaten; it is referred to as *'orlah*. As a demonstration of God's ownership and control over the land, Jews brought the first edible fruit of the vine or tree, that is, all the fruit of the fourth year to the holy city to eat before Him. The fruit of subsequent years could then be consumed at home.

Any agricultural gift which one is required to offer but wishes to exchange incurs a 20 percent redemption fine. This is because the item has been sanctified, *heqdesh*, and redeeming it disturbs that sanctity. What has been put under the ban, *herem*, that is, completely devoted for destruction, may not be redeemed since it is considered "Holy of Holies." One who violates a *herem* is in mortal danger.[44]

Scripture clearly connects the offering of these gifts with the maintenance of holiness in Israel:

> For in my holy mountain, in the mountain of the height of Israel, says the LORD God, there shall all the house of Israel, all of them serve me in the land; there will I accept them, and there will I require your agricultural offerings and the first of your gifts, with all your holy things. With your sweet savor will I accept you, when I bring you out from the peoples, and gather you out of the countries wherein ye have been scattered; and I will be sanctified in you in the sight of the nations.
>
> (Ezek. 20:40–41; 34:24–28)

Some agricultural laws are in place to provide for the poor who cannot work the land or perhaps do not own any, and thus cannot support themselves. A sheaf must be "forgotten" and left for the poor to glean. The corners of a field may not be gleaned but must be left for the poor as well. During the sabbatical year, all produce is ownerless, providing another opportunity for the poor to gather food. Still other agricultrual laws ensure that the land will not be damaged. The Rabbis prohibited the raising of small livestock in agricultural areas so as not to damage the land, "the Land of Israel not be laid waste" (m. *BQ* 6:7; t. *BQ* 8:10).

What is learned about holiness from these agricultural requirements? First, it is the divine ownership which marked the land as special, and agricultural gifts to the priests are in effect gifts to the Holy One himself. They have to be of fine quality and they must be set aside first, that is, before the farmer benefits from any of the rest of his produce. Second, it is clear that God requires Israel to remember and acknowledge his ownership of the land in order for its holiness to be maintained. "Human will is determinative in the process of sanctification."[45] Third, not only the power of holiness is acknowledged but also the goodness inherent within it. It is the goodness of the Holy One which blesses the land and causes it to produce (see pp. 122–8). Many of the holy, agricultural gifts are used to support the poor and less fortunate in the land, thus divine goodness is extended throughout Israel. Charles Primus attempts to define the elusive nature of the agricultural dimension of holiness.

> If we are to understand the qualities attributed to the Land I think we must go further and assert that there is assumed

here some sort of special element: it is substantive, although obviously invisible; it is attached to the soil and is transmitted to crops that grow in the soil, thereby making those crops special, even if exported outside the Land. Following biblical phrasing, we may call this quality an element of holiness, or of sanctity [Lev. 19:8, 24; 22:10, 14; 27:30, 32]. It is affective, that is its effect can be seen in terms of resulting human actions; and therefore I argue that it must be regarded as real, although probably not tangible.[46]

The second category of requirements concerns matters of purity. Strictly speaking the holiness of a place means "that impurity must be kept away from that place."[47] All of the above holy offerings had to be harvested and preserved in a state of purity. Without this precaution the gifts would not be considered holy. Thus, holiness is not simply taken for granted as a sort of magical element in the land but must be guarded in order to be effective.

The holy city must maintain a high standard of purity which will accommodate the divine Temple within it. Most of the purity requirements deal with the Temple and its courts (see Chapter 2). According to the Rabbis, most of the holy meat (e.g. lesser holy sacrifices) could be eaten anywhere in Jerusalem (m. *Zeb*. 5:8). Consequently, the sages prohibited raising chickens in Jerusalem. They might poke into garbage and then come into contact with and contaminate holy food. Jerusalem's streets were swept daily and markets were checked every day for *sheretz*, unclean vermin. Standing piles of garbage, *ashpatot*, were not allowed in the city.[48] While impure persons may enter the city, the most impure sorts, the leper and the dead, were not allowed. The half-shekel required of all Jews for the Temple was used to maintain not only the sacred courts but "the city wall and the towers thereof and all the city's needs" (m. *Sheq*. 4:2). Purity restrictions lessen when one leaves Jerusalem. The dead are buried in other cities, but outside of all walled cities (m. *Kel*. 1:7).

A comparison of these laws with those imposed by the first century Essenes is instructive. The latter regarded Jerusalem at such a holy status, that it was almost equivalent to the Temple itself. Essenes did not bring their wives into Jerusalem. According to Yigael Yadin, Essenes living in Jerusalem were unmarried.[49] No defecation was allowed there, and since they were forbidden to leave Jerusalem on the Sabbath, that meant no defecation on the Sabbath.

The holiness of the land of Israel is also bounded by ethical restraints. Retaining rights to the land is contingent on moral integrity. The standard Jewish liturgy, which includes the phrase, "Because of our sins we were exiled from our land," is based on biblical antecedents like the verse below:

> Ye shall therefore keep all My statutes and all My ordinances, and do them, that the land, wither I bring you to dwell therein, vomit you not out. And ye shall not walk in the customs of the nation which I am casting out before you; for they all did these things, and therefore I abhorred them. But I have said unto you, "Ye shall inherit their land, and I will give it unto you to possess it, a land flowing with milk and honey" I am the LORD your God, who has set you apart from the peoples. And ye shall be holy unto Me.
>
> (Lev. 20:22–26)

The Rabbis comment on this passage:

> The Land of Israel is not like the other lands. It does not suffer transgressors. A parable. It may be compared to a prince who was given something to eat which he could not digest. Therefore he spewed it out. So too the Land of Israel does not suffer transgressors. Thus it says, "So let not the land spew you out for defiling it, as it spewed out the nation that came before you" (Lev. 18:28).
>
> (*Sifra*, Weiss, 93a)

Thus, part of being holy is maintaining God's laws in the land, which will purge itself by expelling disobedient inhabitants. Indeed the Bible refers to the land as a "habitation of righteousness, the mountain of holiness" (Jer. 31:23). Part of the reason God has given the land to Israel is that they will promote divine goodness and justice there (Deut. 4:37–38; 6:18–25; 7–9).[50]

Particular ethical restrictions, like the following, ensure the holiness of the land: no prostitution, "lest the land fall into harlotry and the land become full of wickedness" (Lev. 19:29); no shedding blood (Num. 35:29–34; Deut. 21:6–9); no remarriage with former, divorced and remarried wife (brings guilt upon the land) (Deut. 24:1–4; see also Jer. 3:1). Deuteronomy insists: "You must have completely honest weights and . . . measures, if you are to endure long on the soil that the Lord your God is assigning to you" (Deut. 25:15). Probably more of a purity concern, but nevertheless with ethical overtones, Israel is not allowed to leave a corpse hanging all night on a tree in the land (Deut. 21:22–23).

While this ethical worldview was championed in the Torah, the reality of Jewish life in the early centuries was far from supporting it. Jews had no political control of their homeland and thus could not enforce many of these laws. Nevertheless, the Rabbis did not ignore these socio-ethical ideals and always pointed to the day when the Messiah would rectify the situation. The Messiah was anticipated as a coming Jewish king in Israel, who would establish Jewish political freedom in the land as well as enforce social justice and the rest of the divine law.

Agricultural festivals

Agricultural festivals in Israel are holy.[51] Scripture gives the title, *miqra' qodesh*, "holy proclamation," to each of the major agricultural festivals.[52] Leviticus teaches: "These are the appointed seasons [*mo'adim*] of the Lord, even holy proclamations [*miqra'e qodesh*], which ye shall proclaim in their appointed season" (Lev. 23:4; see also Num. 28–29). The three chief festivals, *regalim*, those requiring all Jewish men to appear before God at the Jerusalem temple, are: *Pesah*, "Passover," *Shavu'ot*, "Weeks," and *Sukkot*, "Booths" (Figure 3.3)

The sanctity of these festivals is apparent in the command to refrain from work, something not stipulated for the more secular, new moon feasts. Passover and Booths were celebrated for at least a week, the first and last days being the most holy; no work could be done on these days. Work necessary for preparing food was allowed on intervening days (except the Sabbath) (*Mekh.* 73; Exod. 12:16; *Sif. Num.* 147). Other light work was allowed as well. However, these days still carry restrictions (e.g. no leaven).

Israel was told to rejoice on these festivals (Deut. 16:14; Amos 8:10; Hos. 2:13[11]; Ezek. 6:22). Joy is an integral part of holiness. *Hag*, festival, literally means "to celebrate," or perhaps "to go round, dance" before the LORD.[53] The prohibition on work and emphasis on joy were strong marks of the holiness of festival days. As Nehemiah tells the Jews on the Feast of Booths: "This day is holy to the LORD your God. You must neither mourn nor weep" (Neh. 8:9). Isaiah testifies to the joy at the feasts, "You shall have a song as in the night when a feast is hallowed; and gladness of heart, as when one goes with a pipe to come into the mountain of the Lord to the Rock of Israel" (30:29). After the destruction of the Temple the festivals were still spent in rejoicing, but also in increased study of the Torah. R. Joshua's opinion "half [time] to the Lord and half for

Figure 3.3   Pilgrims at the Western Wall, Jerusalem, during the festival of
Sukkot.
Source: Palphot Ltd.

yourselves" became the general rule (b. *Pes.* 68b; see also b. *Bezah.*
15b).

The holy character of the feasts is marked by special sacrificial
offerings and rituals in the Temple accompanied by prayers and
hymns.[54] In the Second Temple period tens of thousands of animal
sacrifices were offered during the festivals (Aristeas 88; see also
Philo, *Vit. Mos.*, 2:31). Both congregational and individual offerings

were offered on the festivals. For the congregation, the priests offered sin offerings to ensure the sanctity of the Temple and its vessels (m. *Sheb.* 1:3–5). Since Leviticus teaches, "And they shall not appear before the Lord empty" (16:16), the Sages set a fixed amount for the offering on the pilgrimage festivals (*Sif. Deut.* 143). In addition, individual offerings which one incurs throughout the year (see previous section) were usually brought at the first pilgrimage festival that followed the requirement (b. *RH* 4b).

The holiness of the festival is apparent not only in the rest, joy, and holy gifts but also in Israel's remembrance of divine intervention in her history. Celebration of miraculous, historical events are connected to each festival. Passover celebrates national freedom obtained at the time of the Exodus from Egypt (Exod. 12; m. *Pes.* 10:5). It is also the season for bringing the firstfruits of the barley harvest to the Temple. The Feast of Weeks, or Pentecost, celebrates the divine revelation and giving of the law at Mt. Sinai (b. *Pes.* 68b; b. *Shab.* 88a). It is also the occasion for bringing the firstfruits of the wheat crop to the priests (Exod. 22:29; 23:19; 34:26; Num. 15:20–21; 18:12–13; Deut. 18:4; 26:2–11). The Feast of Booths, also "Feast of Ingathering," remembers the divine protection and provision in Israel's early wilderness journeys (Lev. 23:42–43). It is also the time of rejoicing over the full harvest, praying for the winter rains, as well as giving appropriate gifts to God. Jews came with their families to Jerusalem on these occasions and rejoiced together by sacrificing and feasting in the holy city (Exod. 10:9; 1 Sam. 1; Am. 5:21; Isa. 30:29; Ps. 42:3,5[2,4]; 2 Chron. 5:3).

These festivals were not only rooted in history, but some had eschatological overtones as well. For example, Passover fueled a future hope for the messianic kingdom. Jews began to regard the first national redemption as the occasion on which the Messiah would emerge in the future and bring them redemption from their Roman overlords (*Mekh.* and *Ex. R.* on Exod. 12:42). According to the Prophets, Elijah must precede the Messiah, so the expectancy of Elijah too became part of the Passover tradition. A cup of wine is poured for him at the meal (b. *Pes.* 65b).

All of Israel is required to participate in the holy festivals. They are not for the elite or initiated alone, but the whole community, even slaves, must participate. Care is taken that the helpless, widows, orphans, and needy are not left out (Deut. 16:11, 14; Neh. 8:10–12). As noted above, holiness reaches across class distinctions and socio-economic barriers. Even the stranger who resides among Israel and the animals must rest during these times. The blurring of class lines is apparent at the festivals when all the laity were allowed to form a procession which entered the Court of the Priests, went around the altar, and even afforded a glimpse of the inside of the Sanctuary (m. *Suk.* 4:5; m. *Mid.* 2:6). The laity were allowed to enter the sacred precincts at no other time.

In contrast to at least some of the Graeco-Roman festivals, for example Dionysian banquets, which were characterized by drunken orgies, Jews had to purify themselves for each of their festivals by refraining from sexual intercourse, immersing their bodies in water and laundering their clothes (many also cut their hair); sometimes atoning sacrifices had to be offered as well. The purity restriction at the time of Passover is noted in the New Testament where "many went out of the country up to Jerusalem before the Passover to purify themselves" (John 11:55). Graves were whitened one month before Passover so that pilgrims would be sure to avoid them and not become impure. Jesus was evidently referring to this practice when he called the Pharisees "whited sepulchres . . . full of dead men's bones, and of all uncleanness" (Matt. 23 :27). All Jews who were by chance impure at the time of the feast had to wait one month and celebrate it in purity (Num. 9:9–10; m. *Pes.* 9:1).

In light of Graeco-Roman accounts of the feasts of Dionysus, and others,[55] there must be some truth in the rabbinic description of the difference between the festivals of Israel and those of the Gentiles: "You [God] grant the nations many festivals and they eat, drink, and are wanton, they go to the theater, the circus, and anger You by word and deed; but Israel is not so. You grant them festivals and they eat, drink, and rejoice, and go to the synagogues and *battei midrash* ["houses of learning"] and multiply their prayers, their festival offerings, and their sacrifices" (*PRK* 340–1). Josephus makes the same comparison: "We slaughter the sacrifices not to get ourselves into a drunken state" (*Ag. Ap.* 2.195). Rejoicing however was mandatory at all of the Jewish feasts, and on the Feast of Sukkot a torch dance took place in the Court of the Women which continued until early morning. At times, Israel too is accused of drunkenness, gluttony, and licentiousness (b. Bets. 3a; b. *Qid.* 81a; y. *MQ* 2:3; see also Amos 5:21; Isa. 1:13f.; Mal. 2:3). One might also refer to Rava's statement that on the festival of Purim a man must drink enough wine that he no longer knows if he is blessing Mordecai or cursing Haman (b. *Meg.* 7b). Nevertheless, Purim is not a holy occasion but a minor festival during which work is permitted.

The holiness of the land after 70 CE

The Rabbis discuss the issue of whether or not the sanctification of the land was annulled after the 70 CE destruction of the Temple (m. *Ed*. 8:6; b. *Mak*. 19a; b. *Hul*. 7a; b. *Ar*. 32a; b. *Nid*. 46b). They are not debating the divine designation of the land's holiness because this was guaranteed by a host of biblical promises (see above).[56] Their concern rather is the situation of numerous Jewish deaths and mass exodus from the land brought on by the Roman wars of 70 and 135 CE against the Jews. The issue for the Rabbis is how Israel in exile would be able to fulfill land tithes, sabbatical year, and the other agricultural requirements discussed above, that is, how Israel would be able to fulfill her obligations regarding the holiness of the land.

Away from the holy land, the holiness of the people was at stake. The Rabbis thus offer several substitutes for life in the land. First, the very fact of exile was considered a means of atonement. R. Johanan said exile atones for all sins (b. *San*. 37b). Suffering in general is looked upon as another means of substitution for life in the land (see 4 Macc. 17:20–22). Israel's weeping and suffering on account of the loss of the holy land will be rewarded (*Mekh. Pisha* 1; cf. b. *Ber*. 5a). In the same vein, repentance atones for the defilement of and/or loss of the land. The Rabbis regard repentance as more holy than the Temple service. They ask: "Whence is it derived that if one repents, it is imputed to him as if he had gone up to Jerusalem, built the Temple, erected an altar, and offered upon it all the sacrifices enumerated in the Torah? From the text: 'The sacrifices of God are a broken spirit' (Ps. 51:17)" (*Lev. R.* 7:2).

Among the Jews of Qumran, the existence of a righteous Jewish community provides a holy spirit and a ransom for sin and "acceptance for the land" (1QS 8:10; 9:3). While the physical hope of control over the land was retained, in the interim the life of the community was believed to bring atonement (1QS 9:4–6). Traces of this notion are also apparent among the Rabbis. For example, in more than one source, God says, "The righteousness and justice you perform are dearer to me than the Temple" (*Deut. R.* 5; b. *Shab.* 119b).

The observance of holy days, for example the Sabbath and festival pilgrimages, provides still another way of identifying with those who live in the land and is accepted as a substitution for life in the land (y. *Kil.* 9:6). Already from biblical times, the Sabbath was a mark of Israel's holiness, or ownership by God (Ezek. 20:12ff.).

According to Nehemiah, desecrating the Sabbath was one reason for the exile from the land (Neh. 13:15–22; see also Amos 8:4–6). In the Second Temple period and afterward, Sabbath observance became a weekly declaration of this holy status and a public commitment to loyalty to the Holy One.

The Rabbis offer the converse of Nehemiah: if desecrating the Sabbath decreased the holiness of Israel, observing the Sabbath increases her holiness (*Mekh. ShY* on Exod. 31:15). How does this work? It appears that by observing the Sabbath the holy people create a connection with the Holy One by acknowledging his sovereignty as creator. They imitate, and in a way reenact, the act of creation – a labor of six days with a rest on the seventh (*ibid.*). The text reads: "The Sabbath increases Israel's holiness. . . . Furthermore, whoever keeps the Sabbath testifies of Him at whose word the world came into being; that He created the world in six days and rested on the seventh" (*Mekh. ShY* to Exod. 31:14). Thus, as Jonathan Smith says, "Exile may be overcome in moments of sacred time."[57] On the Sabbath the home of the Jew was transformed into a sort of sacred temple and, according to one tradition, an extra Sabbath soul enters his body.

Pilgrimage to Jerusalem, especially at the time of the feasts, was another way of substitution for residing in Eretz Yisrael, "the land of Israel." Already in the time of Christ, Jerusalem was crowded during the festivals with not only Judeans and Galileans but Diaspora Jews as well (see Acts 2:1, 5–11). This practice continued after the destruction of the Temple as well. The Christian Pilgrim from Bordeaux of the fourth century tells that Jews came annually to the site of the Temple to "bewail themselves with groans, rend their garments, and so depart."[58]

Connection with the Land also continues by holy communication to God, that is, prayer. The eighteen benedictions include a blessing "upon thy city and upon thine inheritance."[59] The daily blessings over food too include prayer for the land. Probably the most sustained remembrance of the land by those in exile is in the daily blessings of food.[60] The blessing, *akhat me'en shalosh*, or "one benediction expressive of three," reads: "Blessed are You . . . for the lovely, good, and spacious Land in which You delighted, bequeathing it to our forefathers, to eat of its fruit and to be satisfied with its goodness. . . . Blessed are You for the Land and for its produce." The ninth of Ab is a day set aside to mourn and reflect upon the destruction of both temples and the decree that the fathers not enter the promised land; it concludes a three-week period of sorrow.

Hope is probably the key element continuing the link of Israel to her land. The Jerusalem Talmud states: "Though soil cannot be stolen, a man can forfeit his right to this soil by giving up hope of ever regaining it" (y. *Orla* 1:2). Lieberman applies this passage to Israel's situation vis-à-vis the land in general.[61] The Bible is explicit that the land remains an eternal, divine promise to Israel (Gen. 13:14–15; 17:8). The prophets promise eschatological fulfillment: "On that day the Lord their God will save them . . . like the jewels of a crown they shall shine on his land" (Zech. 9:16–17; see also Amos 9:14–15). The hope of the transformed, renewed land kept the Jews going and "gave them identity and even sanity in a context where everything was denied" (see Ps. 137:5–6).[62]

The Rabbis emphasize that the Torah is a lifeline for Israel in exile that compensates for the temporary loss of the land: the study of the Torah ensures God's holy presence (m. *Ab.* 3:2). They declared: "Greater is study of the Torah than the rebuilding of the Temple" (b. *Meg.* 16b). The study of Torah too came to be considered a holier enterprise, not only than the maintenance of the holy land but even holier, than the Temple service (see Chapter 4).

GRAECO-ROMAN WORLD

Graeco-Roman festivals

In Greece, as well as the rest of the ancient world, feasts and fasts related to the land were common. In Athens alone over thirty-five festivals or public sacrifices were conducted a year. *Heortai* are festivals which are "organized around communal sacrifices and banquets" and which were also holidays from "civil, business and agricultural affairs."[63] Most of the festivities centered around the agricultural cycle: plowing, harvesting, vintage. The god Demeter was honored with a celebration of the grain crop; the Festival of Dionysos was a time of jubilation over wine. As in Israel, firstfruits (*aparchai*) of various harvests were presented to the gods.[64] Some festivals included great public processions which marked the territory controlled by the city (e.g. the Eleusinian Mysteries). Public games, political pomp, athletic and drama contests, and even ship races often accompanied the festivities.[65]

Hieromenia refers to the sacred time of a festival and signals restrictions on regular daily activity. Although some business life continued, courts and other public administration offices did not hold sessions. Military campaigns were interrupted by important festivals, but sometimes Greeks were attacked just because they were celebrating a festival and so were unprepared for fighting.[66] Criminals were not usually executed or seized during the festivals, but if any violence occurred during the festival, punishments were apparently severe.[67] For example, a person who whipped his enemy during the festival was put to death (Dem. 21.180). Restrictions also affected those invited to the festival. For the *Panathenaia* festival the entire body of citizens is enjoined to participate; the *Thesmophoria* was for women only.

Some festivals were associated with particular military or other victories. "At the Carnea, the Spartans gave thanks to Apollo for bringing them into the land as conquerors. During this festival, the people dwelt in tentlike bowers after the fashion of a military camp."[68] Similarly, the Jews lived in temporary shelters on *Sukkot* in celebration of their miraculous wilderness experience.

Purifications were a part of some festivals. Primarily water and blood were used. Sometimes individuals were expelled from the community as human scapegoats. Other purification rites could include routine annual washing of divine statues or rituals for renewal of the community fire.[69] There was also at Athens a concept of "impure days" on which no activity took place. Temples were closed and "nobody would begin any serious undertaking" (Xen., *Hell.* 1.4.12). A few festival days might be considered impure because of the bizarre rites performed on them. There were also impure days separate from the festivals which were probably connected with unpropitious phases of the moon, for example, warfare at Sparta was interrupted by a lunar omen.[70]

The biggest difference in the overall structure of Roman and Greek festivals, was that the Roman calendar standardized the dates of all of the Roman festivals throughout the empire whereas each Greek city had its own individual calendar of festivals. This connection of the Roman festivals and the empire led to an implicit allegiance to the Roman state when one observed the festivals.[71] These festivals, or *feriae*, stressed the unity and commonality of all of the citizens in the empire. John Ferguson discusses the special days of the Roman calendar: "Each day has attached to it a letter of religious significance, F (*fastus*) means that official business might be transacted on that day with divine blessing. C (*comitialis*) means that the day was *fastus*, but also propitious for the holding of political assemblies. N (*nefastus*) means that the day was utterly unpropitious for the conduct of official business."[72]

Like the Greek festivals, the Roman *feriae* were often agricultural, celebrating the various aspects of the farming cycle, from planting to harvesting. The *Cerealia* in April was the festival of Ceres, the goddess of growth, especially grain. The *Vinalia*, also in April, celebrated the new wine and dedicated libations to Jupiter. In the fall, as expected, various harvest festivals were celebrated.

Other festivals commemorated historical events such as military victories or significant political enactments, or the athletic games. The traditional festivals were celebrated annually, but new ones were continually added. For example, a festival would be inaugurated to celebrate the birthday of the reigning emperor. Sometimes before a major event, a festival would be proclaimed.[73]

Some festivals were purificatory. For example, the *Lupercalia* in February, the month of purification, included a ritual led by the *Luperci*, priests, dressed only in loincloths, with sacred goats and a dog at the *Lupercal* (sacred cave at foot of the Palatine). The priests wiped the sacrificial blood from the knife onto their foreheads and later ran through the streets using leather straps, made from the skins of the slain sacrificial goats, to strike at spectators. These leather strips were called *februae*, instruments of purification.[74] In June, the *Vestalia*, festival of Vesta, celebrated the sacred fire. In October, the festival of *Armilustruium* purified the weapons of the military for winter storage.

Some festivals were restricted to specific classes of people. On March 1 only the men sacrificed to Mars, the god of war, while women celebrated the *Matronalia*, a festival for Juno Lucina, a goddess of childbirth. The *Saturnalia* was a winter festival during which roles of slave and master were reversed. Originally a celebration of jollification and gifts, it was eventually taken over by Christians and reinterpreted as Christmas.

With all of these festivals, the precise significance of the rituals is hard to ascertain. Not having the mythologies Homer and Hesiod provided to the Greeks, it is difficult to know how to interpret Roman festivals. There were no fixed theology or doctrines surrounding them and so the rituals could easily mean different things at different times as new ideas were absorbed.[75]

In comparing the Graeco-Roman festivals with those of the Jews, many similarities are obvious: (1) rejoicing for agricultural bounty; (2) refraining from work; and (3) communal feasting. Nevertheless, there are differences too: (1) lack of class distinction at all Jewish festivals; (2) ritual and ethical purity required at all Jewish festivals; and (3) strong historical, theological, and sometimes even eschatological underpinning to each of the Jewish holy days. In some respects, the differences are ones of degree. Some Graeco-Roman festivals do cut across class distinctions and many require ritual purity; some festivals even have historical, military roots. In some the deity is more prominent than in others. In Israel, nevertheless, all of the festivals are occasions of approach to a holy God, who requires a high standard of purity, in terms of both ritual fitness and righteousness, for this meeting. The lines of connection between the Holy One and the holy people are strictly enforced by specific gifts and rituals. Each occasion is one of thanksgiving and acknowledgment of God as the source of agricultural bounty as well as historical deliverance and protection. Holy produce from his sacred land is brought to him as a gift which acknowledges his sovereignty.

From physical site to spiritual center

Contrary to both the rabbinic as well as classical focus on the significance of a physical, holy center, many people in the Graeco-Roman world of the first Christian centuries promoted spiritualization of sacred sites. The Stoics were a key factor in this shift. Zeno (300 BCE), the founder of Stoicism, emphasized cosmic reason over a physical center. Later Stoicism declared that the whole world was the divine temple (Sen., *Moral Essays,* VII, 7, 3; see also Plut., *Tranq. An.*, 20 (II, 477c)). Sometimes the holy site was related to an inner spirit or magical force, as in Valerius Maximus (31 AD).[76] Thus, there was a growing tendency in the Hellenistic world away from a locative view of the sacred which emphasizes a particular place as the center of the world toward a utopian view which values no particular place but regards the divine spirit as immanent.[77]

The Hellenization upon which the Roman empire was built was especially opposed to the kind of Jewish thought described above, that is, belief in the holiness of a particular country, not necessarily because it was Jewish, but primarily because it was particular and historical.[78] Hellenizers tried to transform Jerusalem, an *ethnos*, a tribal-based covenantal shrine, into a *polis*, a Graeco-Roman cosmopolitan urban center.[79] In Greek, *politeia*, citizenship, "is also the life of the citizen, life in civil order especially participation in state life, political activity in all its forms and stages; 'state order'."[80] While the *polis* was in its original conception a religious society, this connection became for the most part formal and did not, at least in imperial times, affect conduct in an ethical manner.[81] *Politeis* came to mean "fellow-citizen, compatriot" without any religious or ethical overtones.

Hellenization had no place for particular historical remembrance and no doctrine of repentance. Rather, the universal, human person, body, and intellect were stressed. Tolerance, inclusiveness, and the breaking down of barriers across the empire were trademarks of the day. Nevertheless, as Martin Hengel has demonstrated, while Hellenization claimed neutral ideology, it actually reinforced class distinctions. By setting forth new goals, for example urban sophistication, gymnasium education, and political arts, Hellenization favored those who could participate in these realms. The new way allowed land to become accessible in new ways. The notion of inheritance for every Jew through divine right without recourse to any social caste was scorned. In the new order, those with class and financial advantages could easily take advantage of the poor (see 1 Macc. 2:19–22, 27). As Walter Brueggemann states succinctly, Hellenization eroded

> old patterns of inheritance, promise, and gift, all of which depend upon (a) historical particularity which now appeared embarrassing if not scandalous, (b) intergenerational identity as land descended with the family, and (c) a notion of inherited right which needed no political legitimacy or defense.[82]

Some early Jewish writers, writing in Greek for a broad audience, seized the principles of Hellenization and tried to express them in Jewish terms.[83] Josephus, for example, uses the term *polis* to conceal the religious character of Judaism and cast it instead as a philosophy. Also, for obvious political reasons, he ignores the hope of Jerusalem as a future Jewish world capital from which the Messiah will rule. The author of 1 Maccabees bases his claims to the land on both biblical and tenancy claims (1 Macc. 15:33–34).[84] The latter would have appealed to a Hellenistic mind that the Jews had lived on their land as long as anyone could remember and thus were justified in establishing a national presence there. Philo emphasizes cosmopolitanism, using "citizen of the world" language. God moves about within the "soul of the wise"; the divine presence in the holy land is forgotten.

Philo seems to adopt the Hellenistic perspective since in his writings there is a complete lack of interest in the sacred space of the physical land of Israel. The promised land becomes wisdom, virtue, and knowledge of God ("On Abraham," 84; "On the Migration," 28–29).[85] For Philo, the borders of the country which one should seek really include "the better part of ourselves" ("On Dreams," 255). Passions are, like the land of Egypt, to be renounced. A Jew should seek control of body and mind, not of physical territory. The return to the land promised by the prophets is interpreted, not as a physical migration, but as a spiritual return to God, that is, repentance.[86] Both Philo and Josephus read a universalism into the text which does not fit well with the particularism of rabbinic land theology.

Christianity

Christianity inherited both trends, Jewish and Hellenistic, in its theology of land. On the one hand, the Land of Israel has been regarded holy by Christians at least as early as the fourth century CE.[87] *Eretz Yisrael* was the place of both old and new covenants and so was understandably revered by both Christians and Jews. In particular, the life of Jesus, having taken place on the soil of the land of Israel, was always good cause for a pilgrimage. Throughout history, but especially during the Byzantine period, Christian pilgrims have revered the holy land which gave birth to their faith. When remembering Jesus' life, it is impossible to divorce him from the land in which he lived. Ethiopian Christians use the term *qedesht agar*, "holy land," frequently even to calling their ascetics who live there *qeddushan*, "holy ones." This designation was based simply on the fact that the latter resided in the land of Israel, not on the moral quality of their lives.[88]

On the other hand, the New Testament authors seem to agree that Jesus, not any particular physical site, is the "place" of divine worship (see John 1:51; 4;19–24; 10:30).[89] Christianity does not have an earthly center, but is centered in its community of believers. According to John, Jesus said to the Samaritan woman: "Woman, believe me, the hour cometh, when ye shall neither in this mountain [Mt. Gerizim], nor yet at Jerusalem, worship the Father" (John 4:21). Paul too appears uninterested in the physical land of Israel. His mission is outside the land. In his teachings, he emphasizes that God dwells within believers, not in a particular house in a particular land (2 Cor. 6:14–17; 3:16–17; 6:12–19). For John, the person of Christ is the sacred "place" for atonement and reconciliation (John 10:37). For both Paul and John, a reverence for the physical Temple applies, but is overshadowed by the superior work of Christ.

Polis in the New Testament is a non-political term.[90] It is used for the heavenly city "whose builder and maker is God" (Heb. 11:10). The patriarchs were pilgrims throughout their lifetimes *teis geis*, i.e. "on the [physical] land," but God had Heaven waiting (Heb. 12:22–24). Following the Jewish ethical requirements of inheriting the land, spiritual citizenship meant belonging to the *hagioi*, "the holy ones" of Israel (Eph. 2:12, 19). *Politeuma* refers to the "homeland" of Christians in Heaven (Phil. 3:20). The Church Fathers too often used *polis* in the sense of the heavenly world with no political interest (see *Herm. Sim.*, 1, 1, 1–6; see also John's Gospel where Jesus says: "My kingdom is not of this world," John 18:36). Jerusalem in many New Testament passages becomes a symbol for Heaven (Gal. 2:19–21; Phil. 3:20ff.). However, many Christians believed they already lived the life of the New Jerusalem, that is, they were already citizens of Heaven, when they accepted faith in Christ. The full realization of their hope, nevertheless, would come in the next life (Heb. 11:10–14; see also 12:22–24).[91]

Although Jesus and his disciples attended the Jewish festivals (John 7:37f.; Matt. 26:30), Paul protests Christian observance of them as stumbling blocks to the new faith (Gal. 4:10; Col. 2:16). Along with other New Testament writers, Paul reinterprets elements of these holy days in the light of Jesus' person and ministry. For example, "the blood of the covenant which was shed," an allusion to the Israelite covenant sacrifice at Mt. Sinai (Exod. 24:1–10), is interpreted as a new covenant inaugurated by Jesus' death. Jesus as the "Passover lamb" is the sacrificial body (1 Cor. 11:23–29; see also m. *Pes.* 10:3; Rev. 13:8; 1 Pet. 1:20). Instead of eating various foods "in remembrance of Hillel," the early Christians ate symbols of Christ's body and blood in remembrance of him. In fact, according to Paul, Jesus stated clearly that the bread was his body and the wine was his blood. As in the Passover drama, believers consuming these items personally reenacted the moment of Christ's crucifixion and resurrection.

Purity was necessary before eating the Lord's Supper just as it was enjoined before the Passover and other feasts, but the focus is on ethical purity (1 Cor. 11:27–28). The Lord's Supper emphasizes the element of *koinonia*, or fellowship, in 1 Cor. 10:14–22, and as such reminds of the fellowship of the Passover meal. Paul makes this point explicit, "Behold Israel after the flesh: are not they which eat of the sacrifices partakers of the altar," that is, the character of this fellowship is sacred. Like the Jewish festival pilgrims, Christians are actually having fellowship with God as well as with others in the body of believers (1 Cor. 10:16–18).

The festivals of *Shavu'ot* and *Sukkot* too are reflected in the New Testament. According to Luke, 120 followers of Jesus who were in Jerusalem to celebrate the festival of *Shavu'ot*, or Pentecost, experienced the revelation of the Holy Spirit (Acts 1–2). As they were celebrating the divine revelation to Moses in Israelite history, they became the recipients of a direct, new revelation. It was on the last day of the Feast of *Sukkot*, the feast which includes a major water ritual, that Jesus "stood and cried, saying, If any man thirst, let him come unto Me, and drink" for "rivers of living waters flow" from within him (John 7:38). John thus makes a pointed reinterpretation of the water rite of *Sukkot*.

For Paul, Christ is the "first of the new harvest," the "first who had risen from the dead," or the "firstfruits," the first sheaf waved before the Lord on the Feast of Unleavened Bread.[92] Since *Shavu'ot*, which celebrated the firstfruits of the wheat crop, was the occasion for the Holy Spirit's initial outpouring on the Jewish-Christian believers gathered together at the feast, Paul says Christians have received the "firstfruits of the Spirit" (Rom. 8:23). Similarly, the first individuals to be baptized into the new faith in a particular town were called "firstfruits" (1 Cor. 16:15; Rom. 16:5).

Johanine literature too associates Christ with the Passover lamb (John 1:36; see also 1 Pet. 1:19). Jesus is the "lamb" slaughtered on the day of Passover at the same time Jews were sacrificing their Passover lambs in the Temple (John 18:28; 19:14, 31). Jesus himself is the Paschal lamb of the new covenant (John 19:36). The lamb is a central symbol for Jesus not only because of the Passover imagery, but because lambs were the most common Jewish sacrifice in the Temple. Revelation uses the image of the lamb more than any other. "Lamb" is a sort of "code word" for the exalted Christ who, although enthroned in heaven, bears the signs of his sacrificial death on his body.[93]

Pilgrimages to Jerusalem among Christians were apparently common in the first Christian centuries, although many of the church fathers discouraged it. St. Gregory of Nyssa encouraged people to "undertake a pilgrimage out of their body towards God, but not out of Cappadocia towards Palestine" since a change of place "does not bring you any closer to God." (Even Jerome emphasized: "The gates of heaven stand open in Britain quite as well as in Jerusalem.") Nevertheless, in the fourth century it appears that this attitude was by-and-large reversed, and Christians came from all over the world to visit the shrines of the holy land and especially the newly discovered tomb of Christ.[94]

GOODNESS AND THE HOLY LAND

In the previous chapters we have discussed goodness as an integral part of holiness. For Israel, God is holy not only because He is separate from humanity but because He is concerned for human welfare. Is this the case with the holy land? Is it simply a selected, exclusive land separated from all others by virtue of God's designation of it, or does it, because of its holiness, reflect God's goodness in specific ways?

We have pointed out that the land is holy by virtue of God's selection of it and presence there. But we would be remiss if we did not ask, what does this "selection" and "presence" mean in practical terms? We know that divine selection generates holiness, but what guides the selection process? If we could answer this we would have yet another element in the Hebrew concept of holiness.

I suggest that the land's holiness by definition translates into benefit to the holy people living in it. While rabbinic sources are not explicit in connecting the terms holy land and good land, the point is implicit in several places. Take this passage, for example: "The Holy One, Blessed Be He, considered all lands, and found no land suitable to be given to Israel, other than the Land of Israel. This is indicated by what is written: 'He rose and measured the earth' – and He released nations (Hab. 3:6)" (*Lev. R.* 13:2). And in another place:

> The Holy One, Blessed Be He, said, "The Land of Israel is more precious to Me than everything. Why? Because I sought it out." In this strain it [Scripture] says, "In that day I lifted up my hand unto them, to bring them forth out of the land of Egypt into a land that I had sought out for them, flowing with milk and honey, which is the beauty of all lands" (Ezek. 20:6). And in the same strain it says, "And give thee a pleasant land, the goodliest heritage of the nations (Jer 3:19)" . . . No land was so precious as the land of Israel. Said the Holy One, Blessed Be He, to Moses, "The land, surely, is precious to me"; as it says, "A land which the Lord thy God cares for, on which the Lord your God always keeps His eye, from year's beginning to year's

end" (Deut. 11:12); and Israel are precious to Me; as it says, "Because the Lord loved you" (Deut. 7:8). "I shall," said the Holy One, Blessed Be He, "bring Israel, who are precious to Me, into the Land that is precious to Me"; as it says, "When ye come into the land of Canaan . . .".

(*Num. R.* 23:7)

From this text it is clear that God's selection of *Eretz Yisrael* means that He selects only the best and that He selects it only in order to give it to Israel.

Deuteronomy is a rich source for describing the land's good qualities and the Rabbis quote it often (Deut. 8:7/*Sif. Deut.* 31; Deut. 6:4/*Sif. Deut.* 49; Deut. 8:10/*Mekh. Pisha* 16). God acts with goodness to Israel's land because He had long ago promised it to her fathers: "He will love you and bless you and multiply you; He will bless the issue of your womb and the produce of your soil, your new grain and wine and oil, the calving of your herd and the lambing of your flock, in the land that He swore to your ancestors to assign to you" (Deut. 7:13). *Eretz Yisrael* is "a land where you will lack nothing; a land whose rocks are iron and from whose hills you can mine copper. When you have eaten you fill, give thanks to the Lord your God for the good land which He has assigned to you" (Deut. 4:9f.). The assignation of the land to Israel is only for the good of the people of Israel.

The separation of Israel from other lands in terms of receiving this goodness is made clear. The land will produce bountifully for Israel but God will not bless other nations so: "'I will grant your rains in their season' (Lev. 26:4). Not the rains of other lands . . . . There will be plenty in the Land of Israel and famine in other lands so that they will come and purchase food from them, thus enriching them" (*Sifra*, Weiss, 110b). Of course, this goodness is always contingent on Israel's obedience, as Isaiah cautions: "If you are willing and obedient, you shall eat the good of the land" (Isa. 1:19).

We have demonstrated also that God's presence guarantees holiness. God's presence in the land along with his selection of it makes it holy, but what does that mean? Holiness provides power to do good. In the case of the land this means fertility. The above quotations demonstrate that God's continued care of the land causes its abundant fertility, protection, life, and atonement. According to Scripture, lions were killing people in Israel because the new colonists transplanted by Assyria did not "know the God of the Land" (2 Kings 17:25ff.). Even earlier, God dispossessed the

Canaanites on behalf of Israel and gave them the land (Amos 2:9–10; 9:7; Gen. 12). The holiness of God could not co-exist with the evil of the Canaanites.

The Rabbis point out this need for protection in addition to fertility. "'Your threshing shall overtake the vintage' (Lev. 26:5). You will still be threshing when the vintage comes. You may say: what does it matter if there is food and drink if there is no peace? The verse says 'I will grant peace in the land' (Lev. 26:6)" (*Sifra*, Weiss, 110b).

The connection of God's protection of the land and its holiness is made explicit by early Jewish writers: "And the holy land shall have mercy on its own and it shall protect its inhabitants at that time" (2 Bar. 71:1; see also 9:2). "And everyone shall survive from the perils aforesaid and shall see salvation in my land, and within my borders which I have made holy for myself eternally" (4 Ezra 9:7–9). The Rabbis too see God's power exhibited because of the holiness of the land:

> And the Lord said unto Moses, "Why do you cry unto Me? Speak unto the children of Israel that they go forward". . . .
> R. Ishmael, "For the sake of Jerusalem, I will divide the sea for them," for it is said, "Awake, awake, put on thy strength, O Zion; put on thy beautiful garments, O Jerusalem, the holy city; for from now on there will not come into you the uncircumcised and the unclean" (Isa. 52:1).
> (Mekh. Beshallah on Exod. 14:15)

Thus, Jerusalem's holiness is seen as a power which protects the people of Israel, in this case, even outside of the land.

Eretz Yisrael, as a holy land, is characterized by a "superabundance of reality."[95] In other words, in the holy land, the connector between earth and heaven, the heavenly world spills out onto earth in such a way that its residents and pilgrims receive divine blessing. The Rabbis wax eloquent in describing this "superabundance." Before the Temple was built evil spirits used to trouble people, but not afterward (*Num. R.* 12:3); spit in Jerusalem is free from impurity (m. *Sheq.* 8:1); never a fly was seen at the Jerusalem slaughterhouse (m. *Ab.* 5:5); "even the gossip of those who live in the Land of Israel is Torah" (*Lev. R.* 34); "he who lives in the land of Israel leads a sinless life" (b. *Ket.* 110b–111a). "The atmosphere of the Land of Israel makes one wise" (b. *BB* 158b). Israel is the highest point in the world; it only rains in Israel, the rest of the world is watered by run-off (b. *Ta'an.* 10a). Prayer toward the holy land was considered more effective than in any other direction (t. *Ber.* 3:15; see also *Sif. Deut.* 28). In the holy city no woman ever miscarried by smelling the sacred flesh, no demons ever attacked, there were never any accidents or fire, no structures ever collapsed, and no pilgrim was ever turned away (b. *Meg.* 17b-18a; *ARNa* 35:1–8).

Christian pilgrims to the holy land have had similar sentiments. Many tried to transport the holiness of the land to their native homes. As noted above, some claimed that soil from the land had the power to cure disease. These relics were called "blessings" because of the holy power they were believed to contain. Pilgrims took home water from the Jordan river, dried flowers from the garden of Gethsemane, and stones from Golgotha.[96] Others remained in the hope that living in the land would confer spiritual blessing. Cyril of Jerusalem explains that the events of the New Testament happened among his community, identifying the Christians living in Byzantine Jerusalem with the believers on the day of Pentecost. Speaking of the outpouring of the Holy Spirit, Cyril says: "This honor belongs to us, and we speak, not about the good things that have happened to others but *among* us" (Cyr., *Cat. Myst.* 17.13). The blessings of the land which came in the first century were thought to be shared by Christians living in the land during subsequent centuries.

The land's power provides an abundant life not only in this era but also resurrection into the messianic era. In fact, "to inherit the land," in many Jewish sources, Christian and rabbinic, can mean to participate in the next life (see also Matt. 5:5; 1QM. 12:11; 19:4; 1En. 5:7; Ps. of Sol. 14:6; m. *Qid.* 1:10; b. *San.* 110b). The Testament of Job refers to the eternal realm as "the holy land" (Test. Job 33). Already in Isaiah, the concept of the holy land takes on eschatological overtones, for example, new Jerusalem, new heavens/earth (Isa. 60; 65:17). The Rabbis say, "All Israelites have a share in the World To Come, for it is written, 'Thy people also shall be all righteous, they shall inherit the land forever, the branch of my planting, the work of my hands that I may be glorified' (Isa. 60:21)" (m. *San.* 10:1).

For the Rabbis it is God's holy presence in the land which guarantees the resurrection. In fact, it is the holy spirit, which is most active within the borders of the land, which will revive the dead.[97] The resurrection takes place first in the land (*Gen. R.* 96:5):

Why did the Patriarchs long for burial in *Eretz Yisrael*? Because the dead of *Eretz Yisrael* will be the first to be resurrected in the days of the Messiah and to enjoy the years of the Messiah. R. Hanina said: He who dies without the Land and is buried there experiences a twofold death . . . (Jer. 20:6). If so, said R. Simon, the righteous who are buried without the Land have lost thereby? [Surely not.] But what does God do? He makes cavities like channels for them in the earth and they roll along in them until they reach *Eretz Yisrael*, when the Holy One, Blessed Be He, will infuse into them a spirit of life and they will arise. How do we know this? Because it is written, ". . . I am going to open your graves and lift you out of the graves, O My people, and bring you to the Land of Israel. . . . I will put My breath into you and you shall live again, and I will set you upon your own soil . . ." (Ezek. 37:12, 14). Resh Lakish said: There is a text explicitly teaching that when they reach *Eretz Yisrael* God will put a soul into them, for it says, ". . . Who gave breath to the people upon it and life to those who walk thereon".

(Isa. 42:5)

The holiness of the land is apparent not only in its power to produce abundant crops, protect its inhabitants, and give life to both the living and the dead, but also in its ability to atone for those who dwell within its boundaries. "R. Meir was wont to say: Anyone who dwells in the Land of Israel, the Land atones for him . . . and so R. Meir was wont to say: Anyone who lives in the Land of Israel, reads the portions of the *Shema* morning and evening, and speaks the holy language – he is a man of the World To Come" (*Sif. Deut.* 333 (383); see also y. *Shab.* 1, 3b; y. *Sheq.* end of Chapter 3 and b. *Ket.* 111a).[98] According to the Talmud, even a Canaanite girl who dies in the land will share in the resurrection (b. *Ket.* 111a). Even the wicked king Jeroboam will be resurrected simply because he was buried in Palestine (*Pesikta R.* 81a; y. *Ket.* 12:3).

The rabbinic notion that the land possessed a certain holiness which could sanctify wayward Jews is illustrated by the following story:

Rabbi and R. Eliezer were once walking by the gates outside Tiberias, when they saw the coffin of a corpse which had been brought from without the Land to be buried in

Eretz Yisrael. Said Rabbi to R. Eliezer: What has this man availed by coming to be buried in *Eretz Yisrael* when he expired without the Land? I apply to him the verse, "Ye made the heritage an abomination – during your lifetime – and you defiled my land (Jer. 11:7) in your deaths." Yet since he will be buried in *Eretz Yisrael*, God will forgive him, he replied for it is written, "And his land makes atonement for His people" (Deut. 32:43).

(Gen. R. 96:5)

In the first to fourth centuries CE, Beth Shearim was a center for reburial of Jews who had died outside of the land.[99] The power and goodness which were inherent in the holy land were considered so strong as to be able to revive even those reburied in it.

When the requirements/restrictions discussed above have not been met, the holiness of the land is violated and it expels those who are responsible. The pathos of God at the lack of covenant responsibility of Israel is expressed vividly by the prophets. Jeremiah reveals God's disappointment at Israel's lack of reciprocation of his goodness: "I had resolved to adopt you as my child and give you a desirable land – the fairest heritage of all the nations; and I thought you would surely call me Father and never cease to be loyal to Me, instead, you have broken faith" (Jer. 3:19ff.). When Israel transgresses, the "land itself ejects them, as in some passages, or the land suffers under the wrath which they have brought upon it, in which case, as Isaiah 24:4–5 puts the matter: 'The earth mourns and withers, the world languishes and withers; the heavens languish together with the earth. The earth lies polluted under its inhabitants: for they have transgressed the laws, violated the statutes, broken the everlasting covenant.'"[100] Thus, the land suffers when it is defiled, and finally ejects the evil inhabitants from it.

Purification of the land is ethical, not ritual. Therefore, repentance is needed among the erring inhabitants. Ezra's reform is probably the quintessential example of land purification in the Bible. For Ezra the land is unclean because of pollutions and abominations, not least of which was intermarriage with idolatrous women (Ezra 8:11). Purification required radical measures including mandatory divorce (Ezra 9:12). Ezra described the goal of this reform in terms of renewed good terms between the land and its people: "That you may be strong and eat the good of the land and leave it for an inheritance to your children forever" (Ezra 9:12; see also 10:10–11, 44).[101]

Another story illustrates the sanctity of living in the land:

> Two rabbis were once on their way out of the Land of Israel
> to Nisibis, where the great teacher R. Judah ben Bathyrah
> dwelt, to learn Torah from him. They got as far as Sidon
> and there they remembered the Land of Israel. They began
> to weep, they rent their garments, and they remembered
> the biblical verses which promised the land to the seed of
> Abraham. The rabbis turned around and went back to their
> place in the land, pronouncing that dwelling in the Land of
> Israel is in itself an act equal of religious significance to all
> of the Commandments in the Torah.
>
> (*Sif. Deut. Re'eh*, 80; see also y. *Kel.* 9:4; b. *BB* 91a)

CONCLUSION

The Graeco-Roman world's concept of holy land signified the
epicenter of contact between the human and the divine. Holy land,
usually a temple or outdoor shrine, was powerful because it was a
location of divine manifestation and was stamped with the seal of
divine ownership and approval. In the rabbinic understanding of
holy land, however, holiness extends to the borders of the entire
land of Israel. Its center is, of course, at the holy house in Jerusalem,
but it radiates outward from this center to the entire country. All
produce and animals raised within the land were subject to a sort of
holy tax. In addition, all residents were subject to well-defined
restrictions.

From the foregoing analysis of holy land several facts emerge
regarding the rabbinic concept of holiness. First, holiness turns out
to have a decidedly physical orientation. It cannot be loosely defined
as a mystical quality of the divine realm. Rather, it acts within the
human sphere and on *terra firma*. Second, holiness requires human
maintenance in the form of obligations resting on every Jew
residing in *Eretz Yisrael*. Many significant gifts from the human
tenants to the divine landowner were required, as well as strict
purity standards, and specific ethical obligations. These requirements are the most prominent aspect of rabbinic discussions of holy
land because this is where Jewish obligation lies. In various Graeco-
Roman cults, gifts dedicated to the gods were expected and purity
was required before entry into sacred space; however, the rigorous
ethical dimension demanded by the Rabbis is missing. Third, the

holy land purifies what is unacceptable to it. Its power can become dangerous, harming and expelling those who do not meet its requirements. Purification of the land is not accomplished by special rituals, but by the repentance of its people for its violations of the divine law.

In contrast to her Graeco-Roman neighbors, Israel's concept of holiness includes a strong component of goodness. The holy land of Israel is by definition a good land, one which is selected and empowered for the primary purpose of bringing benefit to the holy people. The land's holy power brings fertility to crops and life to its people, but also greater supernatural benefits, such as divine protection, atonement, and even resurrection of the dead within its borders.

Christianity walks a middle ground between its Hellenistic and Jewish parents. Its teachings regarding holy land are no exception. For the most part, the physical character of the holy land, in terms of required residence and agricultural gifts, is discarded. Pilgrimages are more of a spiritual luxury than an obligatory act of holiness. However, traditional Jewish teachings regarding the holy land are transferred in an ideological way to the goal of inheriting eternal life, that is, both a "superabundance" of life on earth (John 17:3) as well as life in the "holy land" of Heaven (Heb. 11:16). Nevertheless, even in Christianity, the holy land has never been completely divorced from its physical roots. Throughout the centuries, Christians have made pilgrimages to the land which gave birth to their faith.

While the Rabbis too associate inheritance of the holy land metaphorically with an enhanced life both now and in the next world, they never relinquish the sanctity of the physical Land of Israel. With the loss of the Temple early in the rabbinic period, the land of Israel remained a precious reminder of divine holiness manifest in Israel's past as well as a visible basis of hope for the revitalized holiness of the nation in the future.

4

THE HOLY WORD

In addition to the manifestation of holiness at sacred sites, there is also the notion in many religions that holiness can be mediated to humanity via the divine word. In some cultures this process is by written texts and in others the transmission of holy words is purely oral. Nevertheless, there is a power which is communicated by engagement with holy words believed to be revealed by the gods and then transmitted to holy human beings who receive them and pass them on to other worthy individuals. In this chapter we want to examine the process of transmission of holiness through holy words. Certain questions will be addressed. How does rabbinic Judaism understand the process of holiness through sacred words? How does this understanding compare with other contemporary views in the first centuries CE?

HOLINESS VIA DIVINE WORD

Holiness, a divine force which transforms human beings, can be transmitted through the divine word. Throughout history people have sought connection with the gods and inner transformation. Several religions focus on the power of the revealed word as the connecting link. At the time of the Roman Empire, this notion was especially prominent among eastern religions as well as among Jews and Christians. Christianity regards the divine word as such a powerful link to God that Christ, who was considered God incarnate, is described as "the Word" (John 1:1).

The strong power of the spoken word is marked in the religions east of Greece and Rome. In Hinduism, Brahman is "the whole of speech" and access to him comes by chanting the words of the sacred tradition.[1] The divine words have a healing and salvific power and it is forbidden to commit them to writing. The *Om* is an especially holy syllable that facilitates this access. The holy words are called Veda and they must be spoken aloud in order to exercise power. Unlike the Jews and their eastern counterparts, Buddha rejected the notion of sacred word.[2] He turned his back on the Veda as divine word and sought personal enlightenment directly. Ironically, his own words later became holy scripture to his followers.

The Rabbis inherited a tradition of divine word as revealed in Scripture as well as in oral traditions. The two together were considered holy word. They constituted "Torah," literally "instruction," which was "received," *kibel*, by Moses from God and then passed on to successive generations down to the time of the Rabbis who continued the process to their disciples (m. *Ab.* 1:1–18). The teachings of R. Akiba, for example, were said to be, "*Halakha* of Moses given at Sinai" (b. *Men.* 29b). Perhaps the earliest reference to Oral Law is in the story of Shammai and the proselyte (b. *Shab.* 31a).[3] The proselyte knows there are traditions held at the level of Torah or he would not ask Shammai: "How many Torahs do you have?" When Shammai says the written and the oral, the proselyte does not want to be taught the oral, but Shammai says, "Just as you have accepted the one in faith so accept also the other in faith." (See also *Sifra Be-huqqotay*, 8, p. 112c: "'These are the statutes and ordinances and Torahs,' this teaches that two Torahs were given to Israel, one in writing and the other orally . . . the Torah with its *halakhot* and details and interpretations were given by Moses at Sinai.")

It is not for nothing that Jews are known as the "People of the Book." Biblical writers already refer to sacred text in written form (Josh. 1:8; 2 Kings). Even God is said to have written his words on stone, and Moses put the holy tablets into the ark in the Holy of Holies in the early sanctuary (Deut. 10:1–5; see also Exod. 34:28). "The term 'bible' is an inheritance from Greek-speaking Jews who referred to their scriptures as *ta biblia ta hagia*, 'the holy books.' "[4] The Mishnah declares, "All the Scriptures are holy" (m. *Yad.* 3:5). By contrast, the Zoroastrian Avesta was not written down until perhaps as late as the sixth century CE, and the Hindu Vedas, while they may go back to the second millennium BCE, are still forbidden by the Vedangas to be written down on pain of hellfire.[5] Thus, holiness in early Judaism is transmitted in a tangible way into the community, even though this is a risk for both God and the people, which is unique. The fact that the sacred word was allowed to be represented in physical form is unusual.

Within the written Torah there is a hierarchy of holiness just as we have seen in other aspects of rabbinic Judaism. There is no doubt that the Pentateuch, "the Five Books of Moses," retained the status of greatest holiness and the other books, the Hagiographa (literally "Holy Writings"), and the Prophets, were subordinate. R. Yohanan says: "The Prophets and the Writings will be annulled, but the Five Books of the Torah will not be abolished" (y. *Meg.* 1:1, p. 70d).

The holy spirit is often associated with the giving of the divine word. The Song of Songs was more readily accepted as canonical than Ecclesiastes because the Song was claimed to have been spoken by the holy spirit, whereas Ecclesiastes seemed more like Solomon's own wisdom. Ben Sira could not be considered a holy text because it was thought that by his time the holy spirit had departed from Israel, and the prophetic period closed (t. *Yad.* 2:13–14).[6] Early Christians too attest to the role of the spirit in the transmission of the divine word: "For the prophecy came not in old times by the will of man: but holy men of God spoke as they were moved by the Holy Ghost" (2 Pet. 1:21). Because the transmission process was believed to be guided by the holy spirit, every word was significant.

As discussed in earlier chapters, holiness can be described as a divine "consuming fire." The words of God are holy and as such are associated with fire. Akiba said, "They saw a word of fire issuing from the mouth of the Almighty and hewn out upon the tablets" (*Mekh.*, *Bahodesh*, 9, p. 235). Ben Azzai, Akiba's student, said that fire flamed around him when he taught words of Torah. He explained, "Primarily when they [the words of Torah] were given at Sinai they were given only in fire, (as it is written), 'and the mountain burned with fire unto the heart of heaven'" (*Lev. R.* 16:4, p. 354). These examples confirm the manifestation of holiness in fire that we have seen in other contexts (e.g. holy fire at the Sinai theophany and holy altar fire). Holiness is more than anything a divine "consuming fire."

Rabbinic midrash connects the fiery, divine word with many components of holiness already identified in this study. The passage below from *Sifrei Deuteronomy* is a fine example:

> A fiery law for them from his right (Deut. 33:2). This informs us that words of Torah may be compared to fire: just as fire comes from heaven, so do words of Torah come from heaven, as it is said, 'You yourselves saw that I spoke to you from the very heavens (Exod. 20:19); just as fire [bestows] life upon the world, so words of Torah [bestow] life upon the world. Just as fire warms one who draws close to it, but one far away is chilled, so it is with words of

Torah – when a man occupies himself with them, they give him life, but when he withdraws from them, they cause his death; just as fire is used in this world and in the world-to-come, so words of Torah are used in this world and in the world-to-come; just as fire leaves a mark on the body of one who uses it, so words of Torah leave a mark on the body of one who uses them; just as fire causes people to recognize those who work with it, so words of Torah cause the disciples of the wise to be recognized by their manner of walking, their speech, and their outer dress.

(*Sif. Deut.* 394)

Primary aspects of holiness, such as its heavenly origin and its life-giving power, are here associated with the fiery word of God. Holiness is transformative; the fiery, divine word transforms. Also central to the definition of holiness is the way in which it separates people, marking those who are holy in distinctive ways.

The letters which comprise the words are each holy and so contain power. According to some of the Rabbis, the order of letters can be combined differently for greater power. Rav said: "Bezalel knew how to combine the letters by which heaven and earth were created" (b. *Ber.* 55a). Similarly, the reason that the present arrangement of the material is not in chronological order is in order to diffuse its power. If the order were correct, says R. Eleazar, "anyone reading them would be able to revive the dead and perform wonders" (*Mid. Tehilim* 3:2, p. 33). The Kabbalists, a later mystic group who emerged from rabbinic circles, concentrated most of their attention on uncovering esoteric meanings in the Torah's structure and letters in order to derive spiritual power.

Even for the earlier Rabbis, the power of the Hebrew alphabet, especially of the letters of the Torah, was cosmic.[7] Tradition says that God created the universe by following the blueprint of the Torah (*Gen. R.* 1:1). Likewise some Rabbis tried to create life by tapping into the power of the Hebrew letters. The Talmud tells of Rav Hanina and Rav Oshayah who spent an entire Sabbath Eve immersed in *Sefer Yetzirah*, a mystical book on creation. They claimed to have created a three-year-old calf and eaten it (b. *San.* 65b). *Sefer Yetzirah* seems to be on the fringe of rabbinic tradition. No rabbis are mentioned in it. However, it provides an example, however extreme, of the early association of Hebrew letters with cosmic power.[8]

The holy word often sanctifies the particular language through which it is transmitted. The Hindu Vedas are transmitted only in

Sanskrit, the language of revelation, which is described as "the breath of the Supreme."[9] According to the Sikhs, "spiritual vibration" only comes in the original languages of Punjabi, Hindi, or Urdu.[10] Hebrew is the "holy tongue," *leshon ha-qodesh*. All of the books of the written canon are in Hebrew except for about half of Ezra and Daniel which are in Aramaic. Nevertheless, Aramaic uses the same script as Hebrew and is considered a holy vehicle as well (m. *Yad.* 4:5).

Because of its holy status, the Bible was the authoritative base for all legal decisions. Often the Rabbis would support the correctness of their decisions with the formula *ka-katub*, "as it is written," or *ke-de-amar*, "as it is said." Quotations beginning with "It is written" are found in the New Testament as well and emphasize the status of the Written Torah among Israel. In fact, the lack of clear biblical support for a decision led to the following critique from the Mishnah which accuses some laws of having no foundation in the Torah: they are "like mountains suspended by a hair; their scriptural basis is scant and the *halachot* are abundant." On the other hand, the regulations of civil and criminal law, Temple worship, purity and incestuous relations have strong support in the Torah and form its core (m. *Hag.* 1:8).[11]

But the written character of the Scripture is not what gives it holiness. Rather it is the infusion of the divine breath. A holy book is in many ways "one complex category of holy words."[12] God spoke his words to Moses and Moses simply recorded them. The prophets' words were God's and their pronouncements often begin with the formula, "Thus says the Lord . . ." Therefore, it is really the direct transmission of the divine word from the mouth of God to the scribe that gives Scripture its holiness. Early Christians attest to the same belief: "All Scripture is given by inspiration [Gk., "breathing"] of God" (2 Tim. 3:16).

The sect of Jews living by the Dead Sea at the turn of the era, at a site now called Qumran (Figure 4.1), believed that God continued to speak to the community as it studied the Torah day and night. For these Jews, who copied and preserved what is known as the Dead Sea Scrolls, the holy revelation was open-ended. As the prophets spoke through the agency of the Holy Spirit (1QS 8:16), the sect believed that their interpreters of Scripture were aided by the Holy Spirit as well (1QH 2:15; 4:10, 20). The instructor of the community was advised by the spirit of holiness (1QH 20:12). The sect was engaged in a continual search for new "words," or illuminations, from God in addition to what had already been written.[13]

Figure 4.1 Qumran Caves.
Source: Karen Ensor

The Rabbis too say that much of the Torah was not included in Scripture, although it was given to Moses on Mt. Sinai along with the Written (m. *Ab*. 1:1). The sayings of sages from biblical to rabbinic times were also considered Torah and shared its holiness.[14]

Oral Torah includes the sages' interpretations and conclusions deduced from the Written Torah as well as those regulations they instituted (b. *Yoma* 28ab). The Talmud claims, "The Holy One, Blessed Be He, speaks Torah out of the mouths of all rabbis" (b. *Hag*. 15b). Thus, the most important principle was the reality of the divine word, whether in writing or not.

Both Written and Oral Torah issued from the sanctuary. The Written Torah was recited by the priest in the Temple, and the enactments of the sages went forth from the chief court, the Sanhedrin, which met within the sacred precincts: "They both came to the Great Court that was in the Chamber of Hewn Stone [in the Temple], whence Torah goes forth to all Israel" (m. *San*. 11:2). Expansions of Written Torah by deduction or precedent if approved by the authorities was considered Mosaic law.[15] The Oral Torah was eventually codified in the Mishnah, Talmuds and midrash collections of the Rabbis.[16] For the Rabbis of the Talmud: "The unwritten law . . . was in no wise inferior in authority to the law written in the Pentateuch, both being God's revealed will. . . . The comprehensive name for the divine revelation, written and oral, in which the Jews possessed the sole standard and norm of their religion is Torah."[17]

In the early period, the oral teachings of the rabbis were not accepted on a par with Scripture. Oral law ws not supposed to be raised to the status of Scripture. R. Judah bar Nahmani says what is orally delivered may not be written down (b. *Git*. 60b). The fear was that the oral tradition would eclipse the Written Torah. There is no question, however, that for the Rabbis of the Talmud this is precisely what did happen.[18] The sacred written words were rendered subject to the words of the holy sages, both being regarded as vehicles for the divine word. Stronger penalties applied to breaking the Oral Torah than to those of the Written Torah (m. *San*. 11:3; see also b. *Yeb*. 90b). Laws admittedly *derabbanan*, that is, enactments of the sages, were invested with the authority and sanctity of the Torah, for example benedictions, ablutions, lighting lamps, recitation of certain praises on holy days, reading Esther on Purim, and so on. Before their observance the formula "who has sanctified us by his commandments and has commanded us to" was recited indicating their holy quality (b. *Shab*. 23a).

Thus, according to the Rabbis, both Scripture (Written Torah) and Oral Torah are needed to mediate the divine word in Israel. Scripture on its own needs interpretation, clarification and application to current situations. This indeed is the role of the oral tradition: to explain and apply the law to the contemporary community. The Oral Torah is inexplicable without the written and the written needs the expertise of the sage. "Holy literature is bipartite. The Written Law must be interpreted and applied in tandem with the Oral, a circumstance which consistently militated against literalistic applications of that law."[19] The holy word is mediated progressively to each generation, and new angles are revealed: "Oral Torah is a progressive unfolding of the mysterious plenitude of the original divine revelation."[20]

Even some customs are considered Torah: "*Minhag abotenu torah hi*, The custom of our fathers is Torah" (b. *Ber.* 45a; b. *Pes.* 66a; y. *Pe'ah* 7:5).[21] In fact, it was on this very issue that the Karaites complained that the rabbinic tradition had extended way beyond the literal meaning of the Written Torah. Not everything in the Oral Torah, however, is claimed by the Rabbis to be from Moses. Some laws are explicitly labeled "Mosaic law from Sinai" and others are admittedly just tradition (b. *RH* 7a).

Thus, it appears that in Second Temple times the oral law was, in principle, dependent on the written. However, over time it became clear that the written law depended on the oral, for without the expertise of the sage the ancient laws could not be applied in contemporary times. R. Samuel b. Nahman (mid third century) taught: "Oral laws have been proclaimed, and written laws have been proclaimed and we cannot tell which of these is more precious; but since it is written, 'For in accordance with [*al pi*, literally ' by the mouth of'] these words I have made a covenant with thee and with Israel,' we may infer that the oral precepts are more precious" (y. *Pe'ah* 2:4, p. 17a).

The Amoraim elevated the sages to the level of prophets and gave the former precedence "Since the destruction of the Temple, prophecy was taken away from the Prophets and given to the Sages" (b. *BB* 12a).[22] In the rabbinic period, Torah was separated from prophecy.[23] Prophets were not allowed to originate laws, only sages. The notion was that God transmits his word through the sage, and this is accomplished through inspired study which is in continuum with what has been taught by earlier sages. No new prophecy or doctrine could be purported, only what was based on the previous revelation.

With the loss of the sanctuary in 70 CE, the Torah became even more sacred in the mind of Israel. Whereas the Temple had been a source of holiness to Israel, this possibility was now erased. The sages focus even greater attention on the power of the holy word.

The greater sanctity of the Torah over the Temple is evident in this rabbinic quote: "Better to me [God] is one day spent in occupation with the Torah than a thousand burnt-offerings which your son Solomon will sacrifice before me upon the altar" (b. *Shab*. 30a). The Mishnah argues that the Torah is greater than the priesthood and the monarchy (m. *Ab*. 6:6).

Among the Greeks and Romans the idea of sacred books or traditions did not reach the same heights as among the Jews and in the east. The Homeric Hymns (ca. fifth century BCE with parts as old as seventh to eighth centuries BCE), for example, are "artificial compositions, intended for recitation at festivals of the god. . . . People could win prizes for making them up. Hesiod says that he won a pot for a new hymn at a gathering at Chalcis."[24] They are definitely religious texts, since they describe the gods and give praise to them, but they do not have a quality of sanctity: they are not revered as holy. The Orphic Hymns were considered a sort of sacred hymn-book of a popular mystery cult, but these writings are lost to us except for a few quotations remaining in some Neo-Platonic writings. We do have hymns of the Orphic cult-fellowship.[25] The Greek philosophical writings too, while they contain much of religious value, never attained to the status of sacred. There is, for example, no *veda* or canon of the Stoics.[26]

An exception to the above denial of holy books among the Greeks and Romans are the Sybilline Oracles. These texts were housed in the temple of Jupiter Capitolinus during the republic and became the official sacred writings in Imperial Rome; they remained authoritative until the fourth century CE.[27] These texts, believed to have been originally uttered by an aged prophetess called the Cumaean Sibyl (sixth century BCE), are mainly predictions of future woes and disasters to come upon the world.[28] The Oracles were preserved by the Septimi XV priesthood who consulted them only by order of the Roman Senate in times of crisis. Most of the contents concerned ritual dismeanors which brought the wrath of the gods. Jews (but not the Rabbis) and Christians took over the genre of the Sybilline Oracles to make predictions pertaining to their religions in the hope of gaining a non-Judeo-Christian witness to their faith, that is, in an effort to establish a "common human basis" which gave credence to their beliefs.[29] The Judeo-Christian group of oracles focuses largely on moral exhortation rather than denunciation of ritual offenses.

Christianity and Islam both acknowledge the power of the divine word and both rely on written and oral traditions. In early

Christianity, the Jewish Scriptures remained the holy books. Christians preferred Psalms and Prophets and often ignored the prescriptive and practical portions of the Torah, especially the ritual sections.[30] Scripture was regularly read and expounded in the manner of the synagogue: readings from the Pentateuch and the Prophets followed by an interpretive exposition.[31] Gradually Christians began to read Christian writings alongside the Jewish Bible in the worship setting. This practice was a strong factor leading to the canonization of Christian writings.

It soon became obvious that the Church and Israel were "as if" reading two different holy books because the interpretation was so different.[32] The Church became in many cases anti-Judaic and Jews began to exclude some of the readings and interpretations previously accepted among them which they felt could be misinterpreted by Christians. For example, they discontinued reading the Decalogue with the daily liturgy because many Christians regarded only this part of the law as valid; they rejected the Septuagint since it was adopted by Christians (*Soferim* 1:8f.) and they disassociated Daniel's "son of man" from any connection with the Messiah (b. *Hag.* 14a; b. *San.* 38b).[33]

Oral tradition was also important. Jesus promotes a sort of Oral Torah when he says: "It was said [in the written Torah] . . . but I say to you . . . ."[34] Islam, which regards the Qu'ran as a holy book, also claims an oral tradition that goes back to Mohammed.

TRANSMISSION OF HOLY WORD

The midrash points out the impossibility of apprehending the holy fire of the divine word. Holiness at this level cannot be grasped. The solution is that the holy word must be transmitted through the vehicle of the sage. This early commentary on Deuteronomy 11 clarifies the matter:

> And holding fast to him [God] (Deut. 11:22). How is it possible for a person to ascend on high and hold fast to fire? For is it not said elsewhere, 'For the LORD your God is a consuming fire' (Deut. 4:24) 'and his throne was tongues of flame: its wheels were blazing fire' (Dan. 7:9)? Rather – hold fast to the Sages and their disciples and I will consider it as if you had ascended on high and received [the Torah] there.
>
> (*Sif. Deut.* 49)

Thus, a truly rabbinic concept emerges: pure holiness must be mediated through the sage to the people of Israel.

The human body is both a repository for the sacred word as well as a channel. Holiness was embodied by the sage who knew the holy word. His disciples were a kind of apprentice who served the master much like a Hellenistic student would serve his philosophy teacher. The student would not simply take in information but would seek to internalize the sage's every gesture as an exemplification of what it means to fully embody wisdom. The Talmud says: "Even greater than the study of the Torah is attendance upon the sages" (b. *Ber.* 7b). In the case of the rabbinic student, the goal was the embodiment of Torah through imitation of the sage and, by proxy, imitation of Moses and of God himself. Imitation of God, as I have argued in other contexts, is the key to holiness. "Like the school (Latin, *schola*) of Graeco-Roman philosophers and other teachers of redemptive truths, the rabbinic schools were organized as communities of disciples supervised by a sage, who was both a teacher of traditional knowledge and a role model of wisdom."[35]

The papal church claimed its traditions were handed down by apostolic succession of bishops. The notion is already in the New Testament where Paul says: "I have received of the Lord, that which also I delivered unto you" (1 Cor. 11:23; see m. *Ab.* 1).[36] For the early Christian communities the Hebrew Bible was much less important than the "direct testimony about Jesus" in word and deed from apostles and other witnesses.[37] Records of Jesus were much more easily canonized if attributed to apostles. The apostolic tradition continued to be the authority for the Church from the writings of the New Testament apostles on to the Apostolic Constitutions with the appended canons in the fourth century.[38] Holy word, even in early Christian ranks, was not simply Scripture but depended on the transmission of testimony and authoritative rulings from generation to generation.

In rabbinic Judaism the sage's holy authority has another dimension. The material he must master is in itself largely centered on matters of holiness and purity.[39] Most of the Mishnah, for example, deals with matters of sacred area, holy offerings, purity codes, sacred time, and similar issues. Mastery of these divine truths about holiness increases the sage's holy status.

In more particular imitation of God, the process of transmitting holy word is oral. Just as God spoke his words to Moses, so the sage speaks his words of Torah to his disciples. The Talmud describes this process: "Rabbi Eliezer said: A man is obliged to repeat for his disciples four times. . . . Rabbi Akiba says: How do we know that a man is obliged to repeat to his disciples until he teaches them? For it is said in Scripture: 'Teach it to the children of Israel' (Deut. 31:19). And how do we know that he does so until it is mastered orally? For it is said in Scripture: 'Place it in their mouths (Deut. 31:19)'" (b. *Erub*. 54b). By the third to fourth centuries, study of the Oral Torah from a written manuscript was forbidden; it must be learned as a disciple from a sage.[40] Even the Written Torah must be taught and recited orally. Holiness is transmitted from person to person, received from the mouth of God along a chain of sages to the mouth of every disciple. The chain of transmission is spelled out in detail in the Mishnah (m. *Ab*. 1).

The importance of oral transmission of the sacred word is a cross-cultural phenomenon. It is prevalent especially in Indian religions. "If there is any point in talking about 'revelation' in the Indian context, it is to revelation in the form of sound, which is transmitted orally, through recitation." Veda must be learned orally:

> The "scriptural" quality of sacredness is established within the relationship between persons and as a part of a continuous tradition . . . the most immediate way of grasping it is through the personal relationship between student and teacher. By ancient custom, if an aging teacher is unable to find a student worthy of inheriting the tradition he guards, he should throw the traditional sacred texts in his possession into the river, as if they were no more than ashes, since, in themselves, lacking the continuity of an oral passage from teacher to disciple, they lack both authority and value.[41]

Similarly, the Zoroastrian Avesta is not regarded as a holy book but as a sacred tradition which is transmitted orally.[42] The power of the holy words is only evinced by recitation aloud. Similarly, Buddha's words were transmitted only orally for hundreds of years.

The most sacred pronouncements in Hinduism are Veda, or Sruti, literally "hearing." "To the Hindu, what has been 'heard' directly has an authority superior to what tradition has simply 'remembered' . . . texts being always regarded as inferior in authority to the living memory of an authoritative recaller."[43] "Veda is truth and power only when spoken; it is not scripture; it is Sruti, 'that which is heard'; heard by the *rishis* [seers] and heard by those to whom the *rishis* articulated it, passed down from master to disciple, generation to generation, for more than 3,500 years."[44]

While the Greeks did have a concept of "unwritten law, *nomos agraphos*," it was neither oral nor based on divine word but rather on living in accordance with the environment.[45] The Greeks' unwritten law is the implicit law which exists in and governs nature. Aristotle said that higher law cannot be opposed to nature. Various Hellenistic Jewish authors try to demonstrate that the Torah too is in accordance with natural law (e.g. 4 Macc. 5:7, 25), but the Rabbis readily admit that their law is often not in accordance with nature but based on divine command (*Sifra Qed.* 11). The notion of received revelation was foreign to the Greeks and the Romans.

There is a certain elitism in holiness. The holy status of the priest, without whom holiness was unavailable to Israel, is taken over in rabbinic tradition by the sage. Holiness is available to all Israel but it must be mediated through the proper channels. Just as there is a hierarchy of holiness in the cult, so this is apparent also in the circles which transmitted holiness through the Torah. One does not truly receive the divine word unless it is by mediation of the holy sage.

This elitism probably explains why some of the holy tradition was left in an oral state. The accepted reason for this is so that the Oral Torah would not taken on the same authority as the Written – although this did happen (see m. *San.* 11:3: "Greater stringency applied to the words of the Scribes than to the words of the Torah"). The Rabbis, however, give another reason: God knew that Gentiles would translate Torah into their language and then claim "we are Israel, we are God's own children," so he kept Mishnah oral as evidence that only those who had all of the revelation were really Israel (*Tanh.* 44b; *Pesikta R.* 14b; b. *Ber.* 5a).[46] The power of the internalization of holy word comes across as a strong emphasis in rabbinic Judaism as in the eastern religions. This internalization, or embodiment, as it were, of both Oral and Written Torah is seen as the distinguishing mark of the Jew. For example, the Rabbis say that God told Moses to keep some of the revelation in oral form: "I do not want you to write it down, for I know that the nations of the world will rule over Israel and attempt to take it from them. I give Israel *mikra* [Bible] in written form, but I give them Mishnah, Talmud and Agada orally, and thus will Israel be distinguished from all other nations" (*Exod. R.* 47; see also y. *Pe'a* 11:6). And, in another place, the Oral Torah was finally redacted and compiled in written form by Judah the Patriarch in the early third century CE because of the danger of losing it due to persecutions.[47]

STUDYING HOLY WORD

Study of the holy word invites the presence of God. "If two sit together and interchange words of Torah, the Shekhinah abides between them; as it is said, 'Then they that feared the Lord spake one with the other; and the Lord hearkened and heard, and a book of rememberance was written before Him for them that feared the Lord and that thought upon his name' (Mal. 3:16)" (m. *Ab.* 3:2). The Rabbis use a radical metaphor, eating with God, to describe the holy activity of studying Torah: "If three have eaten at a table and have spoken there words of Torah, it is as if they had eaten at the table of the All-present, to which the Scripture may be applied, 'And he said unto me, This is the table that is before the Lord' (Ezek. 41:22)" (m. *Ab.* 3:3) and the Rabbis insist further that even if five, three, two, or one persons are studying Torah, God is there (m. *Ab.* 3:6). Studying the Torah was a holy experience which brought the Holy One into the midst of Israel. To this end, schools formed hermeneutical principles for proper interpretation of the Torah.

Through engagement with the holy word, God's presence was invited into the community and the study room, or *beit midrash*. After the destruction of the Temple, the *beit midrash* became the new "meetingplace" between the two. What is significant here is that this holy engagement required mental rigor. Connecting to God through his word was based on study at the foot of a sage. In the context of the Temple, the mediators of holiness were the priests; in the context of the divine word, these people are the sages.

Study of the Torah was considered holy worship. "*Abodah*," literally "service," usually describes proper worship through the Temple service. But the Rabbis regard study of the Torah a holy service, especially since the cultic forms were no longer available to them after 70 CE. Torah study was equal to the Temple service, and it became a surrogate for offering sacrifices (b. *Men.* 110a; *PRK* Buber, 60b; *Tanhuma*, Buber, *Ahare,* sec. 16, f. 35a). It is significant that the evening recitation of the *Shema*, the obligatory daily Torah recitation, was placed at the time of the evening sacrifice (m. *Ber.* 1:1). In the verse, "To love the Lord your God and to serve [*'abad*] him" (Deut. 11:13), *'abad* is interpreted by the Rabbis as the study of the Torah. The explanation given is that just as the *'Abodah*, "service or worship," of the altar is called *'abodah*, so is study of Torah called *'abodah* (*Sif. Deut.*, sec. 41, Friedmann, 80a; see also *Gen. R.* 16:5, Theodor, 149, and notes there). The study of Torah was a commitment to uphold its truths which was tantamount to committing an animal to the priest as a holy offering.

Not only in private or rabbinic study circles, but also in the formal synagogue service, Torah readings, accompanied by a vernacular translation and an expository or edifying discourse, formed a vital component of the worship. The Sabbath lay readers of Torah who represented the congregation were in the same role as the "men of the post" who stood by the public sacrifice offered twice daily on account of the community. The "men of the post" identified the community with the offering so that it counted for each member of Israel. Likewise, the lay readers represented the congregation in the reading of the Torah, an act which acknowledged their submission to it. Through them, the entire people of Israel heard the Torah at Sinai, as it were, and offered to God their acceptance of its yoke.[48] All were included in this experience of holiness since all experienced and internalized the divine word.

The role of reasoning is part of the study process. Memory of the holy word is important, but critical thinking is also vital. "An empty-headed man cannot be a sin-fearing man, nor can a person ignorant of Torah be pious" (m. *Ab*. 2:6). In other words, there is no way individuals can be truly holy at the elite level of the Rabbis unless there is intelligent understanding of the divine word. Study of the holy word was the responsibility of every male Jew beginning at age 5 (m. *Ab*. 5:21).[49] A cursory look at the Talmuds reveals the high level of critical reasoning by the many debates, arguments, hypotheses, and other feats of logic.

Recitation of holy tradition, whether written or oral, is a type of worship not only in rabbinic Judaism, but in various eastern religions, but there is no emphasis on critical reasoning. "In the oral transmission through recitation [found in Vedic tradition] sound is all that counts. The words have to be handed down in exactly the same form in which they have been heard. There is no tradition for the preservation of meaning, a concern regarded as a mere individualistic pastime. The Brahmans' task is more noble: to preserve the sound for posterity, maintain it in its purity, and keep it from the unchecked spread and vulgarization which attaches to the written word."[50] "The orthodox position . . . does not initially think of the Avesta as a text to be read for its doctrinal content, but rather as a transcript of the language spoken in Zoroastrian holy rites."[51] The large part of the Avesta that has survived is liturgical. This "underscores the primacy of those portions of the whole Avesta which were used as holy words to be uttered in the rituals. . . .

Religious meaning fundamentally resides in actions, specifically speech acts intimately related to ritual gestures."[52]

The content of the holy words is not that important in Zoroastrianism and in Hinduism. The three main Zoroastrian sources, Yasna, Yashts, and Venidad, are basically hymns to various spiritual powers.[53] The chanting of the holy words is the way to spiritual power. The orthodox position is that Avesta, probably literally "sacred utterance," is not for doctrinal meanings which enter one into the world of ideas.[54] Rather, Avesta is "holy words to be uttered in a liturgical or ritual context, not principally as a text meant for reflective-critical thinking."[55] Preserving the correct sacred utterances and conducting the necessary rituals which actualize them are the primary functions of the Zoroastrian priests. Zoroastrianism fosters an auditory rather than cognitive approach to religion. The hearing and reciting of the holy words brings power.

Similarly in Hinduism:

> The intelligibility of the texts is not a prior condition for their authoritative status .... The Indian sacred text is wholly open precisely because the role of any particular interpretation of its contents has no special importance. The openness of the Vedic text is not expressed by the multiplicity of legitimate interpretations, but by what may be called the irrelevance of these interpretations. This irrelevance is due to the view that the semantic aspect of the Veda is insignificant. The openness of the text is achieved by disregarding its semantic aspect in favor of reciting, chanting, memorizing it, or performing the ritual motions it prescribes. ... In other words, performance of the texts, together with adherence to the ritualistic injunction and prohibitions that may be found in them, constitute the texts as authoritative, infallible and absolute.[56]

The Hindu *rishis* are "mere channels through which the transcendent word passes to make itself available to humans at the start of each creation cycle."[57] The *rishi* must purge himself of ignorance through yoga so his consciousness is transparent to receive the divine word. Thus he removes "mental obstructions." The Vedic words are believed to purify the conscience so that the disciple can receive the same enlightenment through the divine word that the *rishi* received.[58] The words of Veda are the "ladder" to this transforming experience. Such a notion that Scripture can be transcended to such a degree would be heresy to the Rabbis and the early Christians.

Among the Sikhs too, the guru in ancient times was the channel which brought the divine word into the current community. Later, the sacred book took on this function. Worshipers listen to a randomly chosen text by the priest which through inspiration is expected to meet their needs. To the Sikh, God is choosing the text. Study of the text is useful but is not a religious experience. One should be "losing oneself in the devotional singing of the word."[59] Without negating the value of devotional meditation, rabbinic Judaism also considered serious study of the divine word as a holy experience.

OBSERVANCE OF HOLY WORD

Not only the mental faculties must be engaged by rigorous study, but they must translate into proper behavior in order for holiness to be really created in Israel. Only the person who both studies and practices Torah is truly holy (m. *Ab.* 5:14). By reciting various passages of Torah, the Jew is accepting on himself daily the "yoke of Heaven," that is, the commitment to do what is contained in them.[60]

The Rabbis emphasize that the Torah is the link to holiness in Israel only if its commandments are observed: "Be holy, for as long as you fulfill my commandments you are sanctified, but if you neglect them you become profaned" (*Num. R.* 17:6).[61] Commandments are not stultifying but a channel to the divine holiness: "When the Omnipresent enjoins a new precept upon Israel, he endows them with a new holiness" (*Mekh. de-Kaspa* 20). Graeco-Roman cults, in contrast to Judaism and Christianity, had no organized system of beliefs to which members were asked to submit themselves, nor did they demand exclusive commitment.[62] Holiness was not achieved by keeping civil law, nor was it a goal of the philosophers.

With the destruction of the Temple in 70 CE the notion that Jews could still be holy by observing God's commandments sustained the people. The Qumran community, which had already rejected the Temple priesthood as corrupt, explicitly defined themselves as a "Temple of Men" (4QFlor). Pure deeds were the "sacrifices" in this "Temple." Likewise the Rabbis say, "May God send you help from the sanctuary, that is, from the sanctification of your deeds" (*Lev. R.* 24:4 on Ps. 20:3). A standard benediction purportedly existing even before the Temple's destruction was the *Birkat Hamitsvot*, "Blessed be you God, our God, King of the Universe, who has sanctified us by his commandments . . ." (t. *Ber.* 6[7]:9).[63] Indeed, the Bible already emphasizes that obedience is better than holy offerings (1 Sam. 15:22f.).

After 70 CE, each Jewish home took on added significance as a type of sanctuary where deeds continued the holy relationship. Purifications, benedictions, and other rituals which did not require the Temple took on greater importance as they contributed to holiness in the private sphere. The observance of the divine commandments was always the link between the nation and God, originally centered around the Temple, and after its destruction, centered around the home and the community.

Holiness separates Israel from non-Israel. This is achieved by the observance of the divine word. As a consuming fire, the word separates those who are holy from those who are not. The Rabbis regard the divine commandments as just such a fire: "'Are not my words like fire, says the Lord' (Jer. 23:29); so were the words God spoke to Moses" (*Sif. Num.*, II, 160). As a separating fire, the divine word informs a distinctive lifestyle and erects boundaries which reinforce the difference between Israel and non-Israel. According to the Rabbis, God says: "Even though I am about to exile you from the Land to a foreign land, you must continue to be marked there by the commandments, so that when you return they will not be new to you" (*Sif. Deut.* 43, Hammer, 96).[64] A formidable group identity is formed and maintained by the observance of the Torah.

PURITY RESTRICTIONS

As argued in other chapters, divine holiness is perfection and power. When it is mediated into the human sphere it easily encounters imperfection and impurity and is repulsed or brings dire results. Thus, as its literal meaning implies, holiness must be protected by separation and prohibition. Restrictions apply to all who engage the holy word, whether in recitation, study or chanting. This principle applies not only in Judaism but in other religions as well.

According to rabbinic teaching, the divine word is perfect. The Psalmist said long before the Rabbis, "The Torah of the Lord is perfect, renewing life" (Ps. 19:7). Commenting on Proverbs 27:18, the Rabbis say: "What is the meaning of that which is written, 'Whoso keeps the fig-tree shall eat the fruit of it'? Why is the Torah compared to a fig? In all fruits there is a part which is refuse . . . but the whole of the fig is edible. Similarly in the words of the Torah there is no refuse."[65]

The perfection of divine holiness may serve to explain the Mishnah's cryptic statement (m. *Kel.* 15:6): "all [sacred] scrolls defile the hands except the scroll of the Temple Court." The enigma is how can a holy scroll cause impurity? P. Kyle McCarter may have an answer:

> A Torah Scroll . . . is sacred. For this very reason, then, it is a potential source of defilement. If it is blemished or corrupted, it transmits uncleanness. The Books of the Temple Court were protected from corruption by "The correctors of the Book" (y. *Sheq.* 4, 48a; cf. b. *Ket.* 106a). Other sacred books, however, could not be counted upon to be unblemished and were regarded as sources of defilement . . . they are copies of the scroll of the Temple Court, imitations. The copies are not subject to the vigilance of the correctors, so they are apt to be corrupt.[66]

The argument here is that since the only truly perfect holy scroll was the one preserved and corrected in the Temple, all others were open to imperfection and human error. Only the Temple copy of the holy word was guaranteed to be perfect and so truly holy and free from defilement. Because of its guarded perfection, the scroll of the Temple could be counted on not to cause impurity. Other scrolls, while they were regarded as holy, were still subject to imperfection and impurity. The point that the Mishnah may be making is that holiness in its highest form is perfect and free from all defilement.

Nevertheless, it is still disturbing that the ordinary Torah scroll, which is still considered holy, can cause impurity. The Mishnah offers perhaps the best explanation in terms of protecting restrictions by saying that the sages attributed impurity to the Torah scroll as a restriction that would command respect from those handling the scroll.[67] That is to say, by rendering the Torah scroll potentially defiling, the worshiper will treat it more carefully. The Talmud is clear that one is not supposed to touch a Torah scroll directly (b. *Shab.* 14ab). The actual degree of impurity which the sages assign to the Torah scroll is very low, thus supporting the Mishnah's claim that the ascribed impurity is merely to command the respect of the handler.[68] R. Yohanan b. Zakkai explains to the

Sadducees why both the Torah scroll and a dead body transmit impurity, "Proportionate to the respect one should have for these things is their capacity for defilement, so that one should not make ladles out of the bones of his father or his mother. So is it also with the Holy Writings" (m. *Yad.* 4:6). The point here is that since impurity would apply to the bones of a dead person, one would not make cooking utensils out of them; however, the bones of an animal could be used for such a purpose.[69] Similarly, one would not use the holy books for any secular purpose. Again, the concern is respect for the holy word.

One should not infer from the Mishnah's statement comparing impurity with respect that impurity is somehow precious or a desired condition. The impurity of Torah scrolls is not the only case of impurity decreed to avoid an undesired eventuality. Another example concerns the leftover portions of peace offerings, which are said to "defile the hands" (m. *Pes.* 10:9). How is it possible for peace offerings, holy meat, to cause impurity? The answer is that the law wants to ensure that this meat is not left overnight. The biblical command is clear that the offerer must eat the meat in the one-to-two day time period (Lev. 7:15–18). The intent of the time restriction is to force the offerer to invite others to join him and share the sacred meal since he cannot consume the animal alone in the limited time allowed. The declaration of impurity on the meat after the time limit prevents an undesired situation – that the offerer will selfishly eat his meat alone. The case of impurity of Torah scrolls is analogous. The law was issued in order to protect the scrolls against an undesired eventuality, that is (1) that they might be handled directly or without respect, and (2) that they might be used for a secular purpose.[70]

Holiness is thus defined by its restrictions and holy books are no exception. Holy books must be treated with respect. Maimonides lists twenty defects which disqualify a Torah scroll. Some are related to the form of the letters, but many have to do with the attitudes and qualifications of the scribe.[71] The holy writings require careful handling, copying, storage, and speaking. A Jew is not supposed to live where there is no scribe. The scribe must perform a ritual bath before writing the names of the Lord. His scrolls must be copied from a model copy, not written out from memory. Rules apply to all writing flourishes, illustrations within the text, and even the space between the letters.[72]

The holiness of the Torah is manifest in the separation and reverence of it by the congregation. Worshippers kiss the mantle of the

Torah during the service. Study of Torah is considered equal to honoring parents, doing good deeds, and restoring peace among individuals (m. *Pe'ah* 1:1). Before studying the Torah three benedictions are to be recited. Accidental dropping of it signals a "communal disaster requiring the giving of charity and fasting. . . . As the most holy object for the Jew, the Torah scroll and its reading is hedged about by traditions."[73]

As a cross-cultural, parallel example, Hinduism too reveals a strong battery of restrictions for those chanting Veda. The Hindu prepares himself before reciting sacred words (*mantra*). At dawn, he rises and bathes and concentrates his mind before beginning his chants.[74] There are strict rules for *mantra* chanting. The worshiper must be properly purified, have practical skills of chanting, be intellectually and morally fit, and hold requisite status in the tradition. Also a certain sincerity, volume, and proper breathing must be reflected in the voice.[75] A late Vedic text states that a student cannot recite the Veda after eating meat, seeing blood or a dead body, or after intercourse, or if engaged in writing.[76]

The Rabbis stored the Torah scrolls in a cabinet in the synagogue called an "ark" (Figure 4.2) after the ark in the Holy of Holies where Moses is said to have placed the stone tablets. Just as the ark was the most holy item in the Temple, so the ark in the synagogue is the most revered item there. An interesting parallel to this practice is found among the Sikhs. Their sacred text, *Adi Granth*, "is housed in its own building or room, the *Gurdwara*. It is placed on a cushion, covered by a canopy and wrapped in special cloths."[77] The holy text is elevated, moved by carriage on the head. Worshipers bow to it and do not turn their backs on it. It is ritually put to bed and awakened. Persons entering a *Gurdwara* must first bathe and remove their shoes. Offerings are placed in front of the holy book. Thus, the notion of a holy storage area, marked off by restrictions, which houses the sacred word is not unknown outside of rabbinic Judaism. Reverence for holy word by means of purity and other restrictions is a cross-cultural phenomenon.

When a Torah scroll deteriorates to the point of becoming unusable it must still be treated with respect and cannot be destroyed. It may be placed in a *genizah*, a storeroom for sacred articles, including, scrolls and ritual objects. Alternatively, scrolls may be buried in a cemetery.[78] Torah scrolls may not be destroyed because they contain the holy name of God.

Figure 4.2   Torah Ark from India, from the permanent collection of the
Judah L. Magnes Museum, gift of the Jewish community of
Ernakulam, India.
Source: Courtesy of the Judah L. Magnes Museum.

151

LIFE VIA HOLY WORD

Holiness creates life through the divine word. The divine breath is the holy word which gives life to human beings. It is because of this connection of holy word and the creation of life that the Rabbis insist that the Torah preceded creation (*Sif. Deut.*, sec. 37; 76a; see also *Gen. R.* 8:2: Torah preceded creation by 2,000 years). The holy breath put into human beings at creation gives human life sanctity. In fact, divine breath is the holy word which brought everything into existence. Conversely, the human body, which among all creation best reflects the divine image, is the greatest source of defilement when its divine breath is removed (see Chapter 5).[79] It is the divine breath which makes words holy and gives inert bodies vitality.

While the divine breath gives a certain measure of sanctity to life, the life which is truly holy, according to rabbinic definitions, cannot be described simply as the one which is breathing. Holiness still denotes a certain quality of life. When individuals receive the holy word, recite it and make it their own, they are internalizing life in accordance with God's will. The Mishnah says, "The more Torah the more life" (m. *Ab.* 2:8). By contrast, "He who does not study (Torah) deserves to die" (m. *Ab.* 1:13). The divine breath which infuses the words of Torah with holiness energizes the recipient and provides quality to life. The Talmud says individuals perish when they separate themselves from the Torah, like fish on dry land (b. *AZ* 3b). Lack of engagement with holy word causes the quality of a person's life to deteriorate.

Study of divine word has a salvific function. The sages quote God as saying: "If a man occupies himself with the study of Torah, works of charity, and prays with the community, I account it to him as if he had redeemed me and my children from among the nations of the world" (b. *Ber.* 8a). "Whosoever labors in the Torah for its own sake merits many things .... It clothes him in meekness and reverence, fits him to become just, pious, upright, and faithful; it keeps him far from sin and brings him near to virtue" (m. *Ab.* 6:1). Thus, study and observance of the divine word keeps a person from violating the divine will and evoking God's wrath. Torah provides healing and relief from pain (b. *Erub.* 54a). Like water, it refreshes, renews life, cleanses from defilement and purifes the morally defiled (*Cant. R.* 1:2).

The Rabbis connect the holiness of the divine word with its life-giving power. The following verse, "That ye may remember and do all my commandments and be holy unto your God" (Num. 15:40), is interpreted with an analogy:

> The matter is to be compared to a man drowning in water, to whom the shipmaster threw out a cord, saying unto him, Hold fast to this cord, for if thou permit it to escape thee, there is no life for thee. Likewise the Holy One, blessed be he, said to Israel, As long as you cling to my laws, you cleave unto the Lord your God which means life. ... Be holy for as long as you fulfil my commandments you are sanctified, but if you neglect them, you will become profaned.
>
> (*Num. R.* 17:6)

Thus, holiness is achieved by a life committed to imitating and pleasing God, who is the source of life.[80]

Christianity took up the same principle. Deuteronomy states that "man does not live by bread only, but by every word that proceeds out of the mouth of the Lord does a man live" (Deut. 8:3). This passage is upheld and quoted by Jesus in his arguments with Satan over whether he could turn stones into bread (Matt. 4:4).

The divine word is a powerful agent against danger to life. The Jerusalem Talmud (y. *Ta'an.* 3:8) tells the story of a sage who went up on a roof with the Torah scroll and challenged God: "'Lord of the ages! If a single word of this scroll of the Torah has been nullified [in our town], let them come up against us, and if not, let them go their way.' Forthwith people went looking for the troops but did not find them [because they had gone their way]." Thus, the Torah was considered to contain divine power.

The Torah scroll is not simply a magical amulet against trouble and death. Study and observance of its contents are necessary for its power. "Had Israel reflected upon the words of the Torah that was given them, no nation or kingdom would have had dominion over them" (*Sif. Deut.* on Deut. 32:29, Friedmann, 138b). The observance of the holy word, however, makes the difference as to whether God will "lift up His countenance" upon Israel (*Sif. Num.*, Neusner, 191, 195). God promises: "If you do what is your duty to do, I will do what I made it my duty to do, 'Then will the Lord drive out ...'" (*Sif. Deut.* 49, on Deut. 11:23). Needless to say, transgression of the commandments is dangerous. Deuteronomy warns against violations lest "you perish quickly ... therefore shall ye lay up these my words" (Deut. 11:17–18).

The sage, especially, is protected by his learning. The Talmud says that Rabbis do not need to contribute to the upkeep of a town's walls because they do not need this kind of protection (b. *BB* 8a). While the sage, especially in later writings, was credited, as a holy man, with the ability to perform miracles, it was only through his learning that he could access supernatural power.[81]

The Qumran sect is a prime example of an ancient Jewish group seeking as much holiness as possible through a regimen of Torah study as well as a stringent code of ritual purity (see Chapter 5). But, in the minds of the sectarians, maximum holiness was well worth the effort. In addition to divine revelation which they culled from the holy word, the sectarians needed supernatural, holy power in order to fight a final war against the enemies of God. The Sons of Light, as the sect called themselves, were preparing for a battle against the Sons of Darkness. The holy angels would fight alongside the sectarians (1QM 12:1–8; 11Q13 2:9). In accordance with Deuteronomy 23:14, anything unholy would spoil their chances of victory.

The divine word not only directs and gives quality to life in this world, but assures the obedient disciple of life in the world to come. Although Rabbis and Christians disagreed on what exactly constituted the divine word, both agreed that the word of God was eternal and provided the way to eternal life (see Isa. 40:8; 1 Pet. 1:25; Luke 21:33). It had a supernatural force that could not be destroyed and could offer future life to human beings. The power of the holy word was stronger than death itself.

The holy word contained the energy that would eventually resurrect the dead. "He who has acquired for himself words of Torah has acquired for himself life in the World to Come" (m. *Ab*. 2:8). "Great is the Torah which gives life to those that practice it in this world and in the World to Come" (m. *Ab*. 6:7). Ezekiel's vivid vision of the dry bones provides an excellent analogy of the power of the holy word to renew life. It explains that resurrection comes by the divine breath re-entering dead bodies and connects this breath with the word of God. The prophet is told to prophesy to the bones, "O ye dry bones, hear the word of the Lord. Thus says the Lord God unto these bones; Behold, I will cause breath to enter into you, and you shall live" (Ezek. 37:4f.). Scripture says that while Ezekiel was prophesying (speaking under the influence of the holy spirit) the bones came together and formed living bodies (Ezek. 37:7–10). The point is that, as God's mouthpiece, Ezekiel declares the holy word which has the power to resurrect the dead.

HOLINESS AND MYSTICAL EXPERIENCE

Throughout the ancient world, people sought mystical union with God in various ways. Hellenistic secret societies devoted to experiential knowledge flourished in the time of the Roman Empire. Some of the most popular include: Pythagoras' disciples; Egyptian and Babylonian priesthoods; the Gnostics; and the mystery cults of Dionysus, Mithras, Isis, and Cybele. "Knowledge of a heavenly 'mystery' (Greek, *mysterion*) was a common feature of many Hellenistic religious worlds. People knew about such mysteries. . . . But only the few truly claimed to possess such knowledge (Greek, *gnosis*)."[82] The Rabbis use the term *mistoryn* (Aramaic form of *mysterion*), to denote the Oral Torah which distinguishes Israel from other nations and makes them God's children (*Tanh. Ki-Tissa* 34).

For many Rabbis, the study of Torah is considered a mystical experience which brings holiness to the student through the divine word. As discussed above, studying Torah is considered a holy activity akin to worship in the Temple. The "immediate goal is to confront the fullness of the divine Presence here and now, in one's personal experience."[83] Scripture itself teaches that future generations, not just the current one, were a party to the congregational oath to obey the covenant in the time of Moses (Deut. 29:14–15). The Rabbis interpret "All the statutes and the ordinances which I set before you this day" (Deut. 11:32) as "Let them be as beloved of you as though you received them from Mount Sinai this day, be as conversant with them as though you heard them this day" (*Sif. Deut.* 87a, Friedmann). Each student was considered a participant in the receiving of the Mosaic revelation and each experienced holy power in the process.

The study of the fiery, holy words is the key to this experience, which cannot be attained otherwise. This story of Ben Azzai illustrates this principle:

> Ben-Azzai was sitting and interpreting [making midrash], and fire was all around hm. They went and told Rabbi Akiva, "Rabbi, Ben-Azzai is sitting and interpreting, and fire is burning all around him." He went to him and said to him, "I heard that you were interpreting, and the fire burning all around you." He said, "Indeed." He said, "Perhaps you were engaged in the inner-rooms of the chariot [theosophical speculation]." He said, "No. I was sitting and stringing the words of Torah [to each other], and the Torah

to the Prophets and the Prophets to the Writings, and the
words were as radiant/joyful as when they were given from
Sinai, and they were as sweet as at their original giving.
Were they not originally given in fire, as it is written, 'And
the mountain was burning with fire' [Deut. 4.11]?"

(*Cant. R.* 42)[84]

According to this passage, it appeared to some sages that Ben
Azzai was engaged in the study of mystical, theosophical texts
because he was clearly having a supernatural experience: he is
sitting in the middle of fire, unharmed, studying the Torah.
However, Ben Azzai affirms that his unusual experience is achieved
simply by studying the holy words and linking them with each
other. By reiterating the words of the Torah and connecting them
with each other, that is, finding correspondences between the words
of the text to create new understanding, Ben Azzai is a recipient of
divine revelation. By studying these words and the connections
between them, Ben Azzai can participate in the very reception of
revelation that Moses experienced.[85] The holy fire is the evidence
that the words are the same holy words. The Rabbis believed that,
just as Moses received the fiery words of Torah miraculously on the
burning mountain, so a Jewish sage over a thousand years later
could experience this revelation by studying the same holy words.

Each sage since Moses was considered a mentor not only for the
cognitive education of his student but for the individual's overall
moral development. Imitation was the key. Imitation of God
according to the Torah, his word, was the key to holiness. The Torah
provided the blueprint, the master plan of how an individual could
attain the holiness God required. However, the human model for
the Torah was the sage who was a living example of the divine
blueprint. His very life was instructive of how the Torah could be
translated into human experience. Christians found this blueprint or
model in the person of Jesus, whom they considered the divine word
made flesh (John 1:1, 14). Imitation of him and adherence to his
words, as the divine, master teacher, was the key to maintaining the
sanctified, Christian life (see John 14:23; 1 Cor. 11:1; Phil. 2:5; see
also Rom. 12:2).

In addition to the traditional process of studying and observing the
Torah, there were Rabbis who sought more direct forms of accessing
divine holiness. "At least some Jews both within and beyond the
communities of the *beit midrash* cultivated types of knowledge that
were reserved for a small, select group, cf. the *Hekhalot* literature of

Figure 4.3　Ezekiel's divine chariot vision.
Artist: John Skaggs.

the Divine Chariot." We do not know the origin of this literature, but
rabbinic sages such as Akiba and Ishmael figure prominently and it
appears that those who transmitted these texts were in some kind of
contact with the major rabbinic academies. Some of this material goes
back to the early centuries BCE.[86]

The most famous of these early mystical texts is the mystery of
the Divine Chariot, which reflects on Ezekiel 1 (Figure 4.3). Here

the candidate seeks to gain access to successively higher celestial halls called *"Hekhalot"* and, if fortunate, is led at the end into the divine chariot, *Merkavah*. The traditional rabbinic character of the quest for holiness through studying and practicing the Torah is intertwined with the more direct "ladder" as seen in the following text:

> What is it like to have the ability to descend to the *Merkavah*? It is like having a ladder in one's house. Any person who would descend to the *Merkavah* must be purged and cleansed of idolatry, sexual excess, bloodshed, slander, vain oaths, profanation of the Name of God, haughtiness, and arbitrary hatred. And he must observe every positive and negative commandment.
>
> (*Hekhalot Rabbati* 15:2 [*par.* 199])

The fact that "every positive and negative commandment" must still be observed in the process puts this thinking squarely within rabbinic circles.[87]

In no way is the traditional process of rigorous study discarded in this more direct approach to holiness, illustrated further in the following text:

> Dumiel the Prince guards the sixth *Hekhal* and says to the ascender, "No one descends to the *Merkavah* unless he possess the following two virtues. He must be able to study the Torah, the Prophets, and the Writings, and he must have mastered the Oral Torah, halakhic and aggadic interpretation, and the resolution of legal decisions regarding the permissible and forbidden. Also, he must have fulfilled all that is written in the Torah in its entirety, observing all the warnings, the statutes, the judgments, and the teachings which were given to Moses on Sinai. . . ."
>
> (*Hekhalot Rabbati* 21:3–22:1 [*par.* 233–235])[88]

The Jewish mystic does not deny the holy word in his quest for spiritual mysteries; he is rather seeking a more intimate engagement with it.

The role of holiness in aiding the ascent of the disciple through the heavenly halls is apparent in the following late text from the *Maasei Merkavah* (The Dynamics of the *Merkavah*, *par.* 556). Angelic recitations of the *kedushah* are offered at various stages of the ascent:

In the first *Hekhal, Merkavot* of fire say, "Holy, holy, holy is YHWH of Hosts, the whole earth is full of His Glory" (Isa. 6:3) and their flames spread out and gather together to the second *Hekhal*, and say, "Holy, holy, holy . . . ." In the second *Hekhal, Merkavot* of fire say, "Holy, holy, holy . . .," and their flames gather together and spread out to the third *Hekhal* and say, "Holy, holy, holy . . . .' In the fifth *Hekhal*, *Merkavot* of fire say, "Blessed is the Holiness of His Majesty from the place of His presence (so also in the sixth *Hekhal*)." In the seventh and final *Hekhal*, one says, "Blessed be the King of Kings, *YY* [divine name], Lord of all Power. . . . His praise is in the heavens' heaven, the holiness of His majesty is in the highest chambers . . . ."

In this passage the presence of holiness encased in fire throughout the whole process is quite obvious. The candidate must repeatedly acknowledge the holiness of God in order to proceed to higher levels of heaven. Holiness is the vehicle for the ascent, the agent whereby the mystery will be revealed.

A candidate who succeeds in arriving to the *Merkavah* is seated near the *Cherubim*, the *Ofanim* and the "holy creatures." He will be allowed to gaze directly on the mysteries of God, including his ineffable quality of holiness: "He sees wonders and powers, majesty and greatness, holiness and purity, terror and humility and righteousness at the same time" (*Hekhalot Rabbati* 22:2 [*par.* 236]).[89]

CONCLUSION

The holy word provides a way of gaining access to the Holy One. The word of the Holy One is a sort of extension of himself. In various religions of the ancient world, the search for enlightenment was conducted along the path of holy words. In some of the major Indian religions the divine word was considered too holy to commit to writing and was transmitted only from holy man to disciple. In the more classical domain of Graeco-Roman culture, words did not usually carry such sanctity, and the sacred text is the exception rather than the norm. Situated between east and west, rabbinic Judaism, inherited sacred traditions, both written and oral.

Holy word was powerful and so had to be mediated to Israel. For this, the appropriate vehicle was a sage, one who understood the sacred texts and embodied its teachings. The Rabbis considered themselves the intermediaries between the Holy One and the holy people of Israel.

The transmission of holy word from mentor to disciple was a holy process which imitated the holy transmission of God's word to Moses. Only those who were willing to sit at the feet of the sage could benefit from both the Written Torah and the Oral Torah, that is, the complete experience of the holy word. The process required mental rigor and reasoning skills. Holiness was mediated through the mental faculties not in spite of them, as was often the case in other traditions. For many Rabbis, study of the holy word evoked an experience of the holy presence. It was a way of worship.

Study of the holy word alone would not sustain holiness. Observance of the divine teachings were vital. Many of these concerned ethical relationships within society while others were more private matters. The lifestyle of the Torah had to be embodied by the sage and imitated by his disciples.

Holiness is always power and perfection and, as such, can only be mediated along safe, pure channels. In cultures where the holy word is considered powerful, physical and mental restrictions apply. Holy word must be protected or it may prove dangerous. Its perfection must be guarded by careful transmission from one pure vessel to another. The power of the holy word is best seen in its ability to create and recreate life. The observance of the divine word within the community of Israel guarantees life in God's favor in the present as well as the assurance of life in the next world.

The transmission of holiness through the holy word is not a static but a dynamic process which revitalizes those involved. From sage to disciple throughout the generations holiness is a powerful, mystical force which is transmitted and received many times over. Since the source of the holy word is God himself, both mentor and student are engaged with something much greater than themselves. They seek renewal, inspiration, and empowerment. The goal is not just an explosion of knowledge but an internalization of the power and life of the holy word. By studying the Torah, each sage can participate in the holy revelation given to Moses at Mt. Sinai.

5

THE HOLY PEOPLE

A fundamental principle of rabbinic Judaism is that Israel is a holy people by virtue of election and obedience to God's commandments. While Israel is elected by God to be his holy people, a certain lifestyle is required and well-defined by the commandments. If Israel fails to support her holiness with this way of life, she loses her holy status. Election and responsibility form two sides of a paradox: Israel's holiness is ensured by divine decree but is also dependent upon her daily lifestyle.

The following discussion of holy people highlights four main areas: election; ritual; ethics; and sexuality. Each of these topics reveals a special dimension to the definition and description of holy people in rabbinic Judaism. Holiness comes first of all by divine election, but it is maintained by Israel's responsibility, especially in the areas of ritual, ethics, and sexuality.

The biblical notion of holy people and its continued application in both rabbinic Judaism and Christianity is a unique concept in the ancient world. As discussed in Chapter 2, Greeks and Romans did support holy personnel, for example priests, priestesses, *flamines*. However, these specially appointed persons were considered holy simply by virtue of their authority to perform and maintain the rituals connected to a particular sacred site. Furthermore, the lay worshipper was not considered holy. To my knowledge, no ethnic group in the Roman Empire beside the Jews considered themselves "holy" based on the combination of their ethnicity and religion.

DIVINE ELECTION

The Rabbis ascribe to the biblical principle that Israel is holy by divine election (Deut. 7:6; 14:2, 21; 26:19; 28:9; Isa. 4:3; 6:13)."[1] Deuteronomy perhaps states it best: "You are a holy people to the

Lord your God: of all the peoples on earth the Lord your God chose you to be his treasured people" (Deut. 7:4–6). Quoting Jeremiah 2:3, the Rabbis state that Israel partakes of God's holiness for she is "his hallowed portion" (*Seder Eliyahu* 24, Braude, 329). Some Rabbis even state that Israel was designated as God's own holy people before the creation of the world (*Tanh.*, ed. Buber, 3:37a).

Israel is a holy people because God, as the Holy One, has attached her to himself and designated her to be holy, that is, she partakes of his holiness by her bond with him. This is exemplified by various analogies: Israel is attached to God as a waistband, a wife, and a family.

> One sage said: "Ye shall be holy," and why? "because I am holy," for I have attached you unto me, as it is said, "For as the waistband cleaves to the loins of a man, so I have caused to cleave unto me the whole house of Israel" (Jer. 13:11). Another explained: "The matter is to be compared to a king who sanctified a woman (by wedlock) unto him, and said to her: Since you are my wife, what is my glory is thy glory, "be therefore holy even as I am holy."
>
> (*Tanh.* ed. Buber, 3:37a).

Election entails separation. The Rabbis understand holiness as separation and withdrawal from other nations and their evil practices. They interpret the phrase, "kingdom of priests and a holy nation" (Exod. 19:6) to mean a nation separated from the nations of the world and their abominations (*Mekh.* 63a). Some Rabbis insist that God will not allow Israel to be assimilated among her neighbors: "When you say to yourselves, 'Let us become like the nations and tribes of other lands and worship wood and stone' you are thinking of something that can never be. As I live, says the Lord God, I will reign over you with a strong hand, with arm outstretched and wrath outpoured (Ezek. 20:32–33)" (*Sif. Deut.* 43, Hammer, 96).

Despite the strong avowal that God, by executive decision, designated Israel to be holy, this exclusive status depends on Israel's obedience. The theophany on Mt. Sinai provides the definitive example of Israel's holiness by election and obedience. On this occasion, God designates Israel as a "kingdom of priests and a holy nation" (Exod. 19:6) and appears visibly upon the mountain giving Israel an experience *sine qua non* of holiness. However, the holy theophany was immediately followed by the giving of the law. The point is clear: although holiness in Israel is by divine designation, it must be maintained through obedience to the law.[2]

For the Rabbis, the divine commands were the only way of knowing how to maintain holiness in Israel: "'Ye shall be holy' [Lev. 19:2] – that refers to the holiness [conferred by] all the *mitzvot*, commandments" (*Sifra* on Lev. 20:7, Weiss, 91d; see also Lev. 5:17–19). Israel is exhorted: "Be holy, for as long as you fulfill my commandments you are sanctified, but if you neglect them you become profaned" (*Num. R.* 17:6 on Num. 15:40: "That ye may remember and do all my commandments and be holy unto your God"). In the same vein, the author of Revelation says that the "holy ones" against whom the beast was enraged persevered because of their ability to "keep the commandments of God" (Rev. 14:12; see also John 8:51; 14:15, 21, 23; 15:10; 17:6; 1 John 2:3, 5; 3:22, 24:5:3).[3] Their "righteous deeds" (*dikaiomata*) are their protective, pure outer clothing (Rev. 19:8; see also 22:11; Rom. 6:19).

What does it really mean that Israel is a "kingdom of priests and a holy nation" (Exod. 19:6)? How can all Israel attain priestly holiness? Just as the priests serve in God's presence, so all of Israel enjoys, to some degree, the presence of God and a close bond or relationship with him. The holy people are guaranteed divine access and protection.[4] Both Israel and, to a greater degree, the priests, must ascribe to a certain code of behavior in order to make that presence and power possible, separating themselves from certain norms of life in the ancient world, which God considers offensive. Like the priests, all Israel must realize that holiness is always subject to recall depending on one's actions. Nevertheless, as long as the nation of Israel imitates God via the commandments, it can maintain its holy status.

Thus, there is an interrelationship of election and responsibility in the creation of holiness in Israel. God sanctifies Israel in proportion to Israel's self-sanctification. This holiness, which implies absolute purity both in action and thought, and utter withdrawal from evil, begins with a human effort to reach it and finishes with a gift from heaven bestowed upon human beings by an act of grace.[5] The Talmud asserts: "If a person sanctifies himself a little, they (in heaven) sanctify him much; if a person sanctifies himself below (on earth), they bestow upon him (more) holiness from above" (b. *Yoma* 39a). Rabbi Abin states that the angels were only given one portion of holiness since they are not subject to the evil *yetser*, but that humanity is given two portions of holiness in order to strengthen them against this temptation (*Lev. R.* 24:8, Margulies, 562f.; see also *Lev. R.* 14). Thus, God bestows holiness on his people and aids their efforts to maintain it.

The Rabbis struggle with the issue of why God even created the will to do evil:

> The Holy One, blessed be he, who is called righteous and upright, created man in his image only that he might be righteous and upright like Him. And should you say: Why did he create the will to evil? . . . If you can make the bitter things I have created sweet, for your needs, how much more can you do with the will to evil, which is in your power.
>
> (*Tanh.* on Gen. 3:22, *Yelamdenu* 19f.)

Thus, the answer seems to be that the evil inclination was created to allow human beings to choose to serve God of their own volition. Otherwise, individuals could not demonstrate their desire to reject evil and choose good. The Rabbis typically place much weight on human dignity and responsibility.

Many New Testament writers inherit a belief in the holy elect from their Judaic background and transfer it to their new Christian faith. Quite often, all Christians are called holy by virtue of their election (Acts 20:32; 26:10, 18; see also *Herm. Vis.* 3.6.2; *Herm. Sim.* VIII. 8.1).[6] The disciples are pure because of their association with Jesus (John 15:3) and by the divine word (John 15:3; 17:15ff.; see also 1 John 2:10; 3:6).[7] The Corinthian Christians are "made holy in Christ" (1 Cor. 1:2). Paul says the saints are holy by virtue of their position as children of God (1 Cor. 1:2; see also 3:17) even when he rebukes them for their behavior. As saints they are set apart to God through Christ. The writer of 1 John too emphasizes the dual components of the holy people, election and obedience. He affirms Christian holiness by election but links it to godly conduct (1 John 1:7ff.; 2:1ff.; see also John 13:10f.).

RITUAL

The command to Israel, "Be holy as the Lord your God is holy" is found in two contexts in Leviticus: one is ritual, after a catalog of laws regarding impure foods (Lev.11:44; see also 20:26), and the other is moral, coming after a list of sexual impurities and preceding various ethical commands (19:2).[8] Holy ritual reinforces Israel's separation from other nations and her dedication to God.[9]

To many gentiles, such notions as resting on the Sabbath and refusing to eat pork seemed foolish and irrational. For Cicero,

Jewish religion was a *barbara superstitio*. Plutarch associated Jewish ritual with the hedonism of the *bacchae*. Juvenal regarded such Jewish rituals as abstaining from pork as ridiculous, and he considered resting on the Sabbath as simply encouraging idleness. However, separation from gentiles, a key aspect of Jewish holiness which these rituals enforced, seems to be the real frustration and the heart of the problem.[10]

The Rabbis often found it difficult to prove any ethical or tangible value in the ritual commands. Nevertheless, they countered their opponents by saying that these traditions provided the opportunity to attain added holiness in Israel, simply because they fulfill the wishes of God: "Every transgression has the effect of stupefying the heart (b. *Yoma* 39a), while the observance of the laws in the Torah is productive of an additional holiness" (*Mekh.* 98a and *Sifra* 35a; 91d); and "'So you shall remember and do all my commandments and be holy to your God' (Num. 15:37); 'and be holy to your God,' this refers to the sanctity of all of the religious duties [every one of which falls into the classification of remembering and doing, thus of sanctifying Israel]" (*Sif. Num.*, Neusner, 181 on Num. 15:37).[11]

The underlying premise here is that the laws are of divine origin and thus cannot be annulled. The Rabbis especially focus on the ritual laws as sanctifying since these seem to require explanation. The fact that God ordered these rituals to be performed imbued their observance with sanctifying power just like the moral laws, for which a ready explanation was easy.

Circumcision, food laws, and purifications took on great importance in the rabbinic period as the possibility of holiness through the cult disappeared. These private rituals become central to the continuation of holiness in Israel. Their primary ingredient is separation. These rituals erect boundaries which separate and reinforce the difference between Israel and non-Israel creating a formidable group identity. According to the Rabbis, God says: "Even though I am about to exile you from the Land to a foreign land, you must continue to be marked there by the commandments, so that when you return they will not be new to you" (*Sif. Deut.* 43, Hammer, 96).[12]

This stringent separation of Israel from non-Israel was a huge obstacle for the early Church's mission to the gentiles. The purity laws seem to forbid any non-Jew from entering the community of faith. The New Testament writers emphasize that individuals should seek access to God, not through Jewish purity rituals, but through Christ, who was the great equalizer of all races and who could provide direct access to Heaven. Paul allows gentiles to join the holy community without the usual initiation marker of circumcision, and this later becomes standard Church dogma.

Holiness, maintained by keeping both the ritual and moral law, is more than a state of separation but it is a means to divine power. By perfect, unswerving obedience, God promises access to his power. Israel's holiness is powerful; her boundaries are dangerous to those who would trespass them unworthily or violate her in any way (Exod. 19:10–12). Keeping the physical purity laws of the war camp brought the Holy One into Israel's midst thereby guaranteeing victory in battle (Deut. 23:13–15). In fact, God promises: "If you do what is your duty to do, I will do what I made it My duty to do, 'Then will the Lord drive out . . .'" (Deut. 11:23) (*Sif. Deut.* 49, Hammer, 106).

According to modern anthropologists, a group's rituals support and express its values.[13] As demonstrated in the sections below, Israel's rituals express, illustrate, and reinforce what it means to be a holy people. The rituals of the Rabbis: (1) reenact the exclusive character of the Holy One, and by extension, that of the Jewish people – the holy people is set apart from other nations even by their private customs and eating habits; (2) illustrate and emphasize the purity of body and mind reflected in God's character, and by imitation, Israel's; and (3) reinforce Israel's identification with life and the Creator of life. Jewish ritual affirms that life is not chaos but meaningful. The habitual nature of ritual reinforces Israel's holy relationship with God by remembrance and maintenance of it on a daily basis.

Probably the most important rabbinic rituals in the context of holiness, in addition to the Sabbath and festivals discussed above (Chapters 2–3), were circumcision, food laws, and ritual purity. They were basic to all Jews, even to those living in the Diaspora. The Rabbis sent emissaries to the Diaspora to ensure that proper Jewish ritual was observed outside of the holy land. This is attested by the Talmud, the Theodosian Code, and Christian writers.[14] Even Philo of Alexandria, who interprets Jewish law in terms of cosmic and moral principles, emphasizes the need for retaining the ritual requirements (Philo, *Sp. Laws* 4.110; *Vit. Mos.*, II, 24).

A word about Graeco-Roman sacred rituals provides a context for our discussion. Many initiation rituals are attached to the Hellenistic mystery cults of the Graeco-Roman world, including, shaving the head, dancing, fasting, self-flagellation, and even castration, "the familiar means of working of the body in order to gain spiritual goods which we find mocked in Graeco-Roman sources as 'barbaric.'"[15] The Dionysian mystery is characterized by flagellation: the "road to bliss is through suffering." This test of endurance and ritual death precedes resurrection, enacted by an ecstatic gyrating dance with music. Cybele required the *taurobolium*, baptism in bull's blood. The object of this ritual was the purification of the initiate in order to be reborn into a new life. The initiate to the mystery of Isis must be ritually purified, fast for ten days, shave, and wear special clothes. To join the mystery of Hermes, one had to control the senses by meditation, asceticism, and purity. The goal was religious ecstasy which brought rebirth and bliss in the company of the gods. To enjoy the healing which Asclepius promises, the patient had to walk barefoot and take cold baths. For men only, the cult of Mithras involved endurance tests for the initiate, said to include: branding, hot and cold ordeals, fasting, scourging, and journeying.[16] In comparison to these Hellenistic mystery cults, the Jewish rituals seem quite mild.

Circumcision

Observing the command to circumcise all Israelite males is a significant part of maintaining holiness in Israel. The Rabbis place the observance of circumcision and the Passover at the top of the list of religious deeds which bring holiness to Israel (*Mek. de-Pisha* 5). Attempting to nullify circumcision is included with other violations of holiness, including desecrating holy things and despising holy seasons, which cancel all of a person's good deeds and threatens to drive him out of the world (*Sif. Num.*, Neusner, 170). A biblical indication that the term "circumcision" indicates holiness is found in Leviticus where unholy fruit is referred to as "uncircumcised," the opposite of fruit which has been made holy by setting it aside for God (Lev. 19:23–25). Furthermore, circumcision overrides holy days, including the Sabbath and holy festivals; it must be performed on the eighth day after a boy's birth (see also John 7:21–24).

Circumcision is a mark of initiation into the holy people.[17] After the ritual, the father blesses God, "Who has hallowed us by your commandments and has commanded us to make our sons enter into the covenant of Abraham our father."[18] The child receives a name and identity at the time of circumcision (see Luke 1:59). In Christianity, infant baptism and/or dedication replaced circumcision as a communal act and sign of the community's affirmation to remain true to the Christian covenant and to raise their children in accordance with it.[19]

Circumcision, as a sign which marks the physical member of procreation, emphasizes that Israel's holy election is through genealogy and ethnicity. While Christians insisted that in Christ there was neither Greek nor Jew, male nor female, rabbinic Judaism emphasized the physical body as the means by which Israel's holy election was marked and continued.[20]

As with other Jewish rituals of holiness, separation is a key element. In the early Christian centuries, circumcision was an indelible mark distinguishing Jews from non-Jews. Jewish girls were only allowed to marry circumcised men (*Ant.* 20.139, 145). Josephus says that God gave circumcision to Abraham to keep his descendants from mixing with others (*Ant.* 1.192). Nevertheless, as Josephus well knew, other groups too chose circumcision as an initiation marker, especially Egyptian priests (see Jer. 9:25–26). Circumcision was such a strong dividing line between Jew and gentile that the New Testament writers were hard pressed to nullify it in the minds of their congregants for the sake of the unity of the church (see Eph. 2:11–12).[21] With the annulment of circumcision, the writer of Ephesians can claim that gentiles are no longer second-class citizens but full members of the holy people (Eph. 2:19).

There was always a tension regarding ritual as a means to holy power. In a broad sense, of course, observing circumcision brings holy power into Israel. That is, as the fulfillment of a divine commandment, circumcision brings holiness, a positive divine force into the community; nullification of circumcision brings divine wrath (*Mekh.*, *de-Piska* 5; *Sif. Num.*, Neusner, 170). However, the blood rite of circumcision was considered by some to be an atonement ritual like the holy burnt offerings (see Jub. 16:25–34).

David Flusser and Shmuel Safrai note that many Jews in antiquity associated circumcision and the Passover sacrifice, both blood rites, with holy power which thwarts danger.[22] Indeed, only circumcised Israelites were allowed to eat of the holy Passover lamb and experience the Exodus (Exod. 12:43–49; see also Josh. 5:2 where only circumcised Israelites were allowed to enter into Canaan to engage in superhuman battles against the enemies of God). Those who were circumcised were considered protected by holy power, those who were not circumcised remained dominated by evil.[23] It is only among circumcised Jews that God continues to work. The point for our purposes is that attaining holiness through divinely ordained rituals was not considered a static process but a way of accessing divine power over evil.

This association of circumcision and atoning power was so ingrained among many first-century Jews that Paul declares to the Galatians, "If you receive circumcision, Christ will be of no advantage to you . . . you are severed from Christ . . . you have fallen away from grace" (Gal. 5:2–4). Christ, not circumcision, removes people from the sphere of evil (Gal. 1:4; 4:1–11; Phil. 3:19; cf. 4 Ezra 1:31). In his letter to the Romans, Paul admonishes his Jewish audience for thinking that circumcision produces rather than merely signifies acceptance with God (Rom. 4:9–12): "We have been saying that Abraham's faith was credited to him as righteousness. Under what circumstances was it credited? Was it after he was circumcised, or before? It was not after, but before! And he received the sign of circumcision, a seal of the righteousness that he had by faith while he was still uncircumcised." Thus, for Paul, as for the Rabbis after him, circumcision was only a marker or sign that righteousness had been credited. Faith, in particular faith in Christ, is the real key to the kingdom of God. He is the one who provides atonement, nothing and no one else. Initiation into the holy people is not by physical but spiritual means. The attitude of Paul's audience reveals a strong Jewish undercurrent which regarded rituals, such as circumcision, as powerful initiation rites.

As with other divinely ordained rituals, it would be easy to regard circumcision as a sort of magical, apotropaeic rite. Even the traditional rabbinic blessing praises God for giving Abraham this protective rite to spare him and his descendants. This connection between circumcision and atonement is evident in the later sages' claim that Abraham was circumcised on the 10th of Tishri, the Day of Atonement (PRE 29). Nevertheless, although the Rabbis regard circumcision as a means to holiness, this is because it is an act of obedience to the divine law. They stop short of considering it a sacrament. Circumcision signifies the right to participate within God's sphere of activity, the right to be partners with him in the creation of holiness, but it does not, on its own, create that righteousness.

Food

Scripture explicitly connects its dietary laws with holiness. Exodus 22:30 reads, "You shall be a holy people to me: you must not eat flesh torn by beasts in the field; you shall cast it to the dogs." After a long recital of prohibitions with regard to food, the writer of Leviticus concludes:

> You shall not defile your throats with any creature that swarms. You shall not make yourselves impure therewith and thus become impure, for I the Lord am your God. You shall sanctify yourselves and be holy, for I am holy. You shall not contaminate your throats with any swarming creature that moves upon the earth.
>
> (Lev. 11:43–44)[24]

The use of the imperative as well as the repetition of "holy" accentuates the importance of these laws. Also, by observing the food laws, Israel in some sense imitates God.

The full rationale behind the Jewish food laws would be helpful in unraveling the meaning of holiness, but it has eluded both practitioners and scholars. The Rabbis felt that because God ordered these laws, one should obey even without discovering the rationale. Jews should not say they do not want to eat pork (a favorite food throughout the Graeco-Roman world), but honestly admit that they do want to eat it but will abstain because their Father has so ordered (*Sifra Qed.* 11:22). The Rabbis stress that holiness hinges on the act of obedience to a divine command, not on the content of the command itself.

Holiness and diet are connected also in Leviticus 20. Israel is reminded to observe food purity laws as a reinforcement of their separation from other nations:

> I the LORD am your God who has set you apart from other peoples. So you shall set apart the clean beast from the unclean, the unclean bird from the clean. You shall not draw abomination upon yourselves through beast or bird or anything with which the ground is alive, which I have set apart for you to treat as unclean. You shall be holy to me, for I the LORD am holy, and I have set you apart from other peoples to be mine.
>
> (Lev. 20:24–26)

The act of separating edible from forbidden foods is treated as a metaphor for keeping Israel separate from non-Israel.[25] In addition, Israel's separation from non-Israel imitates God's separateness from all other beings.

The notion that food laws reinforce marriage laws and thus keep Israel's bloodline holy, that is, uncontaminated by gentiles, is corroborated by Exodus 34:15–16: "for they will lust after their gods and sacrifice to their gods and invite you, *and you will eat of their sacrifices.* And when you take wives from among their daughters for your sons, their daughters will lust after their gods and will cause your sons to lust after their gods." Thus, Scripture as well as its interpreters realize that the food laws were a protection against idolatry since they obstructed social intercourse between Jews and pagans (*Sifra* 57b). Christianity knew that food laws had to be broken down in order to break the notion that Israel has a special, holy election. "Israel's restrictive diet is a daily reminder to be apart from the nations" (see Acts 10:9–16, 27–28; 11:4–12).[26] Separation is an essential ingredient of holiness.

In addition to the separation principle, scholars have noticed the "wholeness," or element of completeness and perfection, present in holiness, especially with regard to holy animals. Applying social theory to the laws of Leviticus 11, Mary Douglas explains: "Holiness is exemplified by completeness. Holiness requires that individuals shall conform to the class to which they belong. And holiness requires that different classes of things shall not be confused."[27] Douglas sees the process as follows. Three classifications of elements were established at creation (air, water, and earth) by the process of division and separation. In each category normative habits and means of locomotion were established. Animals that do not conform completely to the norm or type of each division are prohibited. For example, the crab is unclean because it does not have fins and scales like "normative" water creatures. Insects are unclean because they walk on the earth and also fly in the air, thus confusing their classification in terms of locomotion. Physical perfection is, of course, required for all priests and priestly gifts. Additionally, mixed seeds and fabrics of mixed weaves are forbidden. The Rabbis are especially detailed in describing the physical perfection of holy items (see m. *Zeb.* 14:2).

Douglas goes on to give implications of her theory in terms of social values. Theft, lies, fraud, and cheating are "clearly contradictions between what seems and what is. . . . To be holy is to be whole, to be one; holiness is unity, integrity, perfection of the individual and of the kind."[28] Douglas considers the dietary laws as "signs which at every turn inspired meditation on the oneness, purity and completeness of God. By rules of avoidance holiness was given a physical expression in every encounter with the animal kingdom and at every meal." As her critics have demonstrated, wholeness is not the complete definition of holiness nor is it the full rationale of the food laws. Nevertheless, Douglas provides an important insight into holiness.[29]

Life is an important component in the creation of holiness as already demonstrated in earlier sections of this book. Nowhere is this more evident than in the dietary laws. Israel is forbidden to ingest the blood of any animal because blood is central to sanctification. That is, an animal's lifeblood is placed on the holy, sacrificial altar, sprinkled above and drained below it, in order to create and maintain holiness in Israel (Lev. 17:11). Therefore, according to Jewish law, meat must be salted and rinsed to remove all surface and capillary blood.[30] The principle resonates that blood is essential both for the continuance of the life of the body and the life of holiness in Israel. Both the physical and spiritual life of Israel is holy. Israel's neighbors do not have any prohibitions on ingesting the blood of their victims and do not connect blood with life or holiness.[31] In some Graeco-Roman cults, blood was ingested directly, as among the initiates of Mithras.

In the same vein, the Rabbis prescribe slaughter in the most humane way.[32] They demand that the three sides of the knife, sharp edge and the two sides, be examined (b. *Hul.* 17b) before and after slaughtering, and that it is razor sharp for one clean cut across the esophagus and trachea (see *Sif. Deut.* 12:22; m. *Hul.* 2:4). Both the respect for blood because of its association with life and atonement as well as humane slaughter indicate a reverence for life in Israel.

In addition to severe restrictions on blood and slaughter it is important to add that the impure animals are not inherently unclean but are only impure when they are dead. All animal carcasses are defiling (Lev. 11:39–40).[33] The forbidden birds are those which eat carrion. Animals which have died as prey are also forbidden. In fact, the only animals Israel may eat are the herbivores, those which do not eat other animals. Thus, there is a distancing in Israel from those animals which cause or are the result of death. The ban on cooking a young animal in its mother's milk is another indication of reverence for life, this time the life conveyed from mother to offspring. The Rabbis consider this law so important that they prohbit eating any meat with any type of dairy product, since one does not know if the two products came from an animal and its own mother (m. *Hul.* 8:1f.).

A final issue of holiness and food concerns eating in a state of ritual purity (see also next section). Leviticus 11 warns against violating the command to holiness by contaminating one's throat (Lev. 11:44). Unclean pots and vessels would contaminate the food within them (Lev. 11:32–38). So as not to defile the food one was eating and then ingest the impurity, Jews would purify themselves before meals. The practice of eating food in purity was a tenet of early rabbinic Judaism. The Mishnah writer exclaims: "Come and see how far purity has broken out in Israel that everyone eats ordinary food in a state of purity" (m. *Shab.* 13:1). Even the least observant Jew was trusted to protect priestly food as well as liquids and tithes from impurity (m. *Toh.* 8:2).[34]

The Pharisees, the predecessors of the Rabbis, ate together in a state of ritual purity and some performed a full immersion before meals (Luke 11:38; *War* 2.129). Apparently other first century Jewish groups did as well. The Essenes are the quintessential example of purity at meals: men, fully bathed and clothed in white, silently eating a communal meal. Among the disciples of Jesus, the lack of handwashing was conspicuous (Mark 7:3; m. *Hag.* 2:5). In rabbinic Judaism, prior ablutions before meals was a simple expression of the strong belief that the Jewish community in its daily life outside of the Temple was also holy (b. *Hul.* 106a; m. *Ed.* 5:6; see also Matt. 15:2). This conviction sustained Jewish life, especially after the Temple's destruction. When Jesus eats with tax collectors and sinners, people who could not be trusted to keep pure (Mark 2:15–17; Luke 5:1–2), he "provokingly rejects the boundary between what is unclean and what is clean" and he invites into the holy community many who were considered unworthy by others.[35]

On festivals, apparently, all Jews made the effort to eat in a state of purity. The Midrash asks how to make a festival holy and then answers its own question: "Make it holy with food, make it holy with drink, make it holy with clean clothes" (*Mekh. ShY*, ed. Epstein-Melamed). The early Rabbis regarded purity as the model for all times, not just during holy festivals.

Ritual purity

Ritual purity provides a foundation for holiness; the latter cannot exist without the former. In addition to the pure food which Israel must eat in order to be a holy people, there are a number of laws of physical purity which they must observe. In Judaism there is an emphasis on the sanctification of every day and every Jew. For many Jews of the early centuries CE, impurity must be kept away not only from the sacred, but, as far as possible, from the borders of the holy community. Purity is the state of being in which holiness can be active. Pinchas b. Yair sets forth an instructive progression of attributes, including purity and holiness, for which a Jew should strive. He says heedfulness leads to cleanliness (physical) which leads to purity which leads to *perishut* (separation) which leads to holiness, on to humility, shunning of sin, saintliness, the Holy Spirit, and finally to the resurrection of the dead (m. *Sot.* 9:15).

While these impurities concern the body, they are not labeled "impure" because they are physically dirty. A person can be dirty and sweaty from work in the field all day and still not be considered impure by the biblical definition. Most impurities are not diseases either. Thus, as with the forbidden foods, the rationale cannot be found completely in the area of hygiene. Significantly, the Hebrew word *tahor*, "pure," rarely refers to physical cleanliness.[36] The specific ritual impurities which threaten Israel's holiness are discussed in Leviticus 12–15, Numbers 19 and Deuteronomy 23, and can be outlined in three categories: death; leprosy (i.e. various types of scale disease); and bodily emissions. The Mishnah spells out the ramifications of these impurities in its sixth Division, Tohorot, "Purities," in terms of contamination and purification (see Table 5.1; see also Figure 1.2 above). Most of these impurities concern temporary conditions of the body, and are part of the normal course of life.

For Greeks, Romans, and Jews, holiness and impurity were incompatible. Death was the greatest impurity and it had to be kept away from the sacred realm. Artemis abandons Hipplytus on his deathbed with the words, "Farewell. Sacred law forbids me to look upon the dead, or stain my eye with the exhalation of death" (Eur., *Hipp.* 1437ff.). Corpse impurity in all three cultures, as well as in Egypt, temporarily excludes a person from worshipping the gods.[37] Sophocles, in the *Antigone*, described scraps of an unburied corpse being dropped by birds of prey upon sacrificial altars and hence dousing the sacred fire and dooming the city (Soph., *Ant.* 999–1015). Corpses had to be buried; only extreme criminals were thrown out unburied. Nevertheless, because of the sanctity of the island of Delos, no burials were allowed there.

Skin diseases, like biblical leprosy, were incompatible with the sacred sphere throughout the Graeco-Roman world. Scale disease was considered by the Babylonians a curse of God requiring immediate ostracization of the diseased person from society in order to avoid automatic disaster. The Greeks too regarded leprosy as a divine curse. When the people of Delos allowed a burial on their sacred island, they incurred divine wrath and the disease of leprosy.[38] Among the Rabbis, leprosy, the only disease in the levitical list, was definitely considered a punishment from God (t. *Neg.* 6:7; b. *Ar.* 16a; *Lev. R.* 17:3; 18:4; Lev. 14:34; Num. 12:11–12; 2 Chron. 26:23; Job 22:5; 2 Sam. 3:29; see also

Table 5.1 The Mishnaic system of impurity (m. Kel. 1:1–4; Lev. 11–15; Num. 19)

Impurity	Purification
Corpse	hopeless
Human bone	hopeless
Leper	needs healing, 8 days purification, 4 sacrifices
Woman who has just given birth	2 stages; 7/33 days (boy) 14/80 days (girl), sacrifice, bathing
Woman with abnormal menstrual flow	needs healing, 8 days purification, sacrifice
Gonnorrheic	needs healing, 8 days purification, sacrifice
Impure couch	
Impure saddle	washing
Impure flows of gonnorrheic and menstruant	hopeless
Sexual intercourse with a menstruant	7 days purification, sacrifice
Carrion handler; purgation water handler	bathing, evening
Touching a creeper, semen, corpse-contaminated person, purifying leper, insufficient purgation water	bathing, evening

Note: See, also, Hannah Harrington, *Impurity Systems of Qumran and the Rabbis* (Atlanta: Scholars Press, 1993).

4Q266–272; 1QH 1:32) and extensive rites were prescribed for purification, including blood daubings, sacrifices, bathings, and shavings (Lev. 13–14).

Sexual flows, both male and female, were incompatible with holiness and considered a chief cause of impurity. For many Greek societies, contact with the new mother could render a person impure from two to seven days.[39] After a few days, the mother lost her contagion but was still impure until the tenth day when the child was named, a sacrifice offered, and the mother began to return to normal life; still a fortieth day festival is attested marking the final end of the birth period. Similarly, according to rabbinic law, there were two stages to a new mother's impurity. During the first stage of her impurity, seven days (boy) or fourteen days (girl), she contaminated those around her in the common sphere, during the second (the next thirty-three or sixty-six days depending on the sex of the child), she remained contagious only to holy items and persons.

Sexual emissions kept a person from the holy realm. In *Lysistrata*, Myrrhine pleads with her eager husband: "[If I yield to you] I won't be pure enough to go back up to the acropolis." "No trouble about that," answers her husband, "you can wash in the Clepsydra fountain" (Ar., *Lys.* 912f.). Similarly, when Electra tells her brother that her husband has never approached her, her brother asks, "Is he under some sacred requirement of purity?" (Eur., *El.* 256). In Israel, as discussed in Chapter 3, all holy festivals required sexual abstinence as times of sacred encounter with God.

The Essene community at Qumran, which copied the Dead Sea Scrolls, observed some of the strictest standards of purity known anywhere in antiquity. The community was comprised entirely of celibate men. In other cities, Essenes did allow marital relations except for Jerusalem, the holy city (11Q19 45:11–12; CD 12:1–2). The texts from Qumran reveal many stringent purity laws. According to the Temple scroll, double immersions (i.e. on more than one day) were required for entry into Jerusalem (11Q19 45:8–9). Impure persons were denied access to the communal meal until they had purified themselves (1QS 5:13). Hopelessly impure persons, such as lepers, were still required to bathe before eating their own, non-communal food (4Q274). Food had to be pure from the time it was harvested, thus gleaners had to be in a state of purity (4Q284a). The Community Rule gives a rationale for its rules explicitly linking them to holiness: "in accordance with these rules in order to establish the spirit of holiness in truth eternal" (1QS 9:3). Specific laws, for example prohibiting physically impaired persons into the community (CD 15:15–17), forbidding tattoos and gashing (11QT 48:7, 10), and not allowing dogs into Jerusalem (MMT 60ff.), are all linked to maintaining holiness within the community. The rule of celibacy too is clearly an effort to increase the holiness of the sect since sexual intercourse causes impurity (Lev. 15:18).

The early church fathers, influenced by both Jewish and pagan notions of impurity, regarded holiness as incompatible with impurity. Tertullian says prayer and sex are incompatible.[40] In Alexandria one could not receive the sacraments if ritually impure. Some bishops in the early centuries (Bishop Dionysius, second century, and Bishop Timothy, fourth century) forbade sex on weekends and baptism during menstruation. The western church restricted the sexual life of all priests, deacons, and other clerics. The eastern church required celibacy only of bishops and monks.[41]

In the New Testament purity is linked to holiness in the moral sense. Paul uses the familiar dichotomy of *akatharsia*, "impurity," and *hagiamios*, "holiness," but interprets the former as immorality and the latter as purity in sexual relations (2 Cor. 12:21; Gal. 5:19; 1 Thess. 4:7; see also Rom. 6:19). The physical aspect of purity is increasingly reduced to a visual aid for moral exhortation: "Cleanse your hands and sanctify your hearts to draw near to God" (Jas. 4:7f.). 1 Peter 1:22 demands sanctification of soul and love out of a pure heart. Timothy is urged to have a pure heart and pure conscience (1 Tim. 1:5; 3:9; 2 Tim. 2:22; 1:3). Hebrews regards ritual purity as a thing of the past and concludes that only moral purity is perfect since it alone can purge the conscience (Heb. 9:13–14).

For Paul, gentile impurity denotes the immorality of the pre-Christian life typical of many pagans in the Graeco-Roman world. Gentile *akatharsia* [impurity] is the direct opposite of the righteousness of Christian sanctification (Rom. 6:19; 2 Cor. 12:21).[42] It can be counteracted by the force of holiness, which dwells in Christians. This holiness covers unsanctified children and lifts them out of their state of gentile impurity (1 Cor. 7:14).[43]

Ritual purification signifies acceptability for divine holiness. Across the Empire, it was acknowledged that the proper way to approach the gods was in a state of ritual purity. The purification process is a separation ritual. *Katharos* and *Katharizein* denote purification as an attempt to separate oneself from a loathsome situation and thus to appease the deity or demon.

Plato explains: "Of the kind of division that retains what is better but expels the worse, I do know the name . . . every division of that kind is universally known as a purification" (Pl., *Soph.* 226d). For example, purification in water of the entire Athenian assembly was ordered after the news of a murderous slaughter in Argos of 1,500 men.[44] The ritual expressed the horror of the citizens and separated them from the terrible event.

In Latin, the word *lustrum* is especially significant because it not only means "pure" but marks off a period of time. Purification is a way of marking the transition from an undesirable state to a desirable one.[45] It is the access road either back to the normal condition or into a sacred status. The beginnings and ends of military campaigns, for example, are marked by lustrations of the military. Again, purification rites make the individual acceptable to approach the sacred – the realm of the gods. After all, military victories are ascribed to the gods.[46]

Holiness, as the force of the Holy One, is evident in rabbinic rituals of purification. Depending on the degree of impurity, uncleanness is removed by various (usually a combination) purification rituals, for example sacrifices, immersion in water, fire, time lapses.[47] Leviticus (15:13–16; 11:36) indicates that spring water or a natural pool large enough to cover the body was good for purification.[48] For the Greeks too purifying water had to be taken from a flowing source (Aesch., *Eum.* 452; Eur. *El.*, 794; *Hipp.* 653). The Rabbis explain that only water flowing directly from its source, for example rain or spring water, is capable of purifying from impurity because it is given directly by the Holy One.[49] No human intervention, by drawing out or pouring water in vessels, is allowed for ritual immersion (*Sifra Shem. Sher.* 11:7; par. 9:1; m. *Ed.* 1:3; m. *Miq.* 7:2). The symbolism is clear: only the gods, whether the Greek nature gods or the Holy One of Israel, can supply purifying water. Purification which provides access to the divine is enabled by the divine.

Purification in the Bible is sometimes preparatory (as before the theophany at Mt. Sinai) and sometimes restorative (as after impurity or sin). Likewise, the Rabbis teach washing of hands before all formal daily prayers as a preparatory ritual (b. *Ber.* 15a). Purification after impurity restores a Jew to the holy community. Indeed, failure to purify after impurity results in extirpation (Num. 19:20).

Katharizein, "to cleanse," and *hagiazein*, "to sanctify," converge in Ephesians 5:26 in the context of baptism (see also John 3:25; Heb. 1:3; 2 Pet. 1:9; 1 John 1:7,9).[50] "*Bapto*" means "to dip in or under." The ritual promotes the principle that what is unclean in God's sight must be purified before His holiness can be experienced (see Heracl., *Fr.*, 5, Diels).[51] The immersion required for proselytes to Judaism probably influenced Christian baptism as well (see 1 Cor. 6:11; Eph. 5:26; Heb. 10:22; Acts 2:38; 22:16). It signifies a new, innocent beginning for the convert, the start of a way of life activated by holiness.

However, many early Christians regarded baptism as a regenerative rather than a symbolic ritual. In this they were no doubt influenced by Hellenistic mystery cults. In Egypt the dead were purified so that they could enter a new life in the undereworld. The dead Osiris is sprinkled causing blades of grain to sprout from his body. Like Osiris, "to be drowned in the river is to enter into connection with the god and thus to be divinised."[52] Various other mystery cults, for example Eleusis, Bacchus, Isis, and Mithras, required sacral baths. The ultimate goal was eternal life. The initiate is purified from sin and inherits real life from God.[53] Also like the mystery cults, a miraculous change was expected: "We go down into the water full of sins and impurity, but then rise out again laden with fruits" (*Barn.* 11:11). In contrast to this, Paul does not see a magical transformation at baptism (1 Cor. 10:1–13); Paul stays away from the Hellenistic idea of regeneration through baptism. Baptism for him symbolizes rather than creates the purifying work of Christ in the life of the believer. In later Christianity, for example the Mandaean ritual, the sacramental or even magical power of revivification becomes more stressed and ritual cleansing is secondary.

In rabbinic Judaism, immersion remains a symbolic rather than a regenerative act. Purification maintains the holiness of Israel; it is not transformative. Nevertheless, it is still associated with life, and in particular, the life of the holy people of Israel. As discussed earlier (Chapter 1), holiness at its source is life itself – the antonym of death. It is the task of Israel to obey and choose God, represented by life, over pagan gods, represented by death. The purity system illustrates this tension implicitly by its three categories of impure persons:[54] (1) the corpse; (2) the leper, a visibly decaying person; and (3) the loss of sexual flows which create life. As Mary Douglas sums up the matter: "The nature of the living God is in opposition to dead bodies. Total incompatibility holds between God's presence and bodily corruption. God is living, life is his. Other gods belong to death and the contagion of decay."[55]

Douglas, who as an anthropologist has studied numerous tribes and cultures, regards Israel's purity system as unique. She points out that it was common in grave areas throughout the ancient world to worship dead heroes – a fact amply attested but vigorously protested in Israel by the Rabbis.[56] Douglas further points out that taboo systems (e.g. Hinduism) are usually interested in excluding certain social categories; however, the Israelite impurity system, by contrast, is not driven by control of certain classes of people but by a concern for the holiness of the sanctuary and, I might add, for the Jewish people especially after the Temple's demise. Also unlike the Roman world is the Jewish insistence that one's attitude and intention are effectual and a mitigating factor in the process of purification; good intention is necessary for purity.

In further contrast to their neighbors, the Rabbis explicitly deny any connection between demonic forces and impurity. The ancients feared impurity primarily as demonic, even metadivine, capable of attacking the gods. By contrast, in the Bible human beings alone are the cause of the world's ills; only they can contaminate the sanctuary and "force God out."[57] While the Greeks and Romans conceived of impurity as a demonic force which threatened the existence of the community and so must be appeased and curtailed, the Rabbis regarded purification as a neutral but inexplicable divine mandate which was necessary in order to maintain the holy status of Israel (see the discussion of R. Yohanan and his disciples regarding the red cow ritual, Chapter 2, above). The fact that they could not provide a specific rationale for these rituals shows that they did not think of them as containing intrinsic power on their own. Perhaps the most marked point of originality in the rabbinic purity code is that an invisible, aniconic God was considered the inaugurator of it. Other religions do not as a rule connect the need for ritual purity with the commands of a holy God.[58]

ETHICS

Inherent in the rabbinic concept of holiness is a commitment to ethics and morals. These two English words stem from the Greek, *ethos*, and Latin, *mores*, respectively. *Ethos* and *mores* both denote "custom and usage, as well as habit, manners and disposition."[59] Among the Greeks and Romans these terms indicated social norms and had little or nothing to do with the holy sphere. Holiness did not indicate a moral lifestyle prescribed by the Graeco-Roman gods. Greeks and Romans were not asked to submit to an organized system of beliefs or identify with a special "holy people" as among the Jews.[60]

This is not to say that the Greeks and Romans had no morals. They espoused a lifestyle which certainly contained moral principles but these were not dictated or controlled by the gods. Morality was simply not the purview of the priests, who were rather experts in maintaining right relations with the gods through ritual means.[61] As Liebeschuetz says, although the Romans

> were even obsessively convinced of the need to placate the gods, belief in the gods seems to have had little effect on their conduct. The reader of Latin literature feels that fear of divine displeasure was very rarely a motive when a Roman decided on a course of action . . . nor is there much evidence that a divine command was used as an excuse to justify any individual's behaviour retrospectively.[62]

A potentially immoral or aggressive individual would probably not be deterred by reflection on the gods. The emphasis when considering the Graeco-Roman gods was not on their morality but on their power. Cicero may have said it best: Jupiter is the best and greatest "not because he makes us just or sober or wise but healthy and rich and prosperous."[63] Unlike Judaism, societal rules did not carry the backing of divine revelation with accompanying reward and punishment. Judaism and Christianity find their closest Graeco-Roman ethical counterpart among the Stoic philosophers (see below).

Imitatio Dei

The ethical commitment in holiness begins with the principle of *Imitatio Dei*, human imitation of God. The biblical command "Be holy as I the Lord your God am holy" expresses the belief that Israel, because she has been elected by God, is obligated to imitate his holiness. Thus, holiness is not just an elected status but a dynamic force which must be maintained by careful imitation of the Holy One. The Rabbis accentuate Israel's duty to imitate God by using familiar analogies to illustrate God's close relationship to Israel. "Israel is the *familia* of the King (God), whence it is incumbent upon them to imitate the King" (*Sifra* 86c). Israel's imitation of God's holiness is like the identification and solidarity of the royal family with the king, a wife with her husband or children with their parents (*Lev. R.* 24:4). John Gammie calls it *"Noblesse oblige"*; that is, "The nobility to which God summoned Israel obligated her to a social conduct and individual morality befitting the majesty and dignity of the Most High."[64]

How does Israel imitate God? The Rabbis suggest both separation from evil as well as a commitment to ethical goodness. First, since God cannot be credited with evil, it is clear to the Rabbis that holiness involves separation from evil: "By separating oneself from sin, a person can become holy" (*Sif. Qedosh.* 93b; see also *Lev. R.* 23 end). Even the fear of sin leads a person to holiness (b. *AZ* 20b; see also also y. *Sheq.* 3:3).

What is this evil which obstructs holiness? The *Sifra* explains: "As I am separated, so be ye separated: this means separation from things impure and defiling, foremost among which are idolatry [see Chapter 1], adultery and other illicit sexual relations, and murder" (*Sifra* on Lev. 16:16, 57b, Weiss, 81c; see also *Sifra* 81a). In order to save his life a man may violate other laws of the Torah, but never these three prohibitions (b. *San.* 74a). Even gentiles were expected to avoid these sins (b. *San.* 56a). Other sins from which Israel must "separate" include eating meat without draining the blood and theft (m. *Mak.* 3:15). The list continues with sins dealing with business and social improprieties.

Understanding holiness as a positive force is more clear when examining sin, the other side of the coin. Sin is a power which can ultimately dominate individuals and turn them against God: it is "at first called a 'passerby,' then a 'guest,' and finally 'one who occupies the house'" (b. *Ber.* 17a; see also "Do not let your evil inclination persuade you that Sheol is a place of refuge for you" (m. *Ab.* 4:22)). Just as sin is a force influencing a person for evil, so holiness is a force which acts on a person for good. The Talmud regards holiness as the antidote to sin: "Preserve my [God's] Torah in thy heart, and may my fear be present before thy eyes. Guard thy mouth against all sin, and make thyself holy against all sin and injustice, and I will be with thee" (b. *Ber.* 17a).

The dynamic polarity between sin and holiness is apparent in this comment on the holy theophany at Mt. Sinai.

> R. Simeon b. Yohai says, Come and take note of how great is the power of sin. For before the people had laid hands on transgression what is stated in their regard? "Now the appearance of the glory of the Lord was like a devouring fire on the top of the mountain in the sight of the people of Israel" (Exod. 24:17). Nonetheless, the people did not fear nor were they afraid. But once they had laid hands on transgression, what is said in their regard? "And when Aaron and all the people of Israel saw Moses, behold the skin of his face shone, and they were afraid to come near him (Exod. 34:30)."
>
> (*Mek.* on Exod. 34:30)

The point here is that the glory, or manifest holiness (see Chapter 1), of God empowers Israel as long as they are not influenced by evil, which is seen as an ostracizing, negative force. While the Rabbis generally do not personify the evil inclination, they often come close to doing so. R. Simeon b. Lakish, for example, said: "Satan, the *yetser ha-ra*", and the angel of death are one and the same" (b. *BB* 16a).

In contrast to the Holy One of Israel, the traditional Roman gods could not be imitated as models of moral behavior and it was rarely expected of them. In the pursuit of "virtue" Romans were urged to imitate Hercules, but his activities could never be seen as a moral pattern by Judeo-Christian standards. The abstract powers, on the other hand, could be looked to as divine, albeit rather impersonal, models of morality.[65] Fides, "Fidelity," was a keystone of Roman morality; it was always worshipped as a Roman god – even in the fourth century CE.[66] The goddess *Justitia*, "Justice," holds a balance and scales in her hands. Some temples were dedicated to these public moral virtues: Fides, Spes, Honos, Virtus, Pietas, Pudicitia, Libertas. Temples evidently did evoke some sense of purity and justice otherwise Cicero could not say that people would live purer lives if they saw more temples, that the destruction of religion would bring the end of justice, or that crimes are deterred by fear of divine punishment.[67] Nevertheless, these principles remained vague and quite often lacking in the behavior of the Graeco-Roman pantheon. Public disaster was usually considered the result of incorrect ritual not immorality.

Being holy by rabbinic standards is more than abstention from evil. It must include imitation of God's active goodness as well (*Tanh.* 3:37b; *PRK* 111a; *Seder Eliyahu* 133, Braude, 329; *Num. R.* 9:4, 17:6). The Rabbis follow the biblical writers in their insistence that individual integrity and social justice are necessary for the attainment of holiness (see Ps. 24:4; 15:1–5; Isa. 6:5–7; *Seder Eliyahv*, Friedmann, 65 on Ps. 15:2). "Holiness means not only 'separation from' but 'separation to.' It is a positive concept, an inspiration and a goal associated with God's nature and his desire for man."[68] To be holy means to imitate God's goodness as well as his separation, by a life of ethics and kindness. The Hebrew *qadosh* as well as its New Testament translation, *hagiadzo*, indicate both separation and moral goodness.[69] While this imitation is not fully attainable, Israel must continually strive for it. She is elected to represent God, not simply to separate from evil. Separation simply provides the credentials which allow Israel to participate with God in bringing about goodness in the world.

Holiness as an imitation of God is also expressed in the New Testament, but the imitation is first of Jesus Christ who reflects the Father. John often uses the formula, "As I [Jesus] . . . so you . . . .," to illustrate this imitation (John 13:34; 17:18, 23; 20:21). The writer of 1 Peter connects imitation of Christ with holiness: "As he who called you is holy be holy yourselves in all your conduct; because it is written, Be holy, for I am holy" (1 Pet. 1:15). Christ is the perfect image of God, according to Paul, and the one Christians must imitate (2 Cor. 4:4; see also Col. 1:15). Paul urges the Corinthians, "Conform your minds to the mind of Christ" (2 Cor. 3:18; see also Rom. 8:29). He explains that the Spirit is the holy force which can transfigure believers into the image of Christ (2 Cor. 3:18; 1 Cor. 15:49).

Ethical goodness within holiness

What is this ethical goodness which Israel must imitate in order to maintain holiness? There is no single, corresponding Hebrew term for the word ethics. Rather, the Rabbis use several words to describe different types of ethical behavior, for example justice, truth, peace, pillars upon which the world is supported (m. *Ab.* 1:18). The Rabbis do not define ethics or morality. They simply provide terms which reflect aspects of God's goodness and Israel's imitation of it: *gemilut hasadim*, "loving kindness"; *anavah*, "humilty"; *mishpat/din*, "justice"; *emet*, "truth"; *tsedakah*, "charity" [early: "righteousness"]; and *shalom*, "peace." *Hasidut*, "kindness, graciousness," is probably the closest term to *qedushah*, "holiness," since *hasid* and *qadosh* are often used interchangeably in rabbinic literature.[70] Both terms denote the pious, kind person bent on goodness.

Doing good deeds is an effective means of gaining holiness and fighting the temptation of sin (b. *Qid.* 30b). The connection between studying the Torah and holiness is affirmed in the well-known prayer in the Jewish liturgy, "Sanctify us by your commandments."[71] Doing good deeds weighs the balance toward holiness in the community just as committing one sin weights the balance negatively (b. *Qid.* 40a). One Rabbi said, "All according to his deeds does the Holy Spirit rest upon a man." The Rabbis claim that Abraham subdued his evil passions by channeling them into deeds of generosity (y. *Ber.* 9:7, 14b). These deeds of mercy should not be done without *kavanah*, intention. One should be aware that the deed provides access to greater holiness and invites God's activity within Israel.

The Rabbis translate imitation of God's holiness by goodness in specific ways. They exhort, "As he is merciful, you be merciful; as he is gracious, you be gracious" (b. *Shab.* 133b; see also *Mekh. Shira*, par. 3; m. *Ab.* 1:2). Other passages refer to God's patience, forgiveness and kindness as attributes which Israel must emulate. Even specific actions, clothing the naked, burying the dead, nursing the sick, comforting mourners, and the like, are attributed to God in an effort to present the model of goodness which Israel should follow (b. *Sot.* 14a; *Sif. Deut.* on Deut. 11:22).

Rabba defines *hasidut* as carrying out Tractate *Abot*, a section of the Mishnah which deals primarily with ethics.[72] Rab Judah says, "He who is desirous of being a saint, let him fulfil the precepts of that part of the law which deals with 'Damages' (section of the Mishnah on injury to fellowman)" (b. *BQ* 30a; see also m. *Yoma* 8:9). The Talmud exhorts, "make thyself holy against all sin and injustice, and I will be with thee" (b. *Ber.* 17a). Injustice is a definite obstruction to holiness. The Mishnah regards even humiliation of another person in public as a desecration of holiness (m. *Ab.* 3:11). Thus, a sense of goodness and regard for other human beings is inculcated in the rabbinic understanding of holiness.[73] Human life, the focus of holiness, is first of all not the life of the individual, but that of the community.[74] Many of the examples above clearly illustrate this point: injuries, both physical and emotional, to fellow Jews are regarded as desecrations of holiness.

According to the Rabbis, Jews must contribute to the community good, and if they do so they will not sin: "He who brings merit to the community never causes sin, and he who causes the community to sin – they never give him a sufficient chance to attain penitence" (m. *Ab.* 5:18). Jews do not achieve holiness as individuals unless they act on behalf of the group. Holiness is not separation from society but separation from contamination in order to perform acts of goodness among humanity. Holiness requires a commitment to live ethically in a world which often runs along more sordid lines.

Biblical support for the link between ethics and holiness is plentiful. As discussed in a previous chapter, Isaiah states that even God's holiness is manifest by righteousness: "But the LORD of hosts becomes exalted in justice and the Holy God shows himself holy by righteousness" (Isa. 5:16).[75] Injustice is eradicated by positive acts of goodness, and holiness is that force for good (Isa. 1:16–17). The Psalmist speaks of striving for holiness purely in ethical terms: "Who shall ascend the hill of the LORD? And who shall stand in his holy place? The one who has clean hands and a pure heart, who does not lift up his soul to what is false, and does not swear deceitfully" (Ps. 24:3–4).[76] Another Psalm illustrates the same connection: "Who will dwell on thy holy hill? The one who walks with integrity and does justly . . . speaks the truth . . . does no harm . . . does not magnify the shame of the one nearby," keeps his promises, and takes no bribe (Ps. 15). For the Psalmist and the Rabbis holiness requires a complete interweaving of ethics and the cult.

Indeed, the command, "Be holy as I am holy," appears in Leviticus 19:1 beginning a section which primarily legislates ethics in Israel's intra-relationships. The Rabbis refer to this chapter as "the passage on holiness" and debate exactly how many duties are required in it (*Lev. R.* 24:5). The point is that for the Rabbis holiness depended upon fulfilling ethical obligations. Specific and achievable instructions are given in Leviticus 19 concerning the maintenance of holiness. For example, paying wages on time is included in this list of holy obligations (Lev. 19:13).[77] As another demonstration of holiness, farmers must leave a corner of their fields and some gleanings for the poor (Lev. 19:9f.; 23:22). The Rabbis state that the amount left in the field should never be less than one-sixth of harvest (m. *Pe'ah* 1.2). They emphasize that the "forgotten sheaf" of the Torah is an order: make sure to remember to "forget a sheaf" and leave it for the poor (m. *Pe'ah* 6). Social responsibility is not just a vague attitude but is to be expressed by concrete actions. One should never feel self-satisfied that holiness has been once-for-all achieved but must continue to improve relations in society. In fact, this passage (Lev. 19) was the first to promote the ethical ideal, "Love your neighbor as yourself" (v. 18).

It should be noted that the rabbinic laws of ritual purity, discussed above, are subservient to the ethical laws. For example, because of the *kebod ha-beriyyot*, the honor of mankind, even the high priest must become unclean and attend to the burial of a *met mitzvah*, the corpse of a person whose relatives cannot be found. Thus, the attendance to the burial of even a stranger is an overriding *mitzvah*. Even Torah study should be interrupted if one is needed as a funeral escort or as a member of a wedding procession.

Just as the Rabbis see the divine commands as the link to holiness in Israel, so holiness is mediated to Christians through the commandments of Jesus: "For you know what commands we gave you by the Lord Jesus. For this is the will of God even your holiness, that you should abstain from fornication . . . that no man go beyond and defraud his brother in any matter. . . . For God has not called us unto uncleanness, but unto holiness" (1 Thess. 4:2–7).

Righteousness is aligned with holiness by several New Testament writers. Jesus is identified as the "holy and righteous one" by Luke (Acts 3:14: *ho hagios kai dikaios;* see also 4:27, 30). It seems that the two words, "holy" and "righteous," are used to create one title. Paul encourages the Romans to do acts of righteousness (*dikaio*) in order to further holiness in their lives (Rom. 6:19). He points out that in their pre-Christian life the Roman converts had willingly engaged themselves in impure acts, and so now that energy should be channeled into holy activities, that is, righteous deeds. This holiness results in eternal life (Rom. 6:22). The equation of holiness and life is unsurprising in Paul the Jew (see also Rom. 6:23).

In the same vein, it is because of their holy, elect status that the Colossians must demonstrate compassion, kindness, humility of mind, meekness, longsuffering, forbearance, and forgiveness (Col. 3:12f.). The writer of Ephesians insists that Christians, whom he regards as the holy people (1:4), separate themselves from a long list of sins, (5:3–5), and "have no fellowship with the unfruitful works of darkness, rather reprove them" (Eph. 5:11; Gal. 5:19–20). Paul orders the Corinthians not to even eat with Christians who engage in sin (1 Cor. 5:11).

The perfection and completeness noticed earlier in the rabbinic concept of holiness surfaces again in the context of ethics. In the New Testament holy people are those who are perfect in obedience to God and free from sin. As noted above (Chapter 1), the command of Leviticus to be holy is rephrased by Matthew with the word "perfect": "Be perfect, even as your Father who is in heaven is perfect" (Matt. 5:48). This comes after a teaching on love of others, even those who do not give love in return. Indeed, love is a hallmark of the holy ones (Col. 1:4: Eph. 1:15) and the element which perfects them (Col. 3:14).[78] The writer of 1 John links both concepts together, love and obedience to the divine commands: "Whoever keeps his [God's] word, in him is the love of God truly perfected" (1 John 2:5). 1 Peter 1:22 demands sanctification of soul and love out of a pure heart. Other terms signify this holy perfection. Converts should be "blameless" (1 Thess. 3:13; 5:23), "innocent" and "without blemish" (Phil. 2:15). The writer of Ephesians says that Christ's salvific work enables the church to be "without spot or wrinkle . . . holy and without blemish" (Eph. 5:27).

Nevertheless, the endeavor to create perfect holiness and wear down impurity on a daily basis is a lifelong pursuit. Paul stresses perfecting holiness in the area of ethics.[79] This is a continual task, never to be fully achieved (2 Cor. 7:1). In fact, the pursuit of perfection is what the holy ones have been initially selected to work on (Eph. 1:4; 5:6–27). Paul regards the Christian as a holy item, a living sacrifice, which maintains its holiness by being offered daily through a life of goodness (Rom. 12:1–2). Although salvation brings a certain "holiness of the spirit" (2 Thess. 2:13; see also Col. 1:22), this must be followed by adherence to moral traditions (2

Thess. 2:15) and established by "good word and work" (v. 17). In his exhortation to women, the writer of 1 Timothy urges them to "continue" in holiness (1 Tim. 2:15).

Unlike the rabbinic concept, there is among the early Christian Church the notion that a mystical, miraculous transformation happens at conversion which creates a holy person, who is at least equal to the holy status a Jew receives by ethnicity. Believers are "God's temple" and the Holy Spirit dwells in them (1 Cor. 3:16; 5:1; 6:18–19). Paul rebukes the Galatians for relying on the deeds commanded by the law. He challenges them, "Having begun in the Spirit, are you now made perfect by the flesh?" Thus the continuance of the holy people in Christ, just like its creation, is enabled by the Spirit.

Holiness as spiritual transformation and perfection was the goal of many early church fathers. Their belief was that "those who would be perfect must seek divinely given *gnosis*, higher and hidden truth, in their search to know the perfect One, and thereby to participate in divine perfection."[80] Clement, Origen, and Gregory of Nyssa are good examples. Their belief was that spiritual knowledge, *gnosis*, is the key to perfection and it is given by Jesus Christ. Clement says, "We call that perfect which wants nothing. For what is yet wanting to him who knows God?" (Clement, *The Instructor* 1:6). Nevertheless, following the Platonic view of two realms of reality, these men believed that a further perfection is available for the "true gnostics," those who reach beyond the initial salvation experience. *Gnosis* is not just information but entails a mystical progress toward the divine. Nevertheless, the church fathers warned that disreputable conduct would hinder this advancement. The struggle toward perfection, while primarily intellectual and emotional, must generate knowledge generates control of the passions.

Stoicism: ethical goodness without holiness

The Stoics, who enjoyed great popularity in the first centuries CE, developed a closer connection between religion and morality than previously found among the Greeks and Romans. These philosophers conceived of a divine entity that was "the Good" and which should be imitated by humanity. God is not only pure goodness he is also pure reason, and thus conduct guided by pure reason will be good and moral. Virtue is most important in life, not riches or success. Religion should be unemotional because emotional religion is dangerous and even a sign of barbarism.[81] Plato and Aristotle held that the goal of law was to make people good. The highest good humanity could achieve was good citizenship, maintaining one's duties to the state. A good life should be the goal of humanity (Pl., *Crito*, 48; Sen., *Moral Epistles*, 99:1).

What is this virtue? Since all events are predestined, according to Stoicism, the issue is about the way a person handles his fate. The courage to face death was a hallmark of the Stoics (*Moral Epistles* 4:3; 24:5; Epictetus, *Discourses* II.1.13, *Ench.* 21, see also b. *Ber.* 5b; m. *Ab.* 2:1). The best will show emotional indifference, maintain self-respect, and exhibit the traditional behavior espoused by the Roman aristocracy. Cicero's four classes of rules of proper Roman conduct, for example, are: search for truth; preservation of society; achievement of greatness of character; self-control. The Stoics promised no reward or future life, only self-respect. They had a strong sense of ethics, often characterized by their cosmopolitanism and abhorrence of slavery. Seneca (55 CE), one of the most famous of the Stoic philosophers, emphasizes reason and conscience as guides to actions. However, for the Stoics, who were generally resigned to the social state of things in the world, "virtue lay in a disposition of the soul and not in the action."[82] The opposite of virtue appears to be unrestrained pleasure and greed.

The state was the center of a Roman's concern and proper behavior as a good citizen included self-control in all areas. For example, courage in the face of death was evidence of strong character; incest and adultery, on the other hand, were signs of weakness. Influenced in the early Christian centuries by the Stoics, the Roman ideal could be described as free from excessive passion, jealousy, and extremism.

Pliny (ca. 100 CE), a Roman statesman who supported the Stoics, says the gods require uprightness, but his own behavior seems to define this as "fitting conduct."[83] His motives are based on self-respect, self-control, refusal to live a life of disgrace, pain, or bereavement; he is not motivated by hope of immortality nor by the punishment of gods. He is duty oriented and espouses traditional religious rituals. Tacitus, a contemporary of Pliny, was also steeped in Stoic ideas, especially the notion that virtue requires sincere and consistent behavior.[84] Lucan paints a negative picture of morality in the Roman Empire and concludes, "Might became the standard of right."[85]

Stoicism thus recognizes the dignity of individuals and encourages good relationships between people but does not relate these duties to the will of an active, personal God. Stoics were guided by their reason when defining ethics and laid no claim to any external authority or divine revelation. The Generative Reason, which is "the Good," permeates the world and carries life onward, but it is not the same as an active beneficent God intervening in daily life for human welfare.[86] The Stoic's decision is not between God and evil, with heaven the reward of believers and hell that of unbelievers (e.g. Lactantius, *Div. Inst.* 6:3/*P.L.* 6.643), but a choice between virtue and self-respect, on the one hand, and shame and disgrace, on the other, between acting according to reason and acting in opposition to it.

The definition of holiness which brings ethical dealings between human beings into the realm of the sacred is unusual in the ancient world. Greeks and Romans did not regard the two in the same breath. Matters of holiness were connected to the cult, matters of society were discussed by philosophers.[87]

SEXUALITY

Across the Graeco-Roman world sexual activity was generally considered incompatible with the sacred. Sexual intercourse produces impurity, an antonym of holiness. Neither those who have had seminal emissions, nor women who have either engaged in sex or are menstruating, are allowed in shrines throughout the Empire. Birth, death, and sex are excluded from sacred areas. Many Graeco-Roman cults did allow women to serve as priestesses, but these were usually virgins who had in effect given their sexuality to the gods.[88]

Furthermore, Hellenistic philosophers devalued physical passion from an intellectual point of view. Platonists and Stoics set forth the notions that: (1) the physical is just an imperfect shadow of what is really genuine, that which is in the metaphysical sphere; and (2) the ideal man is the one who does not indulge himself in passion but shows restraint, including sexual restraint.[89] Porphyry describes Plotinus, "the philosopher of our times," as seeming "ashamed of being in the body." He says that Plotinus "could never bear to talk about his race or his parents or his native country."[90]

The upper world of the mind and the spirit was considered the world of freedom and enlightenment opposed by the lower world of matter and physical activity, including sexuality. The human being was conceived of as a spiritual being, or soul, which was trapped within a physical container, or body. Sexual activity was a reminder of that physical container with its carnal impulses. Passion was a product of that corporeality and stood in the way of mental and spiritual perfection. Once a person decides that real value rests in the supernatural or metaphysical realm, what is physical and concrete is easily devalued and even disavowed completely.[91]

Asceticism, that is, abstention from accepted human desires ranging from sex, food, and material gain, to any social activity whatever, was promoted among many in the Graeco-Roman world as a means to gaining access to the divine. The logic behind it is simple. By doing without something that is permitted and desired, a person shows his submission and humility before the gods. Also, by separating from things that make one impure or diverting one's focus from human needs, such as sex and food, a person focuses on the spiritual realm. The goal for many was to shed the baggage of the physical body and ascend mystically into the metaphysical sphere. The Stoics and Cynics practiced asceticism in order to control passion, which they found distracting and deleterious, in their effort to develop disciplined lives.[92]

For the Rabbis a paradox is retained. On the one hand, as discussed above, sexual intercourse, by its very nature, causes impurity and is therefore incompatible with the sacred. The Bible and the Mishnah both emphatically claim that sexual intercourse is not a part of the holy cult. The Talmud states that just as the holy theophany at Sinai required abstaining from sexual intercourse, so also those who have had seminal emissions must first purify before reading the Torah (b. *Ber.* 21b).

The passion connected to sexual activity too is recognized as potentially dangerous since it can lead to violation of the law. Extra holiness is required from God in order to deal with it properly. The Rabbis compare the easier status of the angels over humans in maintaining holiness because of their lack of passion (*Lev. R.* 24:8). According to *Leviticus Rabbah*, although humanity has to work harder at being holy, God provides the necessary assistance by giving people two allotments of holiness whereas he gives the angels only one. Again, the reader is reminded of God's willingness and effort to aid Israel in the process of becoming holy.

The impurity connected with sexual activity alone could have moved the Rabbis to equate sex and evil completely, as in many Christian groups. The idea was accepted by many Christians that losing one's virginity in some way re-enacts the Fall of Adam and Eve. As noted above, the Church restricted the sexual life of its clerics.[93] Indeed, several passages in the New Testament reveal a less than positive attitude to the sexual impulse and some regard celibacy as a higher ideal than marriage (Matt. 19:10; 1 Cor. 7).[94] Several of the church fathers were celibate. Even Clement, who was married, treated his wife as a sister rather than engage in conjugal relations.[95] Tertullian says prayer and sex are incompatible. Origen and Gregory of Nyssa were celibate. Under the influence of Neo-Platonism, they believed that the body was an evil material trap, given to humanity as punishment, for the soul.

However, the Rabbis, as a whole, do not make this step. The idea is kept under the surface, simmering on low heat, as it were, and not allowed to boil. The control is the strong orientation toward the physical which is necessary for the holy continuation of Israel. Unlike Hellenistic emphases on the spiritual realm as the ideal state, Israel *in the flesh* is holy.

Thus, on the other side of the paradox, sexuality was seen as a force for good because it was necessary for the continuance of holiness in Israel. Judaism is based on genealogy and ethnicity, and sex, therefore, plays an indispensable role in the continuation of the holy people. *Yetser ha-ra* does not necessarily mean "evil inclination," as in some translations, but rather a positive passion which also holds the potential for negative results. As Daniel Boyarin says: "For the Rabbis, the same desire that leads to Torah study, leads one to procreation: both lead to holiness."[96] In Graeco-Roman mythology, by contrast, sexuality, and in particular female sexuality, seems to be the "root of all evil" exemplified by Pandora to whom the gods gave sexual charms in order to be a pitfall to men and punish them for having stolen the celestial fire.[97]

In opposition to Hellenistic norms, the act of marital sex in rabbinic Judaism is regarded positively because it fulfills a holy commandment (see Gen. 1). The following example from the Talmud places sexual intercourse on a level of obligation commensurate with Torah study:

> Yehuda, the son of Rabbi Hiyya, was the son-in-law of Rabbi Yannai. He went and sat in the House of Study. Every Friday at twilight he would come to his wife, and when he would come they would see in front of him a pillar of fire. One day, he became engrossed in his study and did not come. As soon as they did not see the sign [the pillar of fire], Rabbi Yannai said to them, "Turn over his bed, for were Yehuda alive, he would not fail to fulfill

his sexual obligation," and it was "like an error from the mouth of a ruler" [Eccles. 10:5], and Yehuda died.

(b. *Ket.* 61bff.)[98]

The pillar of fire in this story is reminiscent of the holy fire which led Israel in the wilderness. As we have seen in the previous chapter, fire is also a symbol of the word of God. Indeed, the Consuming Fire is the Holy One (see Chapter 1). In this text from the Talmud, both the study of Torah and marital sex are signified by the pillar of fire and thus both are regarded as holy activities. True enough, they are both competing for the young man's attention, but neither is considered in any way negative, both are a means to holiness in Israel. The Rabbi is punished because he does not realize that his obligation "to sleep with his wife is as holy a commandment as the obligation to study Torah."[99]

The married state was regarded as a security for the continued holiness of Israel because it produced the next generation of the holy people. Marital laws are found in the Talmud under the heading of *Qedushah*. Even the ritual whereby engagement is formalized is called *qiddushin*, an Aramaic term meaning, "sanctification, separation." However, marriage is not a sacrament for the Rabbis. *Qiddushin* is the procedure whereby a wife is *mequddeshet*, literally "consecrated, set aside for, or betrothed," not to God, but to her husband (b. *Qid.* 2ab). This must be clearly stated in writing in a Ketubbah, a marriage contract (see Figure 5.1). Marriage is especially guarded in Judaism, nonetheless, because it is the key to the continuance of the holy people. As such it is protected in rabbinic Judaism by numerous restrictions.[100] For example, a married woman who has sexual relations with anyone but her husband (except in the case of rape) becomes prohibited to both husband and lover (b. *Sot.* 27b). A divorcee who has remarried must never remarry her first husband (Deut. 24:4; see also b. *Yeb.* 61a). Jews must not marry a non-Jew or a person of doubtful parentage. No marriages are allowed within ninety days of a different marital status.

Anthropologists claim that marriage rules, more than any other, effectively draw the boundary lines between groups of people and this was never more true than during the Second Temple period.[101] As the result of decimation and exile by the Babylonians and subsequent intermarriage with foreigners, Israel's holy status was being compromised and the nation in danger of annihilation. Jewish officials complain to Ezra: "The people of Israel and the priests and Levites have not separated themselves from the peoples of the land. ... They have taken their daughters as wives for themselves and for their sons, so that the *holy seed* has become intermingled with the people of the land" (Ezra 9:1–2). Only those who had not intermingled and so had maintained their holiness

Figure 5.1 Ketubbah, Jewish marriage contract from Italy, 1746, from the permanent collection of the Judah L. Magnes Museum, museum purchase, Strauss Collection.

Source: Courtesy of the Judah L. Magnes Museum.

were allowed to celebrate the Passover (Ezra 6:21; see also Isa. 52:11). Ezra and Nehemiah close in the ranks with regard to intermarriage and forbid it entirely (Ezra 9–10; Neh. 13:23–27; see also Mal. 2:11; Josh. 23:12; 1 Kings 11:4; Exod. 34:16). Throughout this period and into the rabbinic era sexuality and, in particular, marriage partners were strictly controlled as the Jews tried to preserve the external boundaries of the holy community.[102] As a New Testament example, Paul warns the Corinthians not to marry outside of the holy community and thus compromise their election.

Marriage was also considered a holy obligation because it provided an outlet for sexual fantasies that could otherwise lead to immorality. In order to truly "study Torah in purity" one must be married and thus have a sexual outlet (b. *Yoma* 72b; see also b. *Pes.* 112b and b. *Men.* 110b).[103] The unmarried person cannot study Torah purely or be a prayer leader (b. *Ta'an.* 16a). The following text from the Talmud illustrates this principle well:

> Rav Huna [the Babylonian] said, "Anyone who is twenty years old and not married, all of his days are sinful." Can you really think that he is sinful? Rather I will say, "All of his days are in thoughts of sin." Rava said, and thus also the One of the House of Rabbi Ishmael teaches, "Until the twentieth year, the Holiness, May it be blessed, waits for the man; when will he marry. When he is twenty and unmarried, He says, 'blast his bones!'" Rav. Hisda said, "I am preferable to my fellows, for I married at sixteen and if I had married at fourteen, I could have said to the Satan, An arrow in your eyes!"
>
> (b. *Qid.* 29b)[104]

Here we see the Rabbis typically objecting to celibacy as an unnatural state leading to sin. Failing to produce children is compared to murder: it is "as if he shed blood, diminished the Image of God, and made the Shekhinah depart from Israel" (*Sh. Ar.*, EH 1:1, based on b. *Yeb.* 63b-64a). The bachelor will have to answer for his actions in the world to come (b. *Shab.* 31a). In addition, suppressing natural instincts can lead to illegitimate forms of sexual activity and, at the very least, create impurity resulting from unrequited sexual fantasies. Paul may reflect the same tradition when he insists that it is better to marry than to burn with passion (1 Cor. 7:9, 36). This concern is not limited to men. A father must similarly find a husband for his daughter while she is young (from 12) lest she become unchaste in the waiting and violate the commandment "Profane not your daughter to make her a harlot" (Lev. 19:29; b. *San.* 76a).

This principle of holiness through marriage is a point of contention between some early Christians and Jews. Aphrahat, a Mesopotamian church father, writes to his congregation as follows:

> I have written to you, my beloved, concerning virginity and holiness because I heard about a Jewish man who has reviled one of our brethren, the members of the church. He said to him, "You are impure for you don't take wives. But we are holy and more virtuous for we bear children and multiply seed in the world."[105]

Aphrahat probably quotes the Jewish man correctly that celibacy leads to impurity, because an unmarried man was assumed to engage in sexual fantasies which could produce both ritual impurity as well as immorality.[106]

The result of this paradox, the impurity of sex and the holiness of the holy people, the product of sex, is the restriction and protection of sexual activity. As others have noted, the concept of holy people in rabbinic literature is connected to sexual purity more than to any other concept.[107] More than any other sin, except for outright idolatry, the Rabbis were concerned to keep Jews separated from sexual immorality. They point to sexual immorality as the divider between heathen and Israel, the object of holiness (*Sifra* 93b; *Num. R.* 9:7; see also *Mekh.*, Friedmann, 63a; Horovitz and Rabin, 209). The Rabbis notice that the command to be holy in Leviticus 19:2 comes immediately after a long catalog of forbidden sexual relations in Chapter 18 and they present numerous prooftexts of the antipathy between holiness and illicit sexual activity (*Lev. R.* 24:6).

This is not to say that there was no asceticism among the Rabbis, simply that it was not the norm. When Rabbi Eleazar notes the conjunction of Genesis 9:6 which forbids murder and Genesis 9:7 which reiterates the command to multiply and concludes, "Whoever does not engage in being fruitful and multiplying is like one who sheds blood," Ben Azzai, who was celibate, responds, "What can I do? My soul clings in love to the Torah; let the world be sustained by others" (b. *Yeb.* 63b). Another Rabbi equated innocence with "a virgin who has never tasted sin"

(*Sif. Deut.* Hammer, 332; see also m. *Sot.* 3:4; b. *Shab.* 87a; *Gen. R.* 35:1; b. *Shab.* 118b; *Gen. R.* 35:1). A third Rabbi suggested a man should "hallow himself," that is, abstain from sex, in the marriage bed (b. *Sheb.* 18b; b. *Shab.* 118b). R. Eleazar endorses asceticism as a means to holiness based on an analogy with the Nazirite's similar abstention from wine, but the other Rabbis disagreed with him (b. *Ta'an.* 11a). There was even an early tradition that Moses was celibate, but the Palestinian midrash tries to ameliorate it (*Sif. Num.* on Num. 12).[108] These examples of asceticism are simply not the recommended or expected lifestyle.

For the writers of the New Testament, all the elect, married or not, are holy and are required to keep certain sexual standards. 1 Thessalonians 4:4–8 puts sexual ethics in the context of holiness: "For this is the will of God, your sanctification: that you abstain from immorality; that each one of you know how to take a wife for himself in holiness and honor, not in the passion of lust like heathen who do not know God. . . . For God did not call us to impurity but in holiness." According to Paul sexual mores distinguish believer from non-believer. "Paul urges that the marital relationship, lived as he encourages them to live it, be seen as a matter of their belonging to God ('their sanctification')" (see 1 Thess. 4:3).[109]

The antagonism between flesh and spirit, or war between the forces of impurity and holiness is acknowledged by many early Jewish writers (see Gal. 5:17; CD). As a holy institution, marriage is considered by the writer of 1 Thessalonians to be a gift from God (v. 7) which is continually aided by the Holy Spirit (1 Thess. 3:8; 4:4). In fact, the body is a container ("temple") of the Holy Spirit. Even an unbelieving partner and impure (*akathartos*) children are made holy through the power of the Spirit residing in the body of the holy spouse (vv. 14–16). On the other hand, Paul equates immorality and unholiness in his first letter to the Corinthians. A "Christian" who is immoral is to be shunned (1 Cor. 5:11), and those who insist on "unholiness" must be expelled to avoid the contamination of the rest of the elect (1 Cor. 5:13; 3:17).

For the Rabbis too, God's presence is invited by the holy commandment of marriage: "If husband and wife are worthy, God will dwell with them; otherwise, there will be a devouring fire between them" (b. *Sot.* 17a; *PRE* 12). Because of sexual immorality God promises to destroy the heathen: "'And because of these abominations the Lord thy God is driving them out from before thee' (18:12). . . . When R. Eliezer would come to this verse, he would say: How unfortunate we are! Since he who clings to anything unclean, the spirit of uncleanness rests upon him, he who clings to the Shekhinah, the holy spirit should surely rest upon him. What causes this (not to happen)? 'But your iniquities have separated between you and your God' (Isa. 59:2)." The Rabbis continue: "'that he see no unseemly thing in thee, and turn away from thee' (23:15), this indicates that unchastity drives away the Shekhinah" (*Sif. Deut.* 173, 258). Thus, illicit sexual activity drives away the holy force which represents God's presence, pleasure, and power among his people.

In rabbinic literature, the *yetzer ha-ra*, is sometimes interpreted "the sexual urge" which is both advantageous to humanity and a dangerous, hard-to-control force. Without it, people woud not build a house, marry or beget children (*Gen. R.* 9:7). On the other hand, the *yetzer* is a power that requires God's help to resist: "It is revealed before thee, God, that we have not the power to resist the evil inclination. May it be thy will to remove it from us, so that we may accomplish thy will with a perfect heart."[110]

Sometimes the Rabbis enjoin a higher level of holiness: "Sanctify yourselves even in what is permitted" (b. *Yeb.* 20a). According to one rabbinic source, like the words of Jesus, even an unchaste look is to be regarded as adultery: those who surround themselves with a "fence" against anything unchaste are called holy (*Lev. R.* 23, 26:6; see also Matt. 5:27–28). By proscribing the lewd stare, a "fence" is erected against the greater offense of immoral acts. Holiness as separation is thought of in severe terms, even to creating unprescribed barriers to protect Israel from violating explicit holy commandments.

However, there is more than just a "fence" mentality here. To sanctify oneself in what is permitted was assumed to increase holiness. Some Rabbis, especially mystics, supported abstinence of various kinds to aid in attaining a holy experience (*Hekh. Rab.* 30; see also y. *Kel.* 9:3). The logic here is that observing more than what is explicitly required will add more holiness to one's "account." Take this passage from the *Mekhilta*, for example: "When the Omnipresent enjoins a new precept upon Israel, he endows them with a new holiness" (*Mekh. de-Kaspa* 20). Also by observing the sabbath and wearing tassels, one increases holiness in Israel (*Mekh. de-Shabbata* 1; *Sif. Num.* 115). Thus, each commandment's observance adds more holiness in Israel.[111] Holiness for the Rabbis was a dynamic force, one which some tried to accumulate to the good of Israel beyond the stated requirements. The celibate Jews of Qumran took an extreme, maximalist approach to holiness as seen in the examples given above. Their rules follow Scripture's principles but, in an effort to amass as much holiness as possible, they go above and beyond the prescribed laws of the Torah.

The dominant trend in rabbinic Judaism is that marriage does not detract from but rather contributes to holiness and is not simply a concession to human desire. The Talmud warns against excessive asceticism which would weaken one's energy to serve God and become a burden to the community (y. *Dem.* 7:4; b. *Ta'an.* 11b; 22b). Steven Fraade, who has done a masterful study on asceticism in the various Judaisms of the post-biblical era, says: "The idea that one could sanctify oneself through engaging in permitted sexual intercourse with a correct religious intention is, to my knowledge, unique among the varieties of ancient Judaism."[112]

Indeed, Judeo-Christian sexual ethics were different from traditional Roman customs. For most people in the Roman empire, incest was a supreme horror.[113] But the idea that marriage was a divinely ordained institution which should be monogamous, lasting, and unviolated by fornication was not a Greek or Roman concept. Whereas Jewish Christians regarded all sex outside marriage as illicit, Roman law allowed it if done by the husband without infringing on the conjugal rights of another man.[114] In 18 BCE Augustus passed a law that adultery by a woman and condonation of it by her husband was a crime; extra-marital intercourse with a woman of high status also became a crime.[115] Thus, under Augustus there was an increased effort in the area of morality, but unlike the equality of the Jewish law, only men and high-ranking women were protected. In the fourth century CE, Constantine made several legal decrees in order to bring the Roman law nearer the Christian ideal; these laws reveal long-entrenched attitudes toward sexual relations in the Roman Empire. According to the new legislation divorce became more difficult, adultery brought death, concubines were prohibited, and there were stiff penalties for abduction/rape and for affairs between free women and slaves.[116]

Various Roman statesmen and philosophers urged moral reforms, including Horace, Cicero, Sallust, and Polybius, but they do not do so in the cause of holiness. Rather they appeal on a secular level that a self-controlled person would be a better citizen than a self-indulgent one.[117] For people of "honor" (full citizen rights) adultery was "out of place."[118] Offenders were considered stripped of their honor; immoral conduct could easily reduce one's social status. The esteem of one's peers was very important and violation of appropriate behavior could lead to censorship and disgrace to one's family.

CONCLUSION

The rabbinic concept of holy people is based on the dual notions of divine election and human responsibility. God has selected Israel to represent him, and as his agents they must reflect his holiness. This election is reinforced in concrete ways through initiation and separation rituals, such as circumcision, dietary and purity laws. Israel's selection as the holy people requires not only separation from certain foreign customs and habits, but also requires a commitment to extend ethical goodness in the world. This ethics is in direct imitation of the Holy One; it is an extension of his holiness into the human realm. Human sexuality is considered a matter of holiness as well. Although a potential force for evil, human passion is the very key to the continuance of the holy people.

Holiness is not a state of being but the power generated by the relationship between Israel and God. First of all, because of her bond with God, dependent upon election and obedience as described above, Israel is holy and can deal with God's powerful presence without being destroyed by it.[119] Second, Israel is invited to participate in the divine will and is empowered by the Holy One himself. Holiness encourages God to be "present" within the community and enhances its potentiality for ethical goodness.[120]

Someone said, "Holiness is the additional strength needed by all life."[121] As discussed in Chapter 1, the God who created life is himself the source of holiness. He is the one who energizes Israel to do good and gives quality to their lives. As an active power which generates blessing and life, holiness is opposed by the forces of evil and impurity. Israel, as the holy people, must fight these negative forces by keeping the divine commandments. By observing the ritual obligations of the Torah, Israel protects her holiness from foreign infiltration. Her customs and practices daily inculcate the notion that she is holy, separated from other people and their pagan ways. These rituals symbolize important truths about Israel's relationship with God. On a very practical level, extended social involvement between Jew and gentile leading to intermarriage and assimilation is automatically curtailed. Observing the ethical commands gives quality to Israel's life by the implementation of principles of ethical goodness. Thus, holiness provides security as well as quality to Israel's life.

Among early Christians God's holy presence is often personified by the Holy Spirit, who initiates and empowers the life of holiness (1 Cor. 6:9; 2 Cor. 3:18; 1 Thess. 4:8). This interior transformation is expected to produce a holy person and consequent goodness in the Christian life.[122] While early Christian writers tend to emphasize the energizing gift of God's holiness and the transformation which takes place upon initiation into the Church, the Rabbis tend to concentrate on the responsibility and role of the people in the achievement of holiness. Every Jew is born into the holy people by natural means and thus the emphasis is not on holy transformation but on the responsibility of the already holy people to maintain their sanctification as the elect by daily fulfillment of the divine commands.

In comparison to Graeco-Roman systems, some stark contrasts are immediately apparent. There is, to my knowledge, no account of another people claiming holiness or any sacred quality on the basis of their race and religion. While rituals abound universally, Jewish ritual serves to reinforce the sacred, separated status of the race from other races, and its umbilical connection to the Holy One of Israel. Ethics, too, while it is an important subject of Greek philosophy and Roman law, is drawn into the realm of what it means to be holy in Israel.

To be holy in the Graeco-Roman world is, first of all, to command divine power. Issues related to morality and kindness do not, as a whole, surface in the context of the sacred. The gods do not exhibit these traits and do not require such from their followers. Ritual, on the other hand, was strictly performed by sacred personnel in an effort to placate the gods and to make sure that power was not unleashed into the community in a destructive manner. Sexuality was considered at best a necessary evil. For the Rabbis, by contrast, sexuality plays a critical role in the discussion of what it means to be holy because, while it is recognized as a potential source of impurity and evil, it is also a gift of God which enables the creation of the next generation of holy people in Israel.

CONCLUSION

We began this study with a question, what did it mean to be holy in the first Christian centuries? We examined the rabbinic model because of the central character of holiness in the rabbinic tradition and the detail with which it is presented and explained in the literature. Rabbinic texts reveal a strong, coherent system against which to compare other notions of holiness in antiquity. As we probed the rabbinic understanding of holiness we made reference to the larger Graeco-Roman context and gave particular attention to holiness in early Christianity. Let us summarize our findings.

Holiness begins within the realm of the divine. Here we find a paradox when comparing rabbinic Judaism with its pagan neighbors. On the one hand, the chasm between humanity and the gods, or between the profane and the sacred, is not near as great when considering Graeco-Roman religion as it is between the Holy One and the people of Israel. Pagan gods share troubles that plague humanity as well. They have problems of trust, love and even death, similar to their human subjects. While they are feared for their power, even that is limited, each god presiding over its own domain. Also, human beings are often allowed to approach the gods more directly than in rabbinic Judaism. Power, perfection and separation are all a part of holiness in both Graeco-Roman cults as well as in rabbinic Judaism, but there seems to be a difference in degree. The rabbinic deity is sole in his power, perfect in knowledge and completely independent of the physical world.

His independence notwithstanding, the rabbinic God is, on the other hand, intimately involved in the affairs of humanity and is especially concerned with the holy people. His holiness, by definition, seeks the good of his people. This is, of course, defined by his terms. Holiness can be a destructive fire as well as a beneficial life force. Justice as well as mercy are under his control. Nevertheless, there is a personal quality to his holiness, absent in traditional Graeco-Roman religion, which is concerned about and actively seeks human welfare. While holiness in its purest form, i.e. as a supernatural energy, is utterly separate from human experience, it also, by rabbinic definition, wishes to be present among human beings. Its focus is not power for power's sake but the empowerment and protection of the holy people.

Rabbinic Judaism shares with its Graeco-Roman neighbors a strong concern for the sacred cult. The cult is the way in which ancient people accessed the gods, and so it was in Israel. Even after the Temple's demise, the cult retained a central focus in rabbinic Judaism and the sages fully expected it to be reinstituted in the future. In the area of holy cult many parallels between the Jews and their neighbors are evident, e.g. in the nature of a sacred site, its personnel and rituals. The contribution of the Rabbis lays in their detailed analysis of the cult in which the observer can detect meaning and rationale at every level. From the many laws appertaining to the cult, principles about holiness are easily brought into sharp relief. The unbending nature of these laws enforces the pillars of holiness they are meant to establish in Israel.

For the Rabbis holiness, that completely other, powerful divine force, is revealed in every aspect of the cult. Through the observance of well-defined rituals the abstract force called holiness is channelled through concrete media and is clarified in ways which human beings can apprehend. By the restrictions it imposes, holiness is defined. It requires perfection in its ministers and gifts, both of which must be without blemish and completely devoted to the Holy One. It requires protection lest it unleash its force destructively upon unwitting violators. It is beautiful since it requires adornment of its house both with costly materials and musical enhancement, but most of all with human praise. Holiness has a jealous streak. It will not tolerate other loyalties and its gifts are meant to be irrevocable. Maintenance of the holy cult must be habitual and perpetual. Holiness nevertheless brings honor to those who are most closely involved with it.

So far, many Graeco-Roman cults would more or less agree with the rabbinic understanding of holiness via the cult. The Romans were noted for their perfection in ritual matters. The primary difference so far lies in the pagan ability to tolerate allegiances to many gods at the same time. Another major difference is in the costly nature of the Israelite cult. Many sacrifices were offered to the Holy One from which humans received little or no benefit. This would have been unusual in pagan circles. However, in Israel, the maintenance of holiness is a costly enterprise.

Unlike their pagan neighbors, the rabbinic cultic system intertwines the matter of ethical relationships into its definition of holiness. In order for sacrifices to be accepted by the Holy One, confession, repentance and restitution must first be made. This linkage of ethics and the cult is unusual in the ancient world. In addition, some sacrifices are given a time limit on consumption for the express purpose of forcing the offerer to invite family and friends to share the feast with him. Thus, rabbinic holiness is interested in and legislates fellowship among the holy people. Social bonding is necessary to holiness.

In the rabbinic system of holiness, land plays a central role. In most cultures there is a geographical center, usually a sacred temple or even a grove or mountain, which is considered a meeting place with the gods. In rabbinic Judaism, while the holy temple is the epitome of sanctity, being the house of God, the entire physical Land of Israel contains a degree of holiness. This is because all of it is owned by the Holy One and is the place of his continued revelation to and communication with Israel. He claims its produce and designates it holy as well.

The land is sanctified further by the blood shed for its possession. To be sure, in the context of war, the Roman army would see the sacrifice of human soldiers necessary for the honor of Rome and even regard the war as sanctioned and empowered by the gods. Nevertheless, the produce of the land itself is not regarded as carrying a sacral quality. In Israel, however, agricultural offerings were required, since the holiness of the land had to be respected and acknowledged in a concrete manner by each farmer offering produce to the Holy One via his agents, the priests. These offerings not only honored God but provided priestly salaries and support for the poor. Fellowship among Israel too is mandated by the requirement to attend three annual festivals in Jerusalem. Class lines were blurred as each one stood representing family and clan in the presence of God at his holy house. Each festival had a historical as well as agricultural character, and Jews were required to remember and rehearse God's past goodness on these occasions in their early history.

God's goodness to Israel is part of his holiness but it is directly related to Israel's behavior in the land. Ethical requirements as well as agricultural ones are stricter in the Land. Because of its holy character, the Land is believed to be fruitful and bounteous, however, it is clear that this benefit depends on Israel's fulfillment of the holy commands. The Land connects the Holy One and the holy people on a regular, recurring basis, with each year's habitual agricultural cycle. It reinforces the notion that Israel is holy only because they have been chosen by the Holy One. They live on his land by his grace and by keeping their promise to render him absolute loyalty and obedience.

Agricultural festivals were not new in the ancient world, and the giving of produce to the priests was a matter of custom. However, these events were not tied into a sophisticated system regulating a people's relationship with a particular God who owned their land and legislated every aspect of their lives.

Furthering the point that holiness is a divine force which is transmitted to Israel by various means, the word of God is holy. It meets the definition described above of both powerfully destructive as well as life-giving. By his word the Holy One destroys nations and creates life. As powerfully holy, the divine word must be protected and mediated. The Rabbis emphasize the mediation of the holy word through the sage. The sage is the embodiment of the holy word not only through his astute cognitive ability, but in his lifestyle as well. The process of studying the divine word is guarded by purity restrictions as one would expect from any transmission of holiness.

In the western Roman empire, religious texts were not usually considered sacred. However, among eastern cults, such as those in India and Persia, there is a strong notion of holy word being transmitted through the vehicle of a holy person and transforming the recipient. The Rabbis differ from the eastern model in requiring the engagement of the student with the word in terms of critical reasoning and argument in addition to strict memorization. Nevertheless, holiness is an active force and its acquisition is not static. The student who engages with holy word is often seeking a mystical experience which brings him into contact with the power of the Holy One.

Finally, each and every Jew is considered a member of the holy people, according to the Rabbis. This is by divine election. This election is supplemented by Israel's commitment to keep the laws placed upon her. The goodness inherent in divine holiness is also apparent in Israel's holiness. After all, Israel's holiness is merely an arm or extension of God's holiness. Just as the holiness of God has humanity at the center of its concern, so the empowerment of the holy people is for the same purpose: to extend ethical goodness among human beings. The laws, which are the means to maintaining holiness in Israel, force her to maintain separation from other forms of religion by legislating distinctive rituals which affect such basic areas of life as food and sex. These laws also enforce goodness within the community. That is to say, it is impossible to fulfill the holy commands without extending ethical goodness to one's neighbor. As we have seen in other areas, ethics is imbedded within holiness. This is a distinctive trait of rabbinic Judaism in that morality, i.e. justice and mercy, is a key component of the sacred. Among pagans, the realm of the sacred was feared and placated but it was not a model for ethics nor was it considered the business of holy personnel to dictate the behavior, private or public, of the laity.

Early Christianity forms a bridge between rabbinic Judaism and the pagan world. It shares with both its pagan and Jewish neighbors the notion of holiness as separation, power and perfection. In all of these forms of religion, holiness is an active and powerful force which originates with the gods. The divine force is personified in Christianity as the Holy Spirit, who brings about the transformation of the initiate. Christianity owes to its Jewish parent its strong emphasis on ethical goodness as a component of holiness, its imitation of the divine model for the acquisition of holiness, and its dependence on the divine word as a guide for becoming holy.

APPENDIX

The rabbinic hierarchy of holiness

The charts below illustrate some of the interrelationships within the rabbinic system of holiness and impurity discussed in this book.[1] The categories on the horizontal spectrum range from "Most Holy" to "Impure," with three intermediate stages between them: "Holy," "Pure," and "Purifying." (While a person's purifying period varies depending on the type of impurity, the most common is the one day impurity of the *Tebul Yom*.)

The terms listed along the left margin of the chart represent primary cultural categories affected by holiness and impurity. The categories of "Space" and "Persons" are constructed in light of who is allowed to enter which space. For example, only the High Priest is allowed into the Holy of Holies, and only Jews, who have completed purification, are allowed beyond the court of the Gentiles into the holier courts.

	I **Most Holy** *Qodesh Qodashim*	II **Holy** *Qodesh*	III **Pure** *Tahor*	IV **Purifying** *Tebul Yom**	V **Impure** *Tame´*
Space	Holy of Holies	Holy Place; Ct. of Priests	Temple Courts	Outside Temple Courts	Outside Jerusalem**
Person	High Priest	Priest	Levites; Pure Israel	*Tebul Yom* Purifying person	Impure person

A hierarchy of sanctity in terms of food is evident as well although it does not correspond exactly with the first two categories. Most holy sacrifices are either consumed entirely on the altar or eaten by priests within the Temple compound. Lesser holy sacrifices may be shared with the laity. According to the Rabbis, a Jew should not only observe the dietary laws but should eat all food in a state of purity. Food itself cannot be purified. If it is impure, it is invalid for the table.

Rituals correspond to the type of food eaten. For holier food, more intense rituals apply. Most holy food is either burned entirely as a sacrifice to God or is eaten by the priests. Lesser sacrifices are shared by the priest and the offerer.

	I Most Holy *Qodesh Qodashim*	II Holy *Qodesh*	III Pure *Tahor*	IV Purifying *Tebul Yom**	V Impure *Tame´*
Food	Most Holy Sacrifices	Lesser Holy Sacrifices (eaten in Jerusalem)	Pure Food	–	Impure Food. Forbidden Meats
Ritual	Totally burnt on altar or eaten by priests	Priest share with laity	Israel eats in purity	Immersion; wait for sunset	Impure food and forbidden meats are disallowed

Finally, time can be considered in terms of holiness as well. Although some Rabbis insist that the Sabbath is the holiest day in Israel, the rituals of the Day of Atonement place it into a holier category. Not only is work forbidden, but many additional restrictions are in effect which do not apply on the Sabbath (see Chapter 2). Festivals too are designated holy times (see Chapter 3). While sacred time is a fact of Jewish culture, the popular Graeco-Roman notion of impure days has no parallel within the rabbinic tradition.

	I Most Holy *Qodesh Qodashim*	II Holy *Qodesh*	III Pure *Tahor*	IV Purifying *Tebul Yom**	V Impure *Tame´*
Time	Day of Atonement	Sabbath/ festivals	Common days	Purifying day	(No impure days in Israel)

*Other common purifying periods include that of the corpse-contaminated person and that of the menstruant. While the rituals vary in these cases, the length of the purification period for both is one week.

**Only major impurity bearers, such as the corpse and the leper, are excluded from Jerusalem.

NOTES

INTRODUCTION

1 Tr. John W. Harvey (Oxford: Oxford University Press, 1928).
2 Baruch Levine, "The Language of Holiness: Perceptions of the Sacred in the Hebrew Bible" in *Backgrounds for the Bible*, ed. Michael P. O'Connor and David N. Freedman (Winona Lake, IN: Eisenbrauns, 1987); Philip Peter Jenson, *Graded Holiness: A Key to the Priestly Conception of the World* (Sheffield: Sheffield Academic Press, 1992); John G. Gammie, *Holiness in Israel* (Minneapolis, MN: Fortress Press, 1989).
3 See, for example, the work of Bruce J. Malina, *The New Testament World: Insights from Cultural Anthropology* (Atlanta: John Knox Press, 1981).
4 Jacob Neusner, *Sifra: An Analytical Translation* (Atlanta: Scholars Press, 1988), 46.
5 Jacob Neusner, *Purity in Rabbinic Judaism* (Atlanta: Scholars Press, 1994), 57.
6 Neusner, *Purity in Rabbinic Judaism*, 58.
7 Reuven Hammer, *The Classic Midrash: Tannaitic Commentaries on the Bible* (New York: Paulist Press, 1995), 14.
8 For more information on these dates and sources, see George Foot Moore, *Judaism in the First Centuries of the Christian Era*, (New York: Schocken Books, 1971) 135–76, and relevant articles in *Encyclopedia Judaica* (Jerusalem: Keter, 1971).

1 THE HOLY ONE

1 Gerardus van der Leeuw, *Religion in Essence and Manifestation: A Study in Phenomenology* (New York: Harper & Row, 1963), 23.
2 Robert Parker, *Miasma* (Oxford: Clarendon Press, 1983), 151.
3 See Gottlob Schrenk, *"Hieros," Theological Dictionary of the New Testament*, III (Grand Rapids, MI: Eerdmans, 1965), 222.
4 Parker, *Miasma*, 149, also mentions a third term, *hosios. Hosios* refers to restoration to religious normality, the sense of clearing oneself; it does not refer to the gods. This term is also more prevalent in later, *koine* Greek and rare in classical texts, Erich Gruen, University of California Berkeley, oral communication.
5 Likewise, the Qumran Community, which preserved the Dead Sea Scrolls, sometimes used *Qodesh, ha-Qodesh*, or *Qodesh Qodashim*, as synonyms for God,

Jacobus Naude, "Holiness in the Dead Sea Scrolls" in *The Dead Sea Scrolls after Fifty Years*, ed. P. W. Flint and J. VanderKam, II (Leiden: E. J. Brill, 1999), 184. See also Ephraim E. Urbach, *The Sages: Their Concepts and Beliefs*, I (Jerusalem: Magnes Press, 1979), 78, who gives further notes regarding *Qodesh* as a title for God, 77.

6 James Muilenburg, "Holiness" in *Interpreter's Dictionary of the Bible*, II (New York: Abingdon Press, 1962), 617.

7 This intimate connection between holiness and divinity is already biblical. Proverbs uses the word as a synonym for God himself: "The beginning of wisdom is reverence to the Lord; and insight is constituted of knowledge of the Holy (One)." Amos refers to God and holiness synonymously: "The Lord, God has sworn by his holiness" (4:2; cf. 6:8). The book of Isaiah is the most obvious source for the rabbinic title, "The Holy One, Blessed Be He," since the writer refers to God repeatedly as the "Holy One" (40:25; 43:15; 49:7) or "Holy One of Israel" (10:20; 41:14, 20; 43:3, 14; 45:11; 47:4; 48:17; 49:7; 54:5). Ben Sirach too refers to God often as "the Holy One" (Sir. 4:14, 23:9; 43:10; 48:20).

8 John Gammie, *Holiness in Israel* (Minneapolis, MN: Fortress Press, 1989), 195.

9 See Samuel S. Cohon, *Essays in Jewish Theology* (Cincinnati: Hebrew Union College Press, 1987), 141, for a similar explanation.

10 The Rabbis note twelve instances in Scripture where God appeared among Israel as fire, six times beneficially (Lev. 9:24; Judg. 6:24; 13:20; 1 Chron. 21:26; 2 Chron. 7:2; 1 Kings 18:38) and six times destructively (Lev. 10:1; Num. 11:1; 16:35; Job 1:16; 2 Kings 1:10, 12) (*Sif. Zuta* on Num. 11:1).

11 Muilenburg, "Holiness," 617.

12 Other forms of the word, *qadosh*, illustrate the separation principle as well. The *pi'el* form indicates action which imposes separation on something or someone else. The *hiph'il* form refers to setting an item apart for God as a gift. The *hithpa'el* form refers to setting oneself apart or purifying oneself from impurity (2 Sam. 11:4). The *niph'al* of *qadosh* refers to God only.

13 Jacob Milgrom, *Leviticus1–16*, The Anchor Bible 3A (Garden City, NY: Doubleday, 1991), 617.

14 John Armstrong, *The Idea of Holiness and the Humane Response* (London: George Allen & Unwin, 1981), 6.

15 John Ferguson, *The Religions of the Roman Empire* (Ithaca, NY: Cornell University Press, 1970), 65–66.

16 Abraham Joshua Heschel, "By denying the pantheistic view of the Deity as essentially immanent and in no way transcendent, it excludes the deification of nature as a whole or of any of her parts which is the outstanding characteristic of paganism and of modern romantic nature worship and cosmic piety," in *Between God and Man: An Interpretation of Judaism from the Writings of Abraham J. Heschel*, ed. Fritz Rothschild (New York: Free Press, 1965), 17.

17 Cohon, *Essays in Jewish Theology* 145.

18 Hero-worship had been common among the Greeks. In legend the hero had a divine father and mortal mother. He was not sacrificed to as a god but the offering was poured down to the ground linking him to the ancestral dead, Ferguson, *Religions*, 88.

19 Ferguson, *Religions*, 96.

20 Urbach, *The Sages*, I, 70–71.

21 Baruch Levine, "The Language of Holiness: Perceptions of the Sacred in the

Hebrew Bible," in *Backgrounds for the Bible*, ed. Michael P. O'Connor and David N. Freedman (Winona Lake, IN: Eisenbrauns, 1987), 241–55.

22 Schrenk, *"Hieios,"* 226. New Testament writers remain faithful to the Septuagint and continue to prefer *hagios* over other Greek terms for holiness. Muilenburg attributes this to a lack of ethics and personality in the Greek terms for holiness, "Holiness," 623.

23 See Solomon Schechter, *Aspects of Rabbinic Theology* (New York: Schocken Books, 1961), 205.

24 Gerhard von Rad, *Theologie des Alten Testaments*, I (Munchen: Kaiser Verlag, 1957), 203–211, 272; trans. D. M. G. Stalker, *Old Testament Theology*, I (Edinburgh–London: Harper, 1962), 203–211, 272.

25 Max Kadushin, *A Conceptual Approach to the Mekhilta* (New York: Jewish Theological Seminary of America, 1969), 43.

26 *"Kedushah"* in *Encyclopedia Judaica*, VIII (Jerusalem: Keter, 1971), 872.

27 Schechter, *Aspects*, 95; Kadushin, *A Conceptual Approach*, 141.

28 Abraham Cohen, *Everyman's Talmud* (New York: Schocken Books, 1975), 23.

29 Mary Douglas, "The Abominations of Leviticus" in *Anthropological Approaches to the Old Testament*, ed. B. Lang (Philadelphia, PA: Fortress Press, 1985), 112.

30 Milgrom, *Leviticus 1–16*, 703.

31 Douglas, "The Nominations," 113. Working in a more philosophical vein, Quentin Smith comes to a similar conclusion to Douglas. Smith says holiness epitomizes perfection in key categories of life: the supreme personality; the supreme morality, the item supremely cherished, and the supreme existent, "An Analysis of Holiness," *Rel. Stud.* 24 (1988), 511–528.

32 Cohon, *Essays in Jewish Theology*, 103.

33 George Foot Moore, *Judaism in the First Centuries of the Christian Era*, I (New York: Schocken Books, 1971), 361, 416.

34 See especially the Septuagint's reading, "This people's heart has become calloused; they hardly hear with their ears and they have closed their eyes" (Isa. 6:10).

35 Armstrong, *The Idea of Holiness*, 6–7.

36 Marcus Jastrow, *A Dictionary of the Targumim, the Talmud Babli and Yerushalmi, and the Midrashic Literature* (New York: The Judaica Press, Inc., 1982), 1314.

37 See Urbach, *The Sages*, I, 40.

38 Cited in Gammie, *Holiness in Israel*, 249.

39 Heschel, *Between God and Man*, 26: The difference between the biblical and Greek concepts of God arise from the Greek understanding of reality as an ordered cosmos while the Bible sees the world as the creation of a divine subject as an event which provided the ground of all reality.

40 Milgrom, *Leviticus 1–16*, 730.

41 Urbach, *The Sages,* I, 67.

42 Urbach's translation from Greek into Hebrew, *The Sages,* I, 86.

43 Urbach, *The Sages,* I, 82–83.

44 Ferguson, *The Religions*, 68.

45 John North, "The Development of Religious Pluralism," in *The Jews Among Pagans and Christians*, ed. Judith Lieu, John North and Tessa Rajak (London: Routledge, 1992), 187.

46 The notion that the name of a god is powerful because it represents the god's nature and identity is a widespread belief in the ancient world. Knowledge of the name of a person/god gives one power over them and forces them to help, G. Foucart, "Names, Egyptian," in *Hastings, Encyclopedia of Religion and Ethics*,

IX, 151; A. H. Gardiner, "Magic, Egyptian," *ibid.*, VIII, 265b; Urbach, *The Sages,* I, 149.

47 There was a growing sense of the transcendence of God in later biblical writings which is seen by the avoidance of the Tetragrammaton. The Septuagint renders it *Kurios* (Gk.)=*Adonai* (Heb.), i.e., "the Lord," Urbach, *The Sages,* I, 148.

48 Cohen, *Everyman's Talmud*, 25.

49 Moore, *Judaism*, I, 426; Urbach, *The Sages,* I, 126. For rabbinic opposition to the theurgic use of the Name, see. m. *Ab.* 1:13, *ARN*, 1, ed. Schechter, 56; b. San. 10:1; b. *AZ* 17b. Nevertheless the practice was widespread among Jews. The four who entered Paradise used the Name to ascend into the divine mysteries, although the consequences were disastrous (b. *Hag.* 12a). The Name can dispel demons (*Midr. Teh.* 36:8; *Tanh.*, ed. Buber, *Va'era'* 5).

50 Schechter, *Aspects*, 95.

51 Cohen, *Everyman's Talmud*, 26.

52 Moore, *Judaism*, I, 379.

53 Milgrom, *Leviticus 1–16*, 730. Likewise, Muilenburg describes holiness as "less a condition or state of being. . .more as an expression of his [God's] will and purpose," "Holiness," 621.

54 Trans. by Jacob Neusner, *Judaism and Scripture* (Chicago: University of Chicago Press, 1986), 433.

55 Cohon, *Essays in Jewish Theology*, 109.

56 Cohon, *Essays in Jewish Theology*, 172.

57 Heschel, *Between God and Man*, 24–25.

58 Cited by J. Abelson, *The Immanence of God in Rabbinical Literature* (New York: Hermon Press, 1969 [first edition, London 1912]), 62.

59 Ferguson, *The Religions*, 193; John H. W. G. Liebeschuetz, *Continuity and Change in Roman Religion* (Oxford: Clarendon Press, 1979), 113–115. Seneca is contradictory in holding to a benign Father God and also to the impersonal divine Reason who has "fixed" the universe (even in the same essay). It appears that Seneca is "not serious when he speaks of the personal god." Liebeschuetz, 117, notes that the emotional aspect can only come in if the God is conceived of personally.

60 Liebeschuetz, *Continuity and Change*, 306–7.

61 Ferguson, *The Religions*, 190f.

62 Urbach, *The Sages,* I, 77–78.

63 Samuel Terrien, *The Elusive Presence: Toward a New Biblical Theology* (New York: Harper & Row, 1978), 145.

64 Edmund Jacob defines glory as "holiness uncovered," *Theology of the Old Testament*, trans. Arthur W. Heathcote and Philip J. Allcock (London: Hodder & Stoughton, 1958), 79–80.

65 Gammie, *Holiness in Israel*, 197.

66 Terrien, *The Elusive Presence*, 1, 119, 194.

67 Trans. by Reuven Hammer, *Sifre: A Tannaitic Commentary on the Book of Deuteronomy*, Yale Judaica Series xxiv (New Haven, CT: Yale University Press, 1986), 376.

68 Urbach, *The Sages,* I, 41–48; Schechter, *Aspects*, 35.

69 In the early Christian centuries, the *Shekhinah* was not considered a separate mystical being, but simply a way of speaking about the divine presence itself, Urbach, *The Sages,* I, 44.

70 Cohen, *Everyman's Talmud*, 45.

71 Abelson, *The Immanence of God*, 82–103.

72 Arthur Marmorstein, *Studies in Jewish Theology* (Oxford: Oxford University Press, 1950), 131.

73 See discussion in Abelson, *The Immanence of God*, 184–285.

74 Abelson, *The Immanence of God*, 379.

75 Abelson, *The Immanence of God*, 230.

76 Gammie, *Holiness in Israel*, 4; cf. Terence E. Fretheim, *The Suffering of God: An Old Testament Perspective*, Overtures to Biblical Theology (Philadephia, PA: Fortress Press, 1984). The holiness of the "Name" in Ezekiel includes both divine immanence and vulnerability as well as divine transcendence.

77 "Word" or "Arm" of God are other examples of indirect speech which personalize God, but are really synonyms for him. Other phrases, such as, "Sanctification of the Name" and "Desecration of the Name" refer to God's reputation in human society, again, his encounter with humanity. A good discussion is found in Jacob Licht, "*Qodesh, Qadosh,Qedushah*," in *Entsiqlopedya Mikra'it*, 44–62, VII, ed. E. Sukenik and Moshe D. Cassuto (Jerusalem: Bialik Institute, 1965), 54.

78 See quotations in Abelson, *The Immanence of God*, 290.

79 Heschel, *Between God and Man*, 24, 51.

80 Trans. by Neusner, *Judaism and Scripture*, 429–30.

81 See John N. Oswalt, *The Book of Isaiah: Chapters 1–39*, The New International Commentary on the Old Testament, ed. R. K. Harrison (Grand Rapids, MI: Eerdmans, 1986), 162.

82 Moore, *Judaism*, I, 388.

83 Solomon Schechter, *Studies in Judaism*, second series (Philadelphia, PA: Jewish Publication Society of America, 1980), 151. Indeed the identification of holiness with beauty is already made in Scripture. The Psalmist, more than once, exhorts Israel to worship God in the "beauty of holiness" (Ps. 29:2; 96:9; seealso 1 Chron. 16:29; see Chapter 2).

84 From *Cant. R.*, see Cohon, *Essays in Jewish Theology*, 194.

85 See Urbach, *The Sages*, II, 842, note 54, for other references.

86 Levine, "The Language of Holiness," 252.

87 Milgrom, *Leviticus 1–16*, 731–33.

88 Milgrom, *Leviticus 1–16*, 731–32; 1002–1003.

89 Milgrom, *Leviticus 17–27*, The Anchor Bible 3B (Garden City, NY: Doubleday Press, forthcoming).

90 Nevertheless, many pagans did not believe that the gods and the idols were one and the same. The power of the god was often considered latent in the idol and could be activated by magical rituals.

91 Hannah Harrington, *The Impurity Systems of the Rabbis and Qumran* (Atlanta, GA: Scholars Press, 1993).

92 Milgrom, *Leviticus 1–16*, 637, 686.

93 D. Davies, cited in Philip J. Budd, "Holiness and Cult," in *The World of Ancient Israel: Sociological, Anthropological and Political Perspectives*, ed. R. E. Clements (Cambridge: Cambridge University Press, 1989), 291–92. Jacob Neusner makes the same claim for rabbinic Judaism, *Purity in Rabbinic Judaism* (Atlanta, GA: Scholars Press, 1994), 34.

94 "Holy Spirit" in *Dictionary of Judaism*, ed. Jacob Neusner (New York: Macmillan, 1996), 298–99.

95 Budd, "Holiness and Cult," 281; Terrien, *The Elusive Presence*, 325.

96 Cohen, *Everyman's Talmud*, 352. The belief in the resurrection of the dead is

repeated in the daily service in one of the eighteen Benedictions, "Blessed are You, O Lord, who revives the dead."

97 "God," in *Encyclopedia Judaica*, VII (Jerusalem: Keter, 1971), 652.

2   THE HOLY HOUSE

1 According to *Mekhilta de-Rabbi Ishmael*, God established the Temple during the week of creation and later showed its plans and procedures to Abraham (Jethro, par. 9, Horowitz, 236). See also Jon D. Levenson, *Sinai and Zion: An Entry into the Jewish Bible*, New Voices in Biblical Studies, ed. Adela Yarbro Collins and John J. Collins (Minneapolis: Winston Press, 1985), 98–99.

2 Philip Peter Jenson, *Graded Holiness: A Key to the Priestly Conception of the World* (Sheffield: Sheffield Academic Press, 1992), 112–113; see also Max Kadushin, *The Rabbinic Mind* (New York: Jewish Theological Seminary of America, 1952), the pilgrims who went up to the Temple in Jerusalem went up to see God, 239ff.

3 Baruch Levine, cited in Jacob Neusner, *A History of the Mishnaic Law of Holy Things*, VI (Leiden: E. J. Brill, 1978–80), 24.

4 See also Robertson Smith cited in P. J. Budd, "Holiness and Cult," in *The World of Ancient Israel*, ed. R. Clements (Cambridge: Cambridge University Press, 1989), 275.

5 Jacob Milgrom, *Leviticus 1–16*, Anchor Bible 3A (Garden City, NY: Doubleday, 1991), 322.

6 Jacob Licht, "Qodesh, Qadosh, Qedushah," in *Entsiqlopedya Mikra'it*, VII, ed. E. Sukenik and Moshe D. Cassuto (Jerusalem: Bialik Institute, 1965), 44–62.

7 See also Jenson, *Graded Holiness*, 17; Menahem Haran, *Temples and Temple Service in Ancient Israel*, (Oxford: Clarendon Press, 1978); Edmund Leach, *Culture and Communication: the Logic by Which Symbols Are Connected* (Cambridge: Cambridge University Press, 1983), 81–93.

8 Susan Guettel Cole, "Greek Cults," in *Civilization of the Ancient Mediterranean*, ed. Michael Grant and Rachel Kitzmyer, II (New York: Charles Scribner & Sons, 1988), 887ff.

9 Susan Guettel Cole, "Temples and Sanctuaries," in *Anchor Bible Dictionary* (New York: Doubleday, 1992), 381.

10 Meir Ben-Dov, *In the Shadow of the Temple: the Discovery of Ancient Jerusalem*, trans. Ina Friedman (New York: Harper & Row, 1985), cited by Carol Meyers, "The Jerusalem Temple," in *Anchor Bible Dictionary*, IV, 365. Jewish tradition, following Ezek. 42:20, refers to the Temple Mount as 500 square cubits (m. *Mid.* 2:1).

11 Meyers, "The Jerusalem Temple," 365.

12 Erich Gruen, Prof. of Roman History, University of California, Berkeley, private communication, 1997.

13 Milgrom, *Leviticus 1–16*, 460.

14 Baruch Levine, "The Language of Holiness: Perceptions of the Sacred in the Hebrew Bible," in *Backgrounds for the Bible*, ed. Michael P. O'Connor and David N. Freedman (Winona Lake, IN: Eisenbrauns, 1987), 244–245.

15 A. Mazar, "The Aqueducts of Jerusalem," in *Jerusalem Revealed: Archaeology in the Holy City 1968–1974*, ed. Yigael Yadin (Jerusalem: Israel Exploration Society, 1975), 79–84.

16 Michael H. Jameson, "Sacrifice and Ritual: Greece," in *Civilization of the Ancient Mediterranean*, II, 962.

17 *"Sacrificium,"* in *Harper's Dictionary of Classical Literature and Antiquities,* ed. Harry T. Peck (New York: Cooper Square Publishers, 1962), 1395–1397.

18 Cole, "Greek Cults," 888.

19 Cole, "Temples and Sanctuaries," 381.

20 Meyers, "The Jerusalem Temple."

21 Gottlob Schrenk, *"Hieros,"* in *Theological Dictionary of the New Testament* (Grand Rapids, MI: Eerdmans, 1965), 243.

22 *The Code of Maimonides,* Book VIII, "The Book of Temple Service" (New Haven: Yale University Press, 1957); cf. b. Ber. 616.

23 Schrenk, *"Hieros,"* 247; "Holiness (NT)," *Anchor Bible Dictionary,* III, 253.

24 Robert Parker, *Miasma: Pollution and Purification in Early Greek Religion* (Oxford: Clarendon Press, 1983), 176; Robert Garland, "Priests and Power in Classical Athens," in *Pagan Priests: Religion and Power in the Ancient World,* ed. Mary Beard and John North (Ithaca, NY: Cornell University Press, 1990), 77. *Mantis,* another term used by Homer, is almost synonymous with *hiereus,* Schrenk, *"Hieros,"* 257.

25 Judy Ann Turner, "Greek Priesthoods," in *Civilization of the Ancient Mediterranean,* II, ed. Michael Grant and Rachel Kitzmyer (New York: Charles Scribner's Sons, 1988), 930.

26 Beard and North, *Pagan Priests,* 11.

27 Garland, "Priests and Power," 81.

28 Richard Gordon, "From Republic to Principate: Priesthood, Religion and Ideology," in *Pagan Priets: Religion and Power in the Ancient World,* 180, 196.

29 Beard and North, *Pagan Priests,* 7.

30 Judy Ann Turner, "Greek Priesthoods," 927f.

31 Judy Ann Turner, "Greek Priesthoods," 928.

32 Solomon Zeitlin, *Studies in the Early History of Judaism* (New York: Ktav, 1973), 213.

33 See also Joachim Jeremias, *Jerusalem z. Zeit Jesu,* II, B, 1 (Gottlingen: Vandenhoeck & Ruprecht, 1962), 11. The rules are even stricter according to Philo and the Qumran community which allow the high priest to marry only a woman of the priestly line (Philo, Fug. 114; 4QMMT B).

34 John Ferguson, "Roman Cults," in *Civilization of the Ancient Mediterranean,* II, 911.

35 Ferguson, "Roman Cults," 911.

36 Mary Beard, "Roman Priesthoods," in *Civilization of the Ancient Mediterranean,* II, 936.

37 Milgrom, *Leviticus 1–16,* 553ff.

38 See also Jenson, *Graded Holiness,* 123.

39 The breastplate formed a pouch which was, in first Temple times, a receptacle for the Urim and Thummim, the oracular means by which the high priest communicated with God. The latter items were discontinued in Second Temple times.

40 Milgrom, *Leviticus 1–16,* 53.

41 Milgrom, *Leviticus 1–16,* 600f.

42 But See also Num. 28:19; *The Code of Maimonides,* tr. Jacob J. Rabinowitz, Yale Judaica Series, Book VIII, "Things Prohibited" (New Haven, CT: Yale University Press), 2:10, that even invisible defects can disqualify a priest.

43 Schrenk, *"Hieron,"* in *TDNT,* III, 70. According to the Gospels, Jesus comes into conflict with a cadre of chief priests, perhaps reflecting the ranks listed by the Talmud.

44 Milgrom, *Leviticus 1–16*, 613.

45 *"Sacerdos," Harper's Dictionary of Classical Literature and Antiquities*, ed. Harry T. Peck (New York: Cooper Square Publishers, 1962), 1394.

46 Judy Ann Turner, "Great Priesthoods," 929–30.

47 Richard Gordon, "The Veil of Power: Emperors, Sacrifices and Benefactors," in *Pagan Priests*,222f.

48 John North, "Diviners and Divination at Rome," in *Pagan Priests*, 65.

49 Gordon, "From Republic to Principate," 194; Gordon, "Veil of Power," 224; North, "Diviners and Divination at Rome," 71.

50 *Maimonides*, Book VIII, "Vessels and Ministers" 4:2.

51 See also Schrenk, *"Hieros,"* 263 and citations there.

52 Jenson, *Graded Holiness*, 128, slightly modified.

53 Milgrom, "Greek Priesthoods," *Leviticus 1–16*, 639.

54 Judy AnnTurner, 928f.

55 Deborah F. Sawyer, *Women and Religion in the First Christian Centuries* (London: Routledge, 1996), 127.

56 Sawyer, *Women and Religion*, 129.

57 Garland, Priests and Power," 181.

58 North, "Diviners and Divination at Rome," 55.

59 Parker, *Miasma*, 176.

60 Ferguson, "Roman Cults," 909.

61 E. E. Evans-Pritchard, *Nuer Religion* (Oxford: Clarendon Press, 1956); Claude Levi-Strauss, *The Savage Mind* (Chicago: University of Chicago Press, 1966), 223–238; for a study of biblical sacrifices from a structural perspective, see D. Davies, "An Interpretation of Sacrifice in Leviticus," *ZAW* 89 (1977), 387–398.

62 Michael H. Jameson, "Sacrifice and Ritual: Greece,' in *Civilization of the Ancient Mediterranean*, II, ed. M. Grant and R. Kitzmyer (New York: Charles Scribner's Sons, 1988), 960.

63 Quote in Jameson, "Sacrifice and Ritual," 976–7.

64 Jameson, "Sacrifice and Ritual," 962.

65 Milgrom, *Leviticus 1–16*, 161f.

66 Milgrom, *Leviticus 1–16*, 205, explains that the suet, *heleb*, refers to layers of fat beneath the animal's skin and around its organs which can be easily peeled off.

67 Milgrom, *Leviticus 1–16*, 478.

68 Walter Burkert, *Creation of the Sacred: Tracks of Biology in Early Religions* (Cambridge, MA: Harvard University Press, 1996), 129, 144f.

69 John Burkert, *Creation of the Sacred*, 135–36.

70 John Ferguson, *The Religions of the Roman Empire* (Ithaca, NY: Cornell University Press, 1970), 156.

71 Edmund Leach, *Culture and Communication: The Logic by which Symbols are Connected* (New York: Cambridge University Press, 1976), 81–93.

72 Jameson, "Sacrifice and Ritual," 964.

73 Neusner, *A History of the Mishnaic Law*, VI, 26f.

74 See also J. Barr, "Sacrifice and Offering," in *Dictionary of the Bible*, ed. J. Hastings, rev. edn. F. C. Grant and H. H. Rowley (New York: Scribners, 1963), 871.

75 Milgrom, *Leviticus 1–16*, 152.

76 Jameson, "Sacrifice and Ritual," 963.

77 Jameson, "Sacrifice and Ritual," 974.

78 Jameson, "Sacrifice and Ritual," 962.

79 Trans. by Jacob Milgrom, *Leviticus 1–16*, 270f.

80 Milgrom, *Leviticus 1–16*, 277, regards the Red Cow rite as a "vestige of a pre-Israelite rite of exorcism" which has taken on new meaning in the Israelite cult and its magical character eradicated.

81 Gordon, "Religion," 248.

82 Gordon, "Religion," 252

83 Much debate has centered on the correct translation of *hatta't* as "sin offering" or "purification offering." On the one hand, some *hatta't* offerings are not brought for sin (Lev. 12; Num. 6; Exod. 20:36–37), but in order to purify the sanctuary. Nevertheless, it seems that the majority of sin offerings are related to guilt (se also Lev. 4:27–29; Num. 15:22–31). The Rabbis definitely associated the offering with sin, see R. Eliezer, "The *hatta't* is brought on account of sin" (m. *Zeb.* 1:1; b. *Ker.* 26a).

84 If one was too poor to afford the necessary goat, a cheaper substitute could be offered (Lev. 5:8, 11).

85 H. Hubert and M. Mauss, *Sacrifice: Its Nature and Function* (Chicago: University of Chicago Press, 1964), 98.

86 Milgrom, *Leviticus 1–16*, 638.

87 Milgrom, *Leviticus 1–16*, 351.

88 Milgrom, *Leviticus 1–16*, 320, 322.

89 Parker, *Miasma*, 186–87.

90 Parker, *Miasma*, 146.

91 Burkert, *Creation of the Sacred*, 149.

92 Burkert, *Creation of the Sacred*, 149; Parker, *Miasma*, 151, 165.

93 Milgrom, *Leviticus 1–16*, 172, 484.

94 Jameson, "Sacrifice and Ritual," 968.

95 Burkert, *Creation of the Sacred*, 148–51.

96 See Frances M. Young, *The Use of Sacrificial Ideas in Greek Christian Writers from the New Testament to John Chrysostom*, Patristic Monograph Series 5 (Cambridge, MA: Philadelphia Patristic Foundation, Ltd., 1979), 223–233.

97 Milgrom, *Leviticus 1–16*, 196.

98 To accompany a lamb offering, about 2.2 liters of fine flour was mixed with 0.9 liters of pure oil and 0.9 liters of wine, Emil Schurer, *The History of the Jewish People in the Age of Jesus Christ*, II, (Edinburgh: T&T Clark, 1979), 300.

99 Jameson, "Sacrifice and Ritual," 965.

100 Quoted in P. J. Budd, "Holiness and Cult," in *The World of Ancient Israel: Sociological, Anthropological and Political Perspectives*, ed. R. E. Clements (Cambridge: Cambridge University Press, 1989), 293.

101 Milgrom, *Leviticus 1–16*, 220.

102 Milgrom, *Leviticus 1–16*, 619f.

103 J. Harrison, *Prolegomena to the Study of Greek Religion* (Cleveland: World; reprint of 3rd ed., Cambridge: Cambridge University Press, 1922), 56; see also *Ody* 24.215.

104 Jameson, "Sacrifice and Ritual," 968.

105 Jameson, "Sacrifice and Ritual," 966–972.

106 Hans-Josef Klauck, "Thusia," in *Theological Dictionary of the New Testament*, III, 891.

107 Robert L. Wilken, *The Land Called Holy: Palestine in Christian History and Thought* (New Haven, CT: Yale University Press, 1992), 199f.

108 Mary Douglas, *In the Wilderness: The Doctrine of Defilement in the Book of Numbers*. (Sheffield: Sheffield Academic Press, 1993), 32; see also Baruch Levine, *In the Presence of the Lord*, (Leiden: Brill, 1974), 77–91.

3   THE HOLY LAND

1 Mircea Eliade, *The Sacred and the Profane: the Nature of Religion*, trans. Willard Trask (New York: Harcourt, Brace & World, 1959), 20, cited in W. D. Davies, *The Gospel and the Land: Early Christianity and Jewish Territorial Doctrine* (Berkeley: University of California Press, 1974), 6. See also Claude Levi-Strauss, *The Savage Mind*, (Chicago: University of Chicago Press, 1966); Emile Durkheim, *The Elementary Forms of the Religious Life* (London: G. Allen & Unwin, 1915); Bronislaw Malinowski, *Magic, Science, and Religion, and Other Essays* (Boston: Beacon Press, 1948), 92–93.

2 "Structures and Changes in the History of Religion" in *City Invincible*, C.H. Kraeling and R. M. Adams, eds. (Chicago: University of Chicago Press, 1960), 366.

3 The concept is already biblical: Ezek. 38:12, Israel "dwells at the centre of the earth" and Ezek. 5:5, Israel is in the center of the nations; see also Jub. 8:19, Mt. Zion is "the centre of the navel of the earth."

4 Joel P. Brereton, "Sacred Space," in *The Encyclopedia of Religion*, ed. Mircea Eliade (New York: Macmillan, 1987), 533.

5 Brereton also describes the Brahmans of South India in the town of Srirangam who live on the "two innermost ring roads closest to the temple" while lower castes live further out. The area of Katmandu in South Asia too reveals concentric circles around the innermost area which is the most holy, the temple to Taleju. A similar situation can be found in Buddhism ("Sacred Space," 531–34).

6 Parke and Wormell, *The Delphic Oracle*, I, 1956, cited in Davies, *Gospel*, 10, note 12.

7 Davies, *Gospel*, 10, note 12. For discussion on the relationship between this myth and the rabbinic foundation stone tradition, see Samuel Terrien, "The Omphalos Myth and Hebrew Religion," *VT*, XX (1970), 315–38.

8 Jonathan Z. Smith, *Map is Not Territory: Studies in the History of Religions* (Leiden: E. J. Brill, 1978), 94.

9 Brereton, "Sacred Space," 526

10 Smith, *Map is Not Territory*, 110.

11 Walter Brueggemann, *The Land: Place as Gift, Promise, and Challenge in Biblical Faith* (Philadelphia: Fortress Press, 1977), 167, land possession is "on the one hand in grasping with courage and on the other hand waiting in confidence for the gift."

12 Robert L. Wilken, *The Land Called Holy: Palestine in Christian History and Thought* (New Haven, CT: Yale University Press, 1992), 8.

13 Wilken, *The Land Called Holy*, 27.

14 Ernst H. Kantorowicz, "Pro Patria Mori," in *Selected Studies* (Locust Valley, NY: J. J. Augustin Publisher, 1965), 310.

15 Conor Cruise O'Brien, *God Land: Reflections on Religion and Nationalism* (Cambridge, MA: Harvard University Press, 1988), 13. The ancient *patria* was not necessarily the full Roman Empire. It could refer to a single city, province or village.

16 See discussion in Wilken, *The Land Called Holy*, 44.

17 O'Brien, *God Land*, 12.

18 Citations in Kantorowicz, "Pro Patria Mori," 310.

19 Kantorowicz, "Pro Patria Mori," 311.

20 Wilken, *The Land Called Holy*, 89.

21 Wilken provides many references to this, *The Land Called Holy*, 95.

22 Wilken *The Land Called Holy*, 124f, 165.

23 Pinhas H. Peli, *Soloveitchik: On Repentance* (New York: Paulist Press, 1984), 313–314. In the Midrashic literature, the Rabbis call Jerusalem the biblical "Camp of Israel," and thus require the strict purity code of the wilderness camp of the Pentateuch in the holy city (*Sif. Num.*, Friedman, 1b). Moving in closer to God's house is the "Camp of Levites," i.e. the Temple Mount, and finally, the "Divine Camp," the Temple itself.

24 See Hermann Strathmann, *"Polis"* in *Theological Dictionary of the New Testament* VI, 524, for references to Jerusalem as the "holy city" or "City of God."

25 Wilken, *The Land Called Holy*, 35.

26 Jacob Neusner, *Purity in Rabbinic Judaism* (Atlanta: Scholars Press, 1994), 34, 38.

27 Shmuel Safrai, "The Land of Israel in Tannaitic Halacha," in *Das Land Israel in biblischer Zeit: Jerusalem-Symposium 1981*, ed. Georg Strecker (Gottingen: Vandenhoeck & Ruprecht, 1983), 206.

28 Gedalyahu Alon, *Jews, Judaism and the Classical World: Studies in Jewish History in the Times of the Second Temple and Talmud* (Jerusalem: Magnes Press, 1977), 183–187.

29 Divine revelations to the prophets in exile are explained as due to the merit of the Fathers only (*Mekh. Pisha* 1).

30 Richard S. Sarason, "The Significance of the Land of Israel in the Mishnah," *The Land of Israel: Jewish Perspectives*, ed. Lawrence A. Hoffman (Notre Dame, IN: University of Notre Dame Press, 1986), 115, and see rabbinic references in notes 20–21.

31 R. Judah the Prince, although opposed by other Rabbis, "exempted extensive areas from the commandments dependent on the Land" including, Caesarea, Beit Guvrin, Beit Shean, Kfar Zemach. Safrai explains, "It may be assumed that Jews living in these areas, as a minority among a Gentile majority, were accorded lenient rulings to enable them to compete with their neighbors who did not have to tithe or keep the Sabbatical Year," Safrai, 207; see P. Neeman, *The Boundaries of Eretz Yisrael according to Hasal* (Jerusalem: R. Mas, 1979).

32 J.D. Eisenstein, "Palestine, Holiness of," in *The Jewish Encyclopedia*, IX, ed. I. Singer (New York: Ktav, 1964), 504.

33 Arthur Hertzberg, "Zionism and the Jewish Religious Tradition," in *The Jerusalem Colloquium on Religion, Peoplehood, Nation, and Land*, ed. Marc H. Tanenbaum and R. J. Zwi Werblovsky (Jerusalem: H.S. Truman Research Institute of the Hebrew University, 1972), 165.

34 Sarason, "The Significance of the Land of Israel," 126.

35 Martin Jaffee, *Early Judaism* (Upper Saddle River, NJ: Prentice Hall, 1997), 117–118.

36 Sarason, "The Significance of the Land of Israel," 114–116.

37 The sabbatical year was kept through the second Temple period and up until the Bar Kochba revolt, S. Safrai, "The Sabbatical Year Commandment in Post-Second Temple Reality" (Heb.) *Tarbiz* 36 (1966), 309–328; 37 (1967), 1–21. Even Alexander the Great and Julius Caesar noted this (no cultivation of fields or harvesting) and freed the Jews from land tax on this year (*Ant.* 11:338; 14:202–206). An inscription from the seventh century on a the mosaic floor of a synagogue near Beth Shean reveals that the sabbatical year was still being observed in the land of Israel during the Byzantine period, Lee I. Levine, *Ancient Synagogues Revealed* (Detroit: Wayne State University Press 1982), 152–153.

38 See numerous rabbinic references to this and the problems attached to the law in "Sabbatical Year and Jubilee," in *Encyclopedia Judaica*, XIV (Jerusalem: Keter, 1971), 580.

39 After the Bar Kochba Revolt (135 CE), the Romans insisted on taxation of Jews even during the sabbatical year in order to support the military. Thus, the observance of the sabbatical year fell into widespread disuse (*Lev. R.* 1:1), and the Rabbis began to relax the law because Jews did not have full control over their land, "Sabbatical Year and Jubilee," 583.

40 Brueggemann, *The Land*, 154.

41 Samuel S. Cohon, *Essays in Jewish Theology* (Cincinnati: Hebrew Union College Press, 1987), 302f.; Philo, On the Virtues and Office of Ambassadors, xxiii; see also Ant. 16:6, 2–7; 18.9.1.

42 Michael H. Jameson, "Sacrifice and Ritual: Greece," in *Civilization of the Ancient Mediterranean*, II, ed. Michael Grant and Rachel Kitzmyer (New York: Charles Scribner & Sons, 1988), 968.

43 Walter Burkert, *Creation of the Sacred: Tracks of Biology in Early Religions* (Cambridge, MA: Harvard University Press, 1996), 136.

44 Jacob Licht, "*Qodesh, Qadosh, Qedushah*," in *Entsiqlopedya Mikra'it*, VII, ed. E. Sukenik and Moshe D. Cassuto (Jerusalem: Bialik Institute, 1965), 51.

45 Neusner, *Polity in Rabbinic Judaism*, 36.

46 Charles Primus, "The Borders of Judaism: The Land of Israel in Early Rabbinic Judaism," in *The Land of Israel: Jewish Perspectives*, ed. Lawrence A. Hoffman (Notre Dame, IN: University of Notre Dame Press, 1986), 105

47 Elisha Qimron, "The Holiness of the Holy Land in the Light of a New Document from Qumran," in *The Holy Land in History and Thought*, ed. Moshe Sharon Johannesburg, (Leiden: E. J. Brill, 1988), 9–13.

48 "*Tahorah*," *Entsiqlopedyah Talmudit*, XIX (Jerusalem: Talmudic Publishing Encyclopedia, 1989), 13–15.

49 Yigael Yadin, *Megillat ha-Migdash* (3 vols. 1977), Eng. trans., *The Temple Scroll*, 3 vols. (Jerusalem: The Israel Exploration Society and the Shrine of the Book, 1983), 288–289.

50 Cohon, *Essays in Jewish Theology*, 289; Walter Wurzburger and R. J. Zvi Werblowsky, "Land, People and Nation in Jewish Perspective," in *Fifteen Years of Catholic Jewish Dialogue: 1970–1985* (Rome: Libreria Editrice Vaticana, 1988), 6.

51 This does not include new moons which were primarily popular festivals rather than cultic ones.

52 J. Milgrom, *Leviticus 17–27*, The Anchor Bible 3B (Garden City, NY: Doubleday, forthcoming).

53 B. Kedar-Kopfstein, "*Hag*," in *Theological Dictionary of the Old Testament*, IV, 201–203.

54 "Festivals" in *Encyclopedia Judaica* (Jerusalem: Keter, 1971), 1242f.

55 Robert Turcan, *The Cults of the Roman Empire*, trans. Antonia Nevill (Oxford: Blackwells, 1996), 291–327.

56 J. D. Eisenstein, "Palestine, Holiness of," in *The Jewish Encylopedia*, IX, ed. Isidore Singer (New York: Ktav, 1964), 502.

57 Smith, *Map is Not Territory*, 124.

58 Hertzberg, "Zionism and the Jewish Religious Tradition," 166, cites *The Bordeaux Pilgrim*, 21–22 and gives other accounts as well.

59 cited in Davies, *Gospel*, 68.

60 Lawrence A. Hoffmann, "Introduction: Land of Blessing and 'Blessings of the

Land',," in *The Land of Israel: Jewish Perspectives*, ed. Lawrence A. Hoffman (Notre Dame, IN: University of Notre Dame Press, 1986), 10, 17.

61 Saul Lieberman, *Proceedings of the Rabbinical Assembly of America*, XII (1949); Davies, *Gospel*, 73, y. *Kil.* 7:5; y. *Orla* 1:2.

62 Brueggemann, *The Land*, 166.

63 Susan Guettel Cole, "Festivals, Greco-Roman," *Anchor Bible Dictionary*, II, 793.

64 Jameson, "Sacrifice and Ritual," 966.

65 Cole, "Festivals," 793.

66 Herodotus 6.87; Thuc. 3.3.3, Xen. *Hell.* 5.2.25–36, but at Athens apparently the festivals could continue even if the military was otherwise occupied (Plut. *Phoc.* 6.7).

67 Parker, 157.

68 Kedar-Kopfstein, "*Hag*", 205.

69 Jameson, "Sacrifice and Ritual," 974.

70 Robert Parker, *Miasma: Pollution and Purification in Early Greek Religion* (Oxford: Clarendon Press, 1983), 158f.

71 Cole, "Festivals," 793f.

72 John Ferguson, *Greek and Roman Religion: A Source Book* (Park Ridge, NJ: Noyes Press, 1980), 43.

73 John A. North, "Sacrifice and Ritual: Rome," in *Civilization of the Ancient Mediterranean*, II, ed. M. Grant and R. Kitzmyer (New York: Charles Scribner's Sons, 1988), 982.

74 North, "Sacrifice and Ritual," 984.

75 North, "Sacrifice and Ritual," 984.

76 "*Hieros*" in *TDNT*, 238, and see references there.

77 Smith, *Map is Not Territory*, 101, emphasizes that while the locative view seems primitive and the utopian view progressive, that is not the case. Both views exist in the modern world.

78 Brueggemann, *The Land*, 159.

79 Martin Hengel, *Judaism and Hellenism* (Philadelphia: Fortress Press, 1974), 74.

80 "*Polis*" in *TDNT*, VI, 519.

81 "*Polis*," 520.

82 Brueggemann, *The Land*, 160.

83 "*Polis*," 527–559.

84 Wilken, *The Land Called Holy*, 29.

85 Betsy Halpern Amaru, "Land Theology in Philo and Josephus," in *The Land of Israel: Jewish Perspectives*, ed. Lawrence A. Hoffman (Notre Dame, IN: University of Notre Dame Press, 1986), 68.

86 Amaru, "Land Theology," 69–71, 85.

87 Kirsten Hoffgren Pedersen, "The Holy Land: History and Reality of the Term," *Immanuel* 22/23 (1989), 35.

88 Pedersen, "The Holy Land," 38.

89 Clemens Thoma, "The Link Between People, Land and Religion in Old and New Testaments," *Service International de Documentation Judeo-Chretienne* 8:2 (1975), 14.

90 "*Polis*" in *TDNT*, VI, 530–35.

91 See W. D. Davies, "Jerusalem and the Land in the Christian Traditions" in *The Jerusalem Colloquium on Religion, Peoplehood, Nation, and Land*, ed. Marc H. Tanenbaum and R. J. Zwi Werblovsky (Jerusalem: Truman Research Institute, 1970); Wilken, *The Land Called Holy*, 150.

92 See also Rom. 11:16 where the patriarchs of Israel are illustrated as the "firstfruits of the dough."

93 Hans Wenschkewitz, *Die Spiritualisierung der Kultusbegriffe Tempel* (Leipzig: Edvard Pfeiffer, 1932), 149–152.

94 Aryeh Grabois, "Medieval Pilgrims, the Holy Land and Its Image in European Civilisation" in *The Holy Land in History and Thought*, ed. Moshe Sharon (Leiden: E. J. Brill, 1988); Wilken, *The Land Called Holy*, 81.

95 Smith, *Map is Not Territory*, 113, uses Eliade's terms.

96 Wilken, *The Law Called Holy*, 191.

97 Several examples and references can be found in Davies, *Gospel*, 61–62. For example, the Rabbis claim, Jonah fled the land because he thought he could escape the spirit of God (*Mekh. Petihata* 25).

98 Quoted in Safrai, "The Land of Israel," 212, 215.

99 Davies, *Gospel*, 65; E. M. Meyers, *BA* 23 (1970, Feb.) no. 1, 1–29 on "Secondary Burials in Palestine," and "Jewish Ossuaries: Reburial and Rebirth," *Biblica et Orientalia* (Rome: Institute Press, 1979), 72ff.

100 Davies, *Gospel*, 35.

101 Brueggemann, *The Land*, 153.

4 THE HOLY WORD

1 Harold Coward, *Sacred Word and Sacred Text: Scripture in World Religions*, (Maryknoll, NY: Orbis Books, 1988),113; Robert C. Lester, "Hinduism: Veda and Sacred Texts", in *The Holy Book in Comparative Perspective*, ed. Frederick Denny and Rodney Taylor (Columbia, SC: University of South Carolina Press, 1985) 128, 131.

2 Coward, *Sacred Word*, 140.

3 See also I. H. Weiss, *Dor Dor ve-Dorshav*, I (Vienna, 1871), 1, who says later Sages put the words into Shammai's mouth. Ephraim E. Urbach, *The Sages: Their Concepts and Beliefs*, I (Jerusalem: Magnes Press, 1979), 290.

4 Martin Jaffee, *Early Judaism* (Upper Saddle River, NJ: Prentice Hall, 1997), 55.

5 James W. Boyd, "Zoroastrianism: Avestan Scripture and Rite," in *The Holy Book in Comparative Perspective*, 136.

6 George Foot Moore, *Judaism in the First Centuries of the Christian Era*, I (New York: Schocker Books, 1971), 243. Most of the books of the Hebrew Bible were considered authoritative by the end of the first century CE and doubts remained only in the case of a few.

7 Jaffee, *Early Judaism*, 235.

8 Jaffee, *Early Judaism*, 233–240.

9 Lester, "Hinduism," 134.

10 Coward, *Sacred Word*, 136.

11 Samuel S. Cohon, *Essays in Jewish Theology* (Cincinnati: Hebrew Union College Press, 1987), 63.

12 "Introduction" by Frederick M. Denny and Rodney L. Taylor, *The Holy Book in Comparative Perspective*,2.

13 Joseph Baumgarten, *Studies in Qumran Law* (Leiden: E. J. Brill, 1977), 29–31.

14 Jonathan Rosenbaum, "Judaism: Torah and Tradition" in *The Holy Book in Comparative Perspective*,10.

15 Moore, *Judaism*, I, 255.

16 The Mishnah was transmitted orally even though its compilation did require writing, at least in notes, long before 200 CE, cf. Jaffee, 220.

17 Moore, I, 262–63.
18 Cohon, *Essays in Jewish Theology*, 65–68; Jacob Neusner, *The Oral Torah: The Sacred Books of Judaism* (San Francisco: Harper & Row, 1986) 148, charts the development of the status of the Oral Torah from the early centuries CD to its fullest expression in the Babylonian Talmud.
19 Rosenbaum, "Judaism," 12.
20 Michael Fishbane, "Jewish Biblical Exegesis: Presuppositions and Principles," in *Scripture in the Jewish and Christian Traditions*, ed. F. E. Greenspan (Nashville: Abingdon, 1982), 94–102.
21 Moore, I, *Judaism*, 254, not all custom was considered divine law.
22 Urbach, *The Sages*, I, 306.
23 Urbach, *The Sages*, I, 304.
24 Alan C. Bouquet, *Sacred Books of the World* (London: Cassell, 1962), 81.
25 Alan C. Bouquet, *Sacred Books of the World* (London: Cassell, 1962), 179.
26 Bouquet, *Sacred Books*, 183, 212.
27 "Sibylline Oracles," in *Encyclopedia of Religion*, XIV, ed. Mircea Eliade (New York: Macmillan, 1987), 306.
28 John J. Collins, "Sibylline Oracles," in James Charlesworth, *The Old Testament Pseudepigrapha*, I (Garden City, NY: Doubleday, 1983), 317–318.
29 Collins, "Sibylline Oracles," 322.
30 Harry Y. Gamble, Jr., "Christianity: Scripture and Canon," in *The Holy Book in Comparative Perspective*, 45.
31 Gamble, "Christianity," 52.
32 F. F. Bruce, "Scripture and Tradition in the New Testament," in *Holy Book and Holy Tradition*, ed. F. F. Bruce and E. G. Rupp (Grand Rapids, MI: Eerdmans, 1968), 69.
33 Bruce, "Scripture and Tradition," 69, 86, 93; Marcel Simon, "The Ancient Church and Rabbinical Tradition," in *Holy Book and Holy Tradition*, 110.
34 Urbach, *The Sages*, I, 295.
35 Jaffee, *Early Judaism*, 215.
36 Simon, "The Ancient Church," 94–95.
37 Gamble, "Christianity," 45.
38 Moore, *Judaism*, I, 257.
39 Jacob Neusner, *From Testament to Torah: An Introduction to Judaism in Its Formative Age* (Englewood Cliffs, NJ: Prentice Hall, 1988), 45.
40 Jacob Weingreen, "Oral Torah and Written Records," in *Holy Book and Holy Tradition*, eds. F. F. Bruce and E. G. Rupp, 57–59; Jaffee, *Early Judaism*, 221.
41 Shlomo Biderman, *Scripture and Knowledge: An Essay on Religious Epistemology* (Leiden: E. J. Brill, 1995), 177–178.
42 George. Widengren, "Holy Book and Tradition in Iran: The Problem of the Sassanid Avesta," in *Holy Book and Holy Tradition*, 52.
43 Biderman, *Scripture and Knowledge*, 175–76.
44 Lester, "Hinduism," 127.
45 Urbach, *The Sages*, I, 291.
46 Translations in Simon, "The Ancient Church," 110–111.
47 Coward, *Sacred Word*, 13.
48 Jaffee, *Early Judaism*, 198.
49 Rosenbaum, "Judiasm." 29.
50 Frits Staal, "The Concept of Scripture in Indian Tradition," in *Sikh Studies: Comparative Perspectives in a Changing Tradition* ed. M. Juergensmeyer and N. G. Barrier (Berkeley, Graduate Theological Union, 1979), 179, cited in Biderman, *Scripture and Knowledge*, 139.

51 Boyd, "Zoroastrianism," 109.

52 Boyd, "Zoroastrianism," 114.

53 Boyd, "Zoroastrianism," 110.

54 Mary Boyce, *Zoroastrians: Their Religious Beliefs and Practices* (London: Routledge & Kegan Paul, 1979), 3.

55 Boyd, "Zoroastrianism," 113–114.

56 Biderman, *Scripture and Knowledge*, 180–81.

57 Coward, *Sacred Word*, 105.

58 Coward, *Sacred Word*, 105.

59 Coward, *Sacred Word*, 135.

60 Max Kadushin, *Worship and Ethics: A Study in Rabbinic Judaism* (Evanston, IL: Northwestern University Press, 1964), 87–88, discusses the example of daily *Shema* recitation.

61 Jacob Milgrom, *Leviticus 17–27*, Anchor Bible Series (Garden City, NY: Doubleday, forthcoming).

62 John North, "The Development of Religious Pluralism," 174–193, in *The Jews Among Pagans and Christians in the Ancient World*, ed. M. Beard and J. North (Ithica, NY: Cornell University Press, 1990), 187.

63 Falk, Ze'ev W. Falk "Spirituality and Jewish Law," *Religion and Law: Biblical-Judaic and Islamic Perspectives*, ed. E. B. Firmage, et al. (Winona Lake: Eisenbrauns, 1990), 133: "By sanctifying one's deeds, a person becomes a sanctuary and a source of salvation. . . . The presence of the Holy Spirit or the Divine Presence depends upon the sanctification of human life by observance of the law."

64 *Sif. Deut.*, 44: All commandments not dependent on the Land (as well as *orlah* and mixed seed) must be done in and out of Israel.

65 Cohen, *Everyman's Talmud* (New York: Schocken Books, 1975), 133f., cites this passage and others on the Torah's perfection.

66 Milgrom, *Leviticus 1–16*, The Anchor Bible 3A (Garden City, NY: Doubleday, 1991), 1004, quotes McCarter.

67 Some have suggested that Torah scrolls were stored alongside *terumah*, food donations to the priests, similar to practices attested in Graeco-Roman temples. The food would attract mice which would damage the scrolls. By declaring the scrolls susceptible to impurity, and thus potentially contaminating to *terumah*, the Rabbis forced them to be kept in a separate location. Discussion is provided in Milgrom, *Leviticus 1–16*, 1004.

68 See Hannah Harrington, *Impurity Systems of Qumran and the Rabbis* (Atlanta: Scholars Press, 1993), 42. The Torah scrolls are only impure in the second degree (m. *Yad.* 3:2).

69 Charles Albeck on m. *Yad.* 4:6, *Shisha Sidrei Mishnah*, VI (Jerusalem: Bialik Institute, 1953), 485.

70 Sid Z. Leiman, *The Canonization of Hebrew Scripture: The Talmudic and Midrashic Evidence* (Hamden, CT: Archon Books, 1976), 118.

71 Rosenbaum, "Judiasm," 24, cites several rules from *Yoreh Deah, Orah Hayyim, Mishnah Berurah* and traditional rabbinic academies. He also cites Maimonides (*Mishneh Torah, Sefer Ahbah, Hilkot Sefer Torah*, 10), 35.

72 "Scribe," in *Encyclopedia Judaica*, XIV (Jerusalem: Keter, 1971), 1043–44; Coward, *Sacred Word*, 6.

73 Coward, *Sacred Word*, 7, 26–27.

74 Lester, "Hinduism," 127.

75 Coward, *Sacred Word*, 113, 122, 148.

76 Biderman, *Scripture and Knowledge*, 139.

77 Coward, *Sacred Word*, 130.
78 "*Genizah*," in *Encyclopedia Judaica*, VII, 404f.
79 cf. Milgrom, *Leviticus 1–16*, 1004.
80 J. Milgrom, *Leviticus 1–16*, 686; see also *Moral Grandeur and Spiritual Audacity: Essays Abraham Joshua Heschel*, ed. Susannah Heschel (New York: Farrar, 1996), 327.
81 Neusner, *From Testament to Torah*, 46.
82 Jaffee, *Early Judaism*, 213–14.
83 Jaffee, *Early Judaism*, 225.
84 Trans. Daniel Boyarin, *Intertextuality and the Reading of Midrash* (Bloomington, IN: Indiana University Press, 1990), 109–110.
85 Boyarin, *Intertextuality*, 110.
86 Jaffee, *Early Judaism*, 223–2 4.
87 Jaffee, *Early Judaism*, 225: Other *Hekhalot* texts do not mention the commandments but require "private prayers as meditative hymns that either aid the traveler's efforts to penetrate the divine realm or serve as exultant signs of his safe arrival."
88 Jaffee, *Early Judaism*, 226f.
89 Texts are taken from Jaffe, *Early Judaism*, 227f.

5   THE HOLY PEOPLE

1 Jacob Milgrom, *Leviticus 1–16*, The Anchor Bible 3A (Garden City, NY: Doubleday, 1991), 687.
2 Ze'ev W. Falk, "Spirituality and Jewish Law," in *Religion and Law: Biblical-Judaic and Islamic Perspectives*, ed. E. B. Firmage, et al. (Winona Lake: Eisenbrauns, 1990), 133.
3 "Holiness (NT)" in *Anchor Bible Dictionary*, ed. David N. Freedman, III (New York: Doubleday, 1992), 253.
4 Milgrom, *Leviticus 1–16*, 637.
5 Solomon Schechter, *Some Aspects of Rabbinic Theology* (New York: Macmillan, 1923), 217.
6 "Holiness (NT)" in *Anchor Bible Dictionary*, II, 250. There are many references to the saints as the holy ones but sometimes they refer to a select group (Eph. 4:11–12; Heb. 13:24; Rev. 11:18). Sometimes only certain righteous people are referred to as holy, just as the priests and prophets of Israel were considered especially holy (Acts 3:21; see also Luke 1:70). John the Baptist, for example, is specially marked as a "righteous and holy [*hagios*] man" (Mark. 6:20; see also Matt. 14:5; Luke 9:7–9).
7 F. Hauck and R. Meyer, "*Katharos*" in *Theological Dictionary of the New Testament*, ed. G. W. Bromley III (Grand Rapido, MI: Eerdmans, 1964–76), III, 426.
8 See Walther Eichrodt, *Theologie des Alten Testaments*, I, trans. J. A. Baker (Philadelphia: Westminster Press,1961), 271. It is erroneous to assume that the prophets but not the priests associated God's holiness with moral qualities (see Lev. 19). As one scholar says, "The prophets deepen and broaden the moral dimension of the divine holiness," "*Kedushah*" in *Encyclopedia Judaica*, X (Jerusalem: Keter, 1971), 868.
9 "Ritual commandments, meaning all action that concerns only the individual and does not affect her or his relation with others," Jacob Milgrom, "Ethics and Ritual: The Foundations of the Biblical Dietary Laws," in *Religion and Law: Biblical-Judaic and Islamic Perspectives*, 160.

10 Deborah F. Sawyer, *Women and Religion in the First Christian Centuries* (London: Routledge, 1996), 34–35. Sawyer supplies references for these Roman writers.

11 Schechter, *Some Aspects*, 208.

12 *Sif. Deut.*, Hammer, 97, P. 44: All commandments not dependent on the Land (as well as *orlah* and mixed seed) must be done in and out of Israel.

13 Philip J. Budd, "Holiness and Cult," in *The World of Ancient Israel*, ed. R. Clements (Cambridge: Cambridge University Press, 1989), 285, quoting Emile Durkheim. Mary Douglas shows that ritual is "preeminently a form of communication, a form which can be highly efficient and condensed," Sheldon R. Isenberg and Dennis E. Owen, "Bodies, Natural and Contrived: The Work of Mary Douglas," *RSR*, 3/1 January (1977), 1–17; see also Edmund Leach, "Culture and Communication: The Logic by Which Symbols are Connected" in *Anthropoogical Approaches to the OT, Issues in Religion and Theology* 8, ed. B. Lang (Philadelphia: Fortress, 1985).

14 Tessa Rajak, "The Jewish Community and Its Boundaries," in *The Jews Among Pagans and Christians*, ed. Judith Lieu, John North and Tessa Rajak (London: Routledge, 1992), 14.

15 Richard Gordon, "Religion in the Roman Empire: The Civic Compromise and Its Limits," in *Pagan Priests: Religion and Power in the Ancient World, ed. Mary Beard and John North* (Ithaca, NY: Cornell University Press, 1990), 248.

16 John Ferguson, *Religions of the Roman Empire* (Ithaca, NY: Cornell University Press, 1970), gives a good discussion of the mystery cults, 99–108.

17 Daniel Boyarin, *Carnal Israel: Reading Sex in Talmudic Culture* (Berkeley: University of California Press, 1993), 232.

18 "Circumcision," in *Encyclopedia Judaica*, V, 572.

19 See John Gammie, *Holiness in Israel* (Minneapolis: Fortress Press, 1989), 25.

20 Boyarin, *Carnal Israel*, 233.

21 Robert Hall, "Circumcision," *Anchor Bible Dictionary*, I, 1031. Nevertheless, the early church council (Acts 15:28) concluded that God accepts both gentiles and Jews as they are.

22 D. Flusser and S. Safrai., "Who Sanctified the Beloved in the Womb?" *Immanuel* 11:46–55 (1980).

23 Hall, "Circumcision," 1028; see also J. J. Collins, "A Symbol of Otherness: Circumcision and Salvation in the First Century," in *To See Ourselves as Others See Us: Christians, Jews and "Others" in Late Antiquity*, ed. J. Neusner and E. S. Frerichs (Chico, CA, 1985), 163–186.

24 Translation by Jacob Milgrom, *Leviticus 1–16*, 645.

25 Early Jewish writers expound on this theme. Aristeas says: "An additional signification [of the diet laws] is that we are set apart from all men, for the majority of remaining persons defile themselves by their promiscuous unions, working great unrighteousness, and whole countries and cities pride themselves on these vices. Not only do they have intercourse with males, but they even defile mothers and daughters. But we have kept apart from these things" (Arist. 151–152; see also Jub. 22:16).

26 Milgrom, "Ethics and Ritual," 183. Nevertheless, Jesus evidently kept the laws regarding forbidden foods because Peter is shocked that God would ask him to eat unclean animals. According to Matthew 23 and Luke 11 Jesus is emphasizing the ethical purity but not completely negating ritual purity.

27 Mary Douglas, "The Abominations of Leviticus," in *Anthropological Approaches to the Old Testament*, ed. Bernhard Lang (Philadephia: Fortress Press, 1985), 112–114.

28 Douglas, "The Abominations of Leviticus," 113–116.

29 Budd, "Holiness and Cult," 286–94 gives a fair evaluation of Douglas' theory.

30 Gene Schramm, "Meal Customs (Jewish)," in *Anchor Bible Dictionary*, IV, 648–650.

31 Milgrom, "Ethics and Ritual," 161–162. The only exception to this claim is the pre-Islamic Arabs, but even they do not connect blood with life force.

32 The slaughtering method fixed by tradition (m. *Hul.* 1:2) may go back to biblical times; the Deuteronomic command, "You may slaughter . . . as I commanded you" may imply a specific method (Deut. 12:21).

33 But note that *nebelah*, "carcass," does not refer to a properly slaughtered clean animal, Milgrom, *Leviticus 1–16*, 681.

34 For more discussion on this issue, see Hannah Harrington, "Did the Pharisees Eat Ordinary Food in a State of Purity?" *JJS* (Spring, 1995).

35 "Unclean and Clean," in *Anchor Bible Dictionary*, VI, 742.

36 In addition to its ritual sense, *tahor* is often used in a figurative sense, like *zakah*, to indicate moral uprightness and ethical goodness (see Job 4:17; 15:14; 25:4). See also H. Ringgren, "*Tahor*," in *Theological Dictionary of the Old Testament*, V, ed. G. J. Botterweck and H. Ringgren, trans. David Green (Grand Rapids, MI: Eerdmans, 1986), 289–290. In "Unclean and Clean," in *Anchor Bible Dictionary*, VI, 729, David Wright provides the complete vocabulary related to purity in the Hebrew Bible.

37 Parker, 34; Ringgren, "Tahor," 288.

38 See Parker, 118 for other examples.

39 Parker, 50–52. Curiously, no Graeco-Roman rituals relating to menstruation are recorded. Nevertheless, this should not be taken as proof that none existed. Aristotle claims that menstruants dim the mirrors in front of them. Roman writers insist that menstrual blood damages wine and blights trees and crops, even blunting knives, killing bees, rusting metals and making dogs crazy, references in Parker, 10.

40 Dorothea Wendebourg, "Die alttestamentlichen Reinheitsgesetze in der fruhen Kirche," *ZKG* 95 (1984), 149–170.

41 Hans Hubner, *Anchor Bible Dictionary*, 745.

42 "*Katharos*," *TDNT*, III, 428.

43 "*Katharos*," *TDNT*, III, 429.

44 Parker, 21–23, 30.

45 Parker, 24.

46 Parker, 23–24, 31.

47 For a complete analysis of each type of impurity and its consequences, see Hannah Harrington, *The Impurity Systems of Qumran and the Rabbis* (Atlanta: Scholars Press, 1993).

48 *Miqva'ot*, immersion pools, found in Israel have several points in common. (1) They are cut into bedrock. (2) They are deep enough for complete immersion and often have steps leading to the bottom. Stepped pools large enough for full immersion, often 7 feet or deeper, have been found in many places, including, the Hasmonean palaces at Jericho, Herod's palaces, the Upper City in Jerusalem, and in ordinary homes in Jerusalem, Sepphoris, Gamla, and Masada. (3) They were filled by means of channels that carried rain or spring water. Synagogues were apparently built near sea water for purification purposes (see Acts 16:13).

49 Jacob Neusner, *Purity in Rabbinic Judaism* (Atlanta: Scholars Press, 1994), 148; Harrington, *Impurity Systems*, 134–135.

50 *Anchor Bible Dictionary*, 743.

51 A. Oepke, "*Bapto*," in *TDNT*, I, 529.

52 Oepke, "*Bapto*," 533–534.

53 Oepke,"*Bapto*," 541.

54 Milgrom, *Leviticus 1–16*; see also the discussion in Jenson, *Graded Holiness*, regarding mourning customs which "provide a controlled framework for the powerful forces [of death] . . . to be acknowledged and brought within the realm of cultural order and control," 83.

55 Mary Douglas, *In the Wilderness: The Doctrine of Defilement in the Book of Numbers*, (Sheffield: Sheffield Academic Press, 1993), 24.

56 See Parker, 39–42; Douglas, *In the Wilderness*, 25–27, 153–158.

57 Milgrom, *Leviticus 1–16*, 259.

58 Douglas, *In the Wilderness*, 25–27, 153–158.

59 Boaz Cohen, *Jewish and Roman Law: A Comparative Study* I (New York: Jewish Theological Seminary of America, 1966), 66.

60 John North, "The Development of Religious Pluralism," in *The Jews among Pagans and Christians*, ed. Judith Lieu, et al. (London: Routledge, 1992), 187.

61 North, "The Development of Religious Pluralism," 188; Erich Gruen, personal communication, 1997. As K. Dowden says, Romans "reckoned their moral behaviour was up to them and what others thought of them" in *Religion and the Romans* (London: Bristol Classical Press, 1992), 8.

62 J. H. W. G. Liebeschuetz, *Continuity and Change in Roman Religion* (Oxford: Clarendon Press, 1979), 3.

63 Cited by Liebeschuetz, *Continuity and Change*, 39; see also 307; North, "The Development of Religious Pluralism," 188.

64 Gammie, *Holiness in Israel*, 195.

65 Liebeschuetz, *Continuity and Change*, 178.

66 Liebeschuetz, *Continuity and Change*, 176.

67 Liebeschuetz, *Continuity and Change*, 54–59.

68 Milgrom, *Leviticus 1–16*, 731.

69 Millard J. Erickson, *Christian Theology* (Grand Rapids, MI: Baker, 1985), 968; Donald G. Bloesch, *Essentials of Evangelical Theology*, II (San Francisco: Harper & Row, 1978), 41.

70 Solomon Schechter, *Studies in Judaism*, second series (Philadelphia: Jewish Publication Society of America, 1908), 151.

71 Schechter, *Some Aspects*, 218.

72 Schechter, *Some Aspects*, 209.

73 Cf. Cohen, *Jewish and Roman Law*, 100 and 105, for rabbinic references and parallels.

74 Baruch Levine, "The Language of Holiness: Perceptions of the Sacred in the Hebrew Bible," in *Backgrounds for the Bible*, ed. Michael P. O'Connor and David N. Freedman (Winona Lake, IN: Eisenbrauns, 1987), 254.

75 See Milgrom, *Leviticus 1–16*, 731. According to Eichrodt, ethics is the primary meaning of holiness and it is a distinctive of the Israelites in contrast to other, older cultures, *Theologie*, I, 270–282.

76 Ps. 15 may be "an entrance ritual and liturgy" which sets forth the conditions for entrance into the Temple, John Hayes, *Understanding the Psalms* (Valley Forge, PA: Judson Press, 1976), 44.

77 Burton Leiser, "The Sanctity of the Profane: A Pharisaic Critique of Rudolf Otto," *Judaism* 20 (1971), 92.

78 For the link between holiness and love in the New Testament, see Steven J. Land, *Pentecostal Spirituality: A Passion for the Kingdom* (Sheffield: Sheffield Academic Press, 1993).

79 E. P. Sanders, "When is a Law a Law? The Case of Jesus and Paul," in *Religion and Law: Biblical-Judaic and Islamic Perspectives*, ed. E. Firmage et al. (Winona Lake: Eisenbrauns, 1990), 154–156.

80 Stanley M. Burgess, "Montanist and Patristic Perfectionism," in *Reaching Beyond: Chapters in the History of Perfectionism*, ed. S. M. Burgess (Peabody, MA: Hendrickson, 1986), 142.

81 Liebeschuetz, *Continuity and Change*, 60.

82 Ferguson, *Religions of the Roman Empire*, 193.

83 Liebeschuetz, *Continuity and Change*, 185–189.

84 Liebeschuetz, *Continuity and Change*, 201.

85 Liebeschuetz, *Continuity and Change*, 143.

86 Ferguson, *Religions of the Roman Empire*, 193.

87 Some exceptions apply. "In Plato's dialogues, Socrates induces Euthyphro to define piety (*to hosion*) as a system of sacrifice and prayer (Euthyphro 14c), but elsewhere (12d) in the same dialogue he suggests to Euthyphro that piety might have some relationship to justice. Euthyphro, who apparently represents the traditional Greek view, is at a loss to characterize the relationship between piety and justice. Some Athenians must have been aware of the connection because it is occasionally implied that piety toward the gods is related to or even dependent upon just actions toward other human beings." Menander fragment 683 reads, "Anyone who believes that he secures the god's favor by sacrifice . . . is in error. For a man must not be useful by not seducing virgins or committing adultery or stealing or killing for money." Susan Guettel Cole, "Greek Cults," *Civilization of the Ancient Mediterranean*, II, ed. Michael Grant and Rachel Kitzmyer (New York: Charles Scribner & Sons, 1988), 889; Cohen, *Jewish and Roman Law*, 74–75.

88 Parker, 93f.

89 David Daube, *The Duty of Procreation* (Edinburgh: Edinburgh University Press, 1977), 29; Boyarin, *Carnal Israel*, 142.

90 Porphyry, *Life of Plotinus*, quoted in Boyarin, *Carnal Israel*, 231; other Hellenistic examples are provided on p. 33. The Stoic Lucan (d. 65 CE) gives a description of virtue through his ideal character, Cato, who is moderate, patriotic, has sex only for procreation, eliminates passion, and is "free from love and free from hate," Liebeschuetz, *Continuity and Change*, 147, 149

91 Daube, *The Duty of Provocation*, 29; Boyarin, *Carnal Israel*, 142.

92 Steven D. Fraade, "Ascetical Aspects of Ancient Judaism," in *Jewish Spirituality from the Bible through the Middle Ages*, ed. Arthur Green (New York: Crossroad, 1986), 257.

93 Robert Hodgson, Jr., "Holiness (NT)," in *Anchor Bible Dictionary*.

94 Celibate tendencies may also be due to Jewish apocalyptic notions which held that in preparation for the age to come (soon), and to diminish anxiety, one should remain single (1 Cor. 7; Rev. 14:4). Paul's approval of celibacy may have been due to this sense that the end time was near and so one should not engage in relationships which would generate further responsibility (1 Cor. 7:12–29).

95 Boyarin, *Carnal Israel*, 41f.

96 Boyarin, *Carnal Israel*, 79, 63.

97 Boyarin, *Carnal Israel*, 85; so also Philo. In *Rereading the Rabbis: A Woman's Voice* (Boulder, CO: Westview Press, 1998), Judith Hauptman argues against those who claim the Rabbis viewed women as inherent temptresses incapable of restraint in sexual matters, 30–31.

98 Boyarin, *Carnal Israel*, 149.

99 Boyarin, *Carnal Israel*, 149–50, following Frankel.

100 "Marriage, Prohibited," in *Encyclopedia Judaica*, XI, 1052f.

101 Mary Douglas, *Natural Symbols: Explorations in Cosmology* (New York: Pantheon Books, 1982), Chs, 2–3, 6, 10; see also Bruce Malina, quoted in Budd, "Holiness and Cult," 283.

102 This separatist attitude continues among Jews throughout the late Second Temple period. Jub. 30:7–11 states that even Moses outlawed intermarriage with all gentiles on the basis of Lev. 18:21. Philo (*De Spec. Leg.* 3:29) as well as Josephus (*Ant.* 8.190–196) argue strongly against intermarriage on the basis of Deut. 7:3–4.

103 Boyarin, *Carnal Israel*, 139.

104 Translation by D. Boyarin in Boyarin, *Carnal Israel*, 140.

105 Translation by D. Boyarin, in Boyarin, *Carnal Israel*, 7.

106 Boyarin, *Carnal Israel*, 139–140, note 10. As it turns out, it was a common Babylonian notion that sexual intercourse was necessary for everyone. Atrahasis: priests/priestesses are forbidden to have children but they are allowed to have sexual intercourse.

107 "*Kedushah:* Rabbinic Literature," in *Encyclopedia Judaica*, X, 871.

108 Boyarin, *Carnal Israel*, 163.

109 Hodgson, "Holiness and Cult," 571.

110 Schechter, *Studies in Judaism*,155.

111 J. Milgrom, *Leviticus 17–27*, Anchor Bible 3B (Garden City, NY: Doubleday, forthcoming), discusses the biblical roots of this approach.

112 Fraade, "Ascetical Aspects," 275. See 286, note 86 where he cites b. *Yeb.* 20a, "Sanctify yourself in what is permitted to you" and b. *Sheb.* 18b; b. *Shab.* 53b.

113 Parker, 98.

114 Liebeschuetz, *Continuity and Change*, 275.

115 Liebeschuetz, *Continuity and Change*, 95.

116 Liebeschuetz, *Continuity and Change*, 295.

117 Liebeschuetz, *Continuity and Change*, 90–91.

118 Parker, 96.

119 Mary Douglas notes that separation from evils will "make it possible for humans to relate to the dread source of power, and to enjoy the benefits of the relations without suffering from unwanted dangerous effects," *In the Wilderness*, 23.

120 Levine, "The Language of Holiness," 250, 254.

121 Budd, "Holiness and Cult," 281.

122 E. F. Harrison, "Holiness; Holy," in *The International Standard Bible Encyclopedia*, ed. G. W. Bromley II (Grand Rapids, MI: Eerdmans, 1982), 728; David McKenna, *Power to Follow, Grace to Lead* (Dallas, TX: Word, 1989), 35; Falk, "Spirituality and Jewish Law," 127–138.

APPENDIX

1 Philip Peter Jenson, *Graded Holiness: A Key to the Priestly Conception of the World* (Sheffield: Sheffield Academic Press, 1992), 17, provides a similar chart for the Priestly system of the Bible.

BIBLIOGRAPHY

Abelson, J., *The Immanence of God in Rabbinical Literature* (New York: Hermon Press, 1969 [first edition, London 1912]).

Albeck, C., *Shisha Sidrei Mishnah*, VI (Jerusalem: Bialik Institute, 1953).

Alon, G., *Jews, Judaism and the Classical World: Studies in Jewish History in the Times of the Second Temple and Talmud* (Jerusalem: Magnes Press, 1977).

Amaru, B. H., "Land Theology in Philo and Josephus," in *The Land of Israel: Jewish Perspectives*, ed. L. A. Hoffman (Notre Dame, IN: University of Notre Dame Press, 1986).

Armstrong, J., *The Idea of Holiness and the Humane Response* (London: George Allen & Unwin, 1981).

Barr, J., "Sacrifice and Offering," in *Dictionary of the Bible*, edn. J. Hastings, rev. ed. F. C. Grant and H. H. Rowley (New York: Scribners, 1963), 871.

Baumgarten, J., *Studies in Qumran Law* (Leiden: E. J. Brill, 1977).

Beard, M., "Roman Priesthoods," in *Civilization of the Ancient Mediterranean*, II, ed. M. Grant and R. Kitzmyer, II (New York: Charles Scribner & Sons, 1988).

Ben-Dov, M., *In the Shadow of the Temple: The Discovery of Ancient Jerusalem*, trans. I. Friedman (New York: Harper & Row, 1985).

Between God and Man: An Interpretation of Judaism from the Writings of Abraham J. Heschel, ed. F. Rothschild (New York: Free Press, 1965).

Biderman, S., *Scripture and Knowledge: An Essay on Religious Epistemology* (Leiden: E. J. Brill, 1995).

Bloesch, D. G., *Essentials of Evangelical Theology*, II (San Francisco: Harper & Row, 1978).

Bouquet, A. C., *Sacred Books of the World* (London: Cassell, 1962).

Boyarin, D., *Intertextuality and the Reading of Midrash* (Bloomington, IN: Indiana University Press, 1990).

——, *Carnal Israel: Reading Sex in Talmudic Culture* (Berkeley: University of California Press, 1993).

Boyce, M., *Zoroastrians: Their Religious Beliefs and Practices* (London: Routledge & Kegan Paul,1979).

231

Boyd, J. W., "Zoroastrianism: Avestan Scripture and Rite," in *The Holy Book in Comparative Perspective.*, ed. F. M. Denny and R. L. Taylor (Columbia, SC: University of South Carolina Press, 1985).

Brereton, J. P., "Sacred Space," in *The Encyclopedia of Religion*, ed. M. Eliade (New York: Macmillan, 1987).

Bruce, F. F., "Scripture and Tradition in the New Testament," in *Holy Book and Holy Tradition*, ed. F. F. Bruce and E. G. Rupp (Grand Rapids, MI: Eerdmans, 1968).

Brueggemann, W., *The Land: Place as Gift, Promise, and Challenge in Biblical Faith* (Philadelphia: Fortress Press, 1977).

Budd, P. J., "Holiness and Cult," in *The World of Ancient Israel: Sociological, Anthropological and Political Perspectives*, ed. R. E. Clements (Cambridge: Cambridge University Press, 1989).

Burgess, S. M., "Montanist and Patristic Perfectionism," in *Reaching Beyond: Chapters in the History of Perfectionism*, ed. S. M. Burgess (Peabody, MA: Hendrickson, 1986).

Burkert, W., *Creation of the Sacred: Tracks of Biology in Early Religions* (Cambridge, MA: Harvard University Press, 1996).

"Circumcision," in *Encyclopedia Judaica*, V (Jerusalem: Keter, 1971).

The Code of Maimonides, trans. J. J. Rabinowitz, Yale Judaica Series, Book VIII (New Haven: Yale University Press, 1957).

Cohen, A., *Everyman's Talmud* (New York: Schocken Books, 1975).

Cohen, B., *Jewish and Roman Law: A Comparative Study*, I (New York: Jewish Theological Seminary of America, 1966).

Cohon, S. S., *Essays in Jewish Theology* (Cincinnati: Hebrew Union College Press, 1987).

Cole, S. G., "Greek Cults," in *Civilization of the Ancient Mediterranean*, ed. M. Grant and R. Kitzmyer, II (New York: Charles Scribner & Sons, 1988).

——, "Festivals, Greco-Roman," *Anchor Bible Dictionary*, II, (New York: Doubleday, 1992).

——, "Temples and Sanctuaries," *Anchor Bible Dictionary* (New York: Doubleday, 1992).

Collins, J. J., "Sibylline Oracles," in *The Old Testament Pseudepigrapha*, ed. James Charlesworth, I (Garden City, NY: Doubleday, 1983).

——, "A Symbol of Otherness: Circumcision and Salvation in the First Century," in *To See Ourselves as Others See Us: Christians, Jews and "Others" in Late Antiquity*, ed. J. Neusner and E. S. Frerichs (Chico, CA: Scholars Press, 1985).

Coward, H., *Sacred Word and Sacred Text: Scripture in World Religions* (Maryknoll, NY: Orbis Books, 1988).

Daube, D., *The Duty of Procreation* (Edinburgh: Edinburgh University Press, 1977).

Davies, D., "An Interpretation of Sacrifice in Leviticus," *ZAW* 89 (1977), 387–398.

Davies, W. D., "Jerusalem and the Land in the Christian Tradition," in *The*

Jerusalem Colloquium on Religion, Peoplehood, Nation, and Land, ed. M. H. Tanenbaum and R. J. Zwi Werblovsky (Jerusalem: Truman Research Institute, 1970).

———, *The Gospel and the Land: Early Christianity and Jewish Territorial Doctrine* (Berkeley: University of California Press, 1974).

Denny, F. M. and R. L. Taylor, "Introduction," in *The Holy Book in Comparative Perspective*, ed. F. M. Denny and R. L. Taylor (Columbia, SC: University of South Carolina Press, 1985).

Douglas, M., *Natural Symbols: Explorations in Cosmology* (New York: Pantheon Books, 1982).

———, "The Abominations of Leviticus," in *Anthropological Approaches to the Old Testament*, ed. B. Lang (Philadelphia: Fortress Press, 1985).

———, *In the Wilderness: The Doctrine of Defilement in the Book of Numbers.* (Sheffield: Sheffield Academic Press, 1993).

Dowden, K., *Religion and the Romans* (London: Bristol Classical Press, 1992).

Durkheim, E., *The Elementary Forms of the Religious Life* (London: G. Allen & Unwin, 1915).

Eichrodt, W., *Theologie des Alten Testaments*, I, trans. J. A. Baker (Philadelphia: Westminster Press, 1961).

Eisenstein, J. D., "Palestine, Holiness of," in *The Jewish Encyclopedia*, IX, ed. I. Singer (New York: Ktav, 1964).

Eliade, M., *The Sacred and the Profane: The Nature of Religion*, trans. W. Trask (New York: Harcourt, Brace & World, 1959).

Erickson, M. J., *Christian Theology* (Grand Rapids, MI: Baker, 1985).

Evans-Pritchard, E. E., *Nuer Religion* (Oxford: Clarendon Press, 1956).

Falk, Z. W. "Spirituality and Jewish Law," *Religion and Law: Biblical-Judaic and Islamic Perspectives*, ed. E. B. Firmage, B. G. Weiss and J. W. Welch (Winona Lake: Eisenbrauns, 1990).

Ferguson, J., *The Religions of the Roman Empire* (Ithaca, NY: Cornell University Press, 1970).

———, *Greek and Roman Religion: A Source Book* (Park Ridge, NJ: Noyes Press, 1980).

———, "Roman Cults," in *Civilization of the Ancient Mediterranean*, II, ed. M. Grant and R. Kitzmyer, II (New York: Charles Scribner & Sons, 1988).

"Festivals," in *Encyclopedia Judaica* (Jerusalem: Keter, 1971).

Fishbane, M., "Jewish Biblical Exegesis: Presuppositions and Principles," in *Scripture in the Jewish and Christian Traditions*, ed. F. E. Greenspan (Nashville: Abingdon, 1982).

Flusser, D. and S. Safrai, "Who Sanctified the Beloved in the Womb?" *Immanuel* 11:46–55 (1980).

Foucart, G., "Names, Egyptian," in *Encyclopedia of Religion and Ethics*, ed. J. Hastings (New York: Charles Scribner's Sons, 1911–22), IX, 151.

Fraade, S. D., "Ascetical Aspects of Ancient Judaism" in *Jewish Spirituality from the Bible through the Middle Ages*, ed. A. Green (New York: Crossroad, 1986), 257.

Fretheim, T. E., *The Suffering of God: An Old Testament Perspective*, Overtures to Biblical Theology (Philadephia: Fortress Press, 1984).

Gamble, Jr., H. Y., "Christianity: Scripture and Canon," in *The Holy Book in Comparative Perspective*, ed. F. M. Denny and R. L. Taylor (Columbia, SC: University of South Carolina Press, 1985).

Gammie, J., *Holiness in Israel* (Minneapolis, MN: Fortress Press, 1989).

Gardiner, A. H., "Magic, Egyptian," *Encyclopedia of Religion and Ethics*, VIII.

Garland, R., "Priests and Power in Classical Athens," in *Pagan Priests: Religion and Power in the Ancient World*, ed. M. Beard and J. North (Ithaca, NY: Cornell University Press, 1990).

"Genizah," in *Encyclopedia Judaica*, VII (Jerusalem: Keter, 1971).

"God," in *Encyclopedia Judaica*, VII (Jerusalem: Keter, 1971).

Gordon, Richard, "From Republic to Principate: Priesthood, Religion and Ideology," in *Pagan Priests: Religion and Power in the Ancient World*, ed. M. Beard and J. North (Ithaca, NY: Cornell University Press, 1990).

——, "Religion in the Roman Empire: the Civic Compromise and Its Limits," in *Pagan Priests: Religion and Power in the Ancient World*, ed. M. Beard and J. North (Ithaca, NY: Cornell University Press, 1990).

——, "The Veil of Power: Emperors, Sacrifices and Benefactors," in *Pagan Priests: Religion and Power in the Ancient World*, ed. M. Beard and J. North (Ithaca, NY: Cornell University Press, 1990).

Grabois, A., "Medieval Pilgrims, the Holy Land and Its Image in European Civilisation," in *The Holy Land in History and Thought*, ed. M. Sharon (Leiden: E. J. Brill, 1988).

Hall, R., "Circumcision," *Anchor Bible Dictionary*, I (New York: Doubleday 1992).

Hammer, R., *Sifre: A Tannaitic Commentary on the Book of Deuteronomy*, Yale Judaica Series xxiv (New Haven, CT: Yale University Press, 1986).

——, *The Classic Midrash: Tannaitic Commentaries on the Bible* (New York: Paulist Press, 1995).

Haran, M., *Temples and Temple Service in Ancient Israel*, (Oxford: Clarendon Press, 1978).

Harrington, H., *The Impurity Systems of the Rabbis and Qumran* (Atlanta: Scholars Press, 1993).

——, "Did the Pharisees Eat Ordinary Food in a State of Purity?" 26 *JSJ* (April, 1995), 42–54.

Harrison, E. F., "Holiness; Holy," in *The International Standard Bible Encyclopedia*, ed. G. W. Bromley II (Grand Rapids, MI: Eerdmans, 1982).

Harrison, J., *Prolegomena to the Study of Greek Religion* (Cleveland: World; reprint of 3d edn, Cambridge: Cambridge University Press, 1922).

Hauck, F. and R. Meyer *"Katharos"* in *Theological Dictionary of the New Testament*, III, ed. G. W. Bromley (Grand Rapids, MI: Eerdmans, 1964–76).

Hauptman, J., *Rereading the Rabbis: A Woman's Voice* (Boulder, CO: Westview Press, 1998).

Hayes, J., *Understanding the Psalms* (Valley Forge, PA: Judson Press, 1976).

Hengel, M., *Judaism and Hellenism* (Philadelphia: Fortress Press, 1974).

Hertzberg, A., "Zionism and the Jewish Religious Tradition," in *The Jerusalem Colloquium on Religion, Peoplehood, Nation, and Land*, ed. M. H. Tanenbaum and R. J. Zwi Werblovsky (Jerusalem: H.S. Truman Research Institute of the Hebrew University, 1972).

Heschel, A. J., *Moral Grandeur and Spiritual Audacity: Essays by Abraham Joshua Heschel*, ed. S. Heschel (New York: Farrar, 1996).

Hodgson, Jr., Robert, "Holiness (NT)," in *Anchor Bible Dictionary*, ed. D. N. Freedman, III (New York: Doubleday, 1992).

Hoffmann, L. A., "Introduction: Land of Blessing and 'Blessings of the Land," in *The Land of Israel: Jewish Perspectives*, ed. L. A. Hoffman (Notre Dame, IN: University of Notre Dame Press, 1986).

"Holy Spirit," in *Dictionary of Judaism*, ed. J. Neusner (New York: Macmillan, 1996).

Hubert, H. and M. Mauss, *Sacrifice: Its Nature and Function* (Chicago: University of Chicago Press, 1964).

Hubner, Hans, "Unclean and Clean (NT)," in *Anchor Bible Dictionary*, VI, ed. D. N. Freedman (New York: Doubleday, 1992).

Isenberg, S. R. and D. E. Owen, "Bodies, Natural and Contrived: The Work of Mary Douglas," *RSR*, 3/1 January (1977), 1–17.

Jacob, E., *Theology of the Old Testament*, trans. A. W. Heathcote and P. J. Allcock (London: Hodder & Stoughton, 1958).

Jaffee, M., *Early Judaism*, (Upper Saddle River, NJ: Prentice Hall, 1997).

Jameson, M. H., "Sacrifice and Ritual: Greece," in *Civilization of the Ancient Mediterranean*, II, ed. M. Grant and R. Kitzmyer (New York: Charles Scribner & Sons, 1988).

Jastrow, M., *A Dictionary of the Targumim, the Talmud Babli and Yerushalmi, and the Midrashic Literature* (New York: The Judaica Press, Inc., 1982).

Jenson, P. P., *Graded Holiness: A Key to the Priestly Conception of the World* (Sheffield: Sheffield Academic Press, 1992).

Jeremias, J., *Jerusalem z. Zeit Jesu*, II, (Gottingen: Vandenhoeck and Ruprecht, 1962).

Kadushin, M., *The Rabbinic Mind* (New York: Jewish Theological Seminary of America, 1952).

——, *Worship and Ethics: A Study in Rabbinic Judaism* (Evanston, IL: Northwestern University Press, 1964).

——, *A Conceptual Approach to the Mekhilta* (New York: Jewish Theological Seminary of America, 1969).

Kantorowicz, E. H., "Pro Patria Mori," in *Selected Studies* (Locust Valley, NY: J. J. Augustin, 1965).

Kedar-Kopfstein, B., "*Hag*," in *Theological Dictionary of the Old Testament*, IV, ed. G. J. Botterweck and H. Ringgren, tr. D. Green (Grand Rapids, MI: Eerdmans, 1986).

"*Kedushah*," in *Encyclopedia Judaica*, X (Jerusalem: Keter, 1971).

Klauck, H.-J., "*Thusia*," in *Theological Dictionary of the New Testament*, III, ed. G. W. Bromley (Grand Rapids, MI: Eerdmans, 1964–76).

Kraeling, C. H. and R. M. Adams (eds), *City Invincible* (Chicago: University of Chicago Press, 1960).

Land, S. J., *Pentecostal Spirituality: A Passion for the Kingdom* (Sheffield: Sheffield Academic Press, 1993).

Leach, E., *Culture and Communication: The Logic by Which Symbols Are Connected* (Cambridge: Cambridge University Press, 1983).

——, "Culture and Communication: The Logic by Which Symbols are Connected," in *Anthropological Approaches to the OT, Issues in Religion and Theology* 8, ed. B. Lang (Philadelphia: Fortress, 1985).

Leeuw, G. van der, *Religion in Essence and Manifestation: A Study in Phenomenology* (New York: Harper & Row, 1963), 23.

Leiman, S. Z., *The Canonization of Hebrew Scripture: The Talmudic and Midrashic Evidence* (Hamden, CT: Archon Books, 1976).

Leiser, B., "The Sanctity of the Profane: A Pharisaic Critique of Rudolf Otto," *Judaism* 20 (1971), 87–92.

Lester, R. C., "Hinduism: Veda and Sacred Texts," in *The Holy Book in Comparative Perspective*, ed. F. M. Denny and R. L. Taylor (Columbia, SC: University of South Carolina Press, 1985).

Levenson, J. D., *Sinai and Zion: An Entry into the Jewish Bible, New Voices in Biblical Studies*, ed. A. Y. Collins and J. J. Collins (Minneapolis: Winston Press, 1985).

Levi-Strauss, C., *The Savage Mind*, (Chicago: University of Chicago Press, 1966).

Levine, B., *In the Presence of the Lord*, (Leiden: Brill, 1974).

——, "The Language of Holiness: Perceptions of the Sacred in the Hebrew Bible," in *Backgrounds for the Bible*, ed. M. P. O'Connor and D. N. Freedman (Winona Lake, IN: Eisenbrauns, 1987).

Levine, L. I., *Ancient Synagogues Revealed* (Detroit: Wayne State University Press, 1982).

Licht, J., "*Qodesh, Qadosh, Qedushah*," in *Entsiqlopedya Mikra'it*, VII, ed. E. Sukenik and M. D. Cassuto (Jerusalem: Bialik Institute, 1965).

Lieberman, S., *Proceedings of the Rabbinical Assembly of America*, XII (New York: Rabbinical Assembly, 1949).

Liebeschuetz, J. H. W. G., *Continuity and Change in Roman Religion* (Oxford: Clarendon Press, 1979).

McKenna, D., *Power to Follow, Grace to Lead* (Dallas, TX: Word, 1989).

Malina, B. J., *The New Testament World: Insights from Cultural Anthropology* (Atlanta: John Knox Press, 1981).

Malinowski, B., *Magic Science, and Religion, and Other Essays* (Boston: Beacon Press, 1948).

Marmorstein, A., *Studies in Jewish Theology* (Oxford: Oxford University Press, 1950).

"Marriage, Prohibited," in *Encyclopedia Judaica*, XI (Jerusalem: Keter, 1971).

Mazar, A., "The Aqueducts of Jerusalem," in *Jerusalem Revealed: Archaeology in the Holy City 1968–1974*, ed. Yigael Yadin (Jerusalem: Israel Exploration Society, 1975).

Meyers, C., "The Jerusalem Temple," in *Anchor Bible Dictionary*, IV (New York: Doubleday, 1992).

Meyers, E. M., "Secondary Burials in Palestine," *BA* 23 (1970, February) no. 1, 1–29.

——, "Jewish Ossuaries: Reburial and Rebirth," *Biblica et Orientalia* (Rome: Institute Press, 1979), 72ff.

Milgrom, J., "Ethics and Ritual: The Foundations of the Biblical Dietary Laws," in *Religion and Law: Biblical-Judaic and Islamic Perspectives*, ed. E. B. Firmage, B. G. Weiss and J. W. Welch (Winona Lake: Eisenbrauns, 1990).

——, *Leviticus 1–16*, The Anchor Bible 3A (Garden City, NY: Doubleday, 1991).

——, *Leviticus 17–27*, The Anchor Bible 3B and 3C (Garden City, NY: Doubleday, forthcoming).

Moore, G. F., *Judaism in the First Centuries of the Christian Era*, I (New York: Schocken Books, 1971).

Muilenburg, J., "Holiness," in *Interpreter's Dictionary of the Bible*, II (New York: Abingdon Press, 1962).

Naude, J., "Holiness in the Dead Sea Scrolls," in *The Dead Sea Scrolls after Fifty Years*, ed. P. W. Flint and J. VanderKam, II (Leiden: E. J. Brill, 1999).

Neeman, P., *Boundaries of Eretz Israel according to Hasal* (Jerusalem: R. Mas, 1979).

Neusner, J., *A History of the Mishnaic Law of Holy Things*, VI (Leiden: E. J. Brill, 1978–80).

——, *Judaism and Scripture* (Chicago: University of Chicago Press, 1986). .

——, *The Oral Torah: The Sacred Books of Judaism* (San Francisco: Harper & Row, 1986).

——, *From Testament to Torah: An Introduction to Judaism in Its Formative Age* (Englewood Cliffs, NJ: Prentice Hall, 1988).

——, *Sifra: An Analytical Translation* (Atlanta: Scholars Press, 1988).

——, *Purity in Rabbinic Judaism* (Atlanta: Scholars Press, 1994).

North, J., "Diviners and Divination at Rome," in *Pagan Priests: Religion and Power in the Ancient World*, ed. M. Beard and J. North (Ithaca, NY: Cornell University Press, 1990).

——, "The Development of Religious Pluralism," in *The Jews Among Pagans and Christians*, ed. J. Licu, J. North and T. Rajak (London: Routledge Press, 1992).

O'Brien, C. C., *God Land: Reflections on Religion and Nationalism* (Cambridge, MA: Harvard University, 1988).

Oepke, A., "*Bapto,*" in *Theological Dictionary of the New Testament*, I, ed. G. W. Bromley (Grand Rapids, MI: Eerdmans, 1964).

Oswalt, J. N., *The Book of Isaiah: Chapters 1–39*, The New International Commentary on the Old Testament, ed. R. K. Harrison (Grand Rapids, MI: Eerdmans, 1986).

Otto, R., *The Idea of the Holy*, trans. J. W. Harvey (Oxford: Oxford University Press, 1928).

Parke, H. W. and D. E. W. Wormell, *The Delphic Oracle*, I (Oxford: Blackwell, 1956).

Parker, R. *Miasma: Pollution and Purification in Early Greek Religion* (Oxford: Clarendon Press, 1983).

Pedersen, K. H., "The Holy Land: History and Reality of the Term," *Immanuel* 22/23 (1989), 35.

Peli, P. H., *Soloveitchik: On Repentance* (New York: Paulist Press, 1984).

Primus, C., "The Borders of Judaism: The Land of Israel in Early Rabbinic Judaism," in *The Land of Israel: Jewish Perspectives*, ed. L. A. Hoffman (Notre Dame, IN: University of Notre Dame Press, 1986).

Qimron, E., "The Holiness of the Holy Land in the Light of a New Document from Qumran," in *The Holy Land in History and Thought*, ed. M. Sharon (Leiden: E. J. Brill, 1988).

Rad, G. von, *Theologie des Alten Testaments*, I (Munchen: Kaiser Verlag, 1957), English trans. by D. M. G. Stalker, *Old Testament Theology*, I (New York: Harper, 1962–65).

Rajak, T., "The Jewish Community and Its Boundaries," in *The Jews Among Pagans and Christians*, ed. J. Lieu, J. North and T. Rajak (London: Routledge, 1992).

Ringgren, H., *"Tahor,"* in *Theological Dictionary of the Old Testament*, V, ed. G. J. Botterweck and H. Ringgren, trans. D. Green (Grand Rapids, MI: Eerdmans, 1986).

Rosenbaum, J., "Judaism: Torah and Tradition," in *The Holy Book in Comparative Perspective*, ed. F. M. Denny and R. L. Taylor (Columbia, SC: University of South Carolina Press, 1985).

"Sabbatical Year and Jubilee," in *Encyclopedia Judaica*, XIV (Jerusalem: Keter, 1971).

"Sacerdos," *Harper's Dictionary of Classical Literature and Antiquities*, ed. H. T. Peck (New York: Cooper Square Publishers, 1962).

"Sacrificium," in *Harper's Dictionary of Classical Literature and Antiquities*, ed. H. T. Peck (New York: Cooper Square Publishers, 1962).

Safrai, S., "The Sabbatical Year Commandment in Post-Second Temple Reality" (Heb.), *Tarbiz* 36 (1966), 309–328; 37 (1967), 1–21.

——, "The Land of Israel in Tannaitic Halacha," in *Das Land Israel in biblischer Zeit: Jerusalem-Symposium 1981*, ed. G. Strecker (Gottingen: Vandenhoeck & Ruprecht, 1983).

Sanders, E. P., "When is a Law a Law? The Case of Jesus and Paul," in *Religion and Law: Biblical-Judaic and Islamic Perspectives*, ed. E. Firmage, B. G. Weiss and J. W. Welch (Winona Lake: Eisenbrauns, 1990).

Sarason, R. S., "The Significance of the Land of Israel in the Mishnah," *The Land of Israel: Jewish Perspectives*, ed. L. A. Hoffman (Notre Dame, IN: University of Notre Dame Press, 1986).

Sawyer, D. F., *Women and Religion in the First Christian Centuries* (London: Routledge, 1996).

Schechter, S. *Studies in Judaism*, second series (Philadelphia: Jewish Publication Society of America, 1908).

——, *Aspects of Rabbinic Theology* (New York: Schocken Books, 1961).

Schramm, G., "Meal Customs (Jewish)," in *Anchor Bible Dictionary*, IV (New York: Doubleday, 1992).

Schrenk, G., "*Hieros*," in *Theological Dictionary of the New Testament*, III (Grand Rapids, MI: Eerdmans, 1965).

Schurer, E. *The History of the Jewish People in the Age of Jesus Christ*, II (Edinburgh: T. & T. Clark, 1979).

"Scribe," in *Encyclopedia Judaica*, XIV (Jerusalem: Keter, 1971).

"Sibylline Oracles," in *Encyclopedia of Religion*, XIV, ed. M. Eliade (New York: Macmillan, 1987).

Simon, M., "The Ancient Church and Rabbinical Tradition," in *Holy Book and Holy Tradition*, ed. F. F. Bruce and E. G. Rupp (Grand Rapids, MI: Eerdmans, 1968).

Smith, Q., "An Analysis of Holiness," *Rel. Stud.* 24 (1988), 511–528.

Smith, J. Z., *Map is Not Territory: Studies in the History of Religions* (Leiden: E. J. Brill, 1978).

Staal, F., "The Concept of Scripture in Indian Tradition," *Sikh Studies: Comparative Perspectives in a Changing Tradition* in ed. M. Juergensmeyer and N. G. Barrier, eds., (Berkeley: Graduate Theological Union, 1979).

Strathmann, H., "*Polis*," in *Theological Dictionary of the New Testament*, VI (Grand Rapids, MI: Eerdmans, 1968.

"*Tahorah*," *Entsiqlopedyah Talmudit*, XIX (Jerusalem: Talmudic Publishing Encyclopedia, 1989).

Terrien, S., "The Omphalos Myth and Hebrew Religion," *VT*, XX (1970), 315–338.

——, *The Elusive Presence: Toward a New Biblical Theology* (New York: Harper & Row, 1978).

Thoma, C., "The Link Between People, Land and Religion in Old and New Testaments," *Service International de Documentation Judeo-Chretienne* 8:2 (1975).

Turcan, R. *The Cults of the Roman Empire*, trans. A. Nevill (Oxford: Blackwell, 1996).

Turner, J. A., "Greek Priesthoods," in *Civilization of the Ancient Mediterranean*, II, ed. M. Grant and R. Kitzmyer (New York: Charles Scribner & Sons, 1988).

Urbach, E. E., *The Sages: Their Concepts and Beliefs*, I (Jerusalem: Magnes Press, 1979).

Weingreen, J., "Oral Torah and Written Records," in *Holy Book and Holy Tradition*, eds. F. F. Bruce and E. G. Rupp (Grand Rapids, MI: Eerdmans, 1968).

Weiss, I. H., *Dor Dor ve-Dorshav*, I (Vienna: Hertsfeld and Boyer, 1871).

Wendebourg, D., "Die alttestamentlichen Reinheitsgesetze in der fruhen Kirche," *ZKG* 95 (1984), 149–170.

Wenschkewitz, H., *Die Spiritualisierung der Kultusbegriffe Tempel* (Leipzig: Edvard Pfeiffer, 1932).

Widengren, G., "Holy Book and Tradition in Iran: The Problem of the

Sassanid Avesta," in *Holy Book and Holy Tradition*, eds. F. F. Bruce and E. G. Rupp (Grand Rapids, MI: Eerdmans, 1968).

Wilken, R. L., *The Land Called Holy: Palestine in Christian History and Thought* (New Haven, CT: Yale University Press, 1992).

Wright, D. P., "Unclean and Clean (OT)," in *Anchor Bible Dictionary*, VI (New York: Doubleday, 1992).

Wurzburger, W. and R. J. Z. Werblowsky, "Land, People and Nation in Jewish Perspective," in *Fifteen Years of Catholic-Jewish Dialogue: 1970–1985* (Rome: Libreria Editrice Vaticana, 1988).

Yadin, Y., *Megillat ha-Migdash* (3 vols. 1977), Eng. trans., *The Temple Scroll*, 3 vols. (Jerusalem: The Israel Exploration Society and the Shrine of the Book, 1983).

Young, F., *The Use of Sacrificial Ideas in Greek Christian Writers from the New Testament to John Chrysostom*, Patristic Monograph Series 5 (Cambridge, MA: The Philadelphia Patristic Foundation, 1979).

Zeitlin, S., *Studies in the Early History of Judaism* (New York: Ktav, 1973).

INDEX